Moving Your Library

Getting the Collection from Here to There

Steven Carl Fortriede

American Library Association
Chicago   2010

Steven Carl Fortriede retired as associate director of the Allen County Public Library in Fort Wayne, Indiana, after more than forty years in the library profession. Fortriede received a BS in education from Ball State University and an MLS from Western Michigan University in 1971. A year later he was assigned, rather abruptly, to move his first library. Since that time he has directed, or consulted for, more than twenty moves for libraries ranging from a few thousand to nearly four million items. He has also been responsible for many space planning and library design projects.

While extensive effort has gone into ensuring the reliability of information appearing in this book, the publisher makes no warranty, express or implied, on the accuracy or reliability of the information and does not assume and hereby disclaims any liability to any person for any loss or damage caused by errors or omissions in this publication.

The paper used in this publication meets the minimum requirements of American National Standard for Information Sciences—Permanence of Paper for Printed Library Materials, ANSI Z39.48-1992. ∞

Library of Congress Cataloging-in-Publication Data
Fortriede, Steven Carl.
    Moving your library : getting the collection from here to there / Steven Carl Fortriede.
       p.   cm.
    Includes bibliographical references and index.
    ISBN 978-0-8389-0994-2 (alk. paper)
    1. Library moving. 2. Library moving—United States. I. Title.
Z703.5.F67 2010
025.1—dc22   2009003943

Copyright © 2010 by the American Library Association. All rights reserved except those which may be granted by Sections 107 and 108 of the Copyright Revision Act of 1976.

ISBN-13: 978-0-8389-0994-2

Printed in the United States of America
14 13 12 11 10   5 4 3 2 1

To my father, who taught me how to eat an elephant

Contents

Preface　vii

PART I　PLANNING

Chapter 1	Overview of a Move	3
Chapter 2	Planning the Process	6
Chapter 3	Selecting a Method	27
Chapter 4	Measuring the Collection and Designing the Shelving Layout	34
Chapter 5	Interfiling and Dividing Collections	52
Chapter 6	Recruiting and Training Move Workers	62
Chapter 7	Assembling Tools and Supplies	70
Chapter 8	Preparing the Workspaces	82
Chapter 9	The Other Move	89

PART II　MOVING

Chapter 10	Preparing to Move	99
Chapter 11	Moving with Carts	106
Chapter 12	Moving with Boxes	112
Chapter 13	Balancing the Move	129
Chapter 14	Moving Microforms	135
Chapter 15	Special Situations	148
Chapter 16	Finishing Up	158

APPENDIXES

A　Specifications for Boxes　161

B　Specifications for Move Carts and Sorting Trays　165

C　Worksheet to Calculate Shelving Layout and Growth Rates　170

D　Signage　181

E　Sample Request for Quotes for an Office Move　184

Index　187

Additional material can be found on the book's website, at www.ala.org/editions/extras/fortriede09942. Look for website material wherever you see this symbol: **WEB**

Preface

The decision to write this book came about because of a phone call. We were in the late stages of planning the return move of the Allen County Public Library from its temporary location into a brand-new 390,000-square-foot building. The move plan covered nearly four million items of all kinds going onto more than fifty miles of shelving. We had one collection we had to divide, part to open shelves, the rest to basement storage; many collections we had to combine from storage and other temporary locations; and nearly a million items in boxed storage in the basement.

The planning area, a 1,200-square-foot two-room complex, was lined with file cabinets and papered with floor plans, shelving charts, route maps, layout drawings, and timetables. Shelf counts, pallet logs, staffing tables, inventories, and task lists covered the two boardroom-size planning tables.

An experienced seven-person move team met regularly. All had helped plan the move into the temporary building. Three had been involved in other moves at various times. Among the seven of us, we had experience in more than thirty moves. Although the scene may have appeared chaotic from the outside, those of us on the team saw a place of calm progress, on many fronts at once, toward a known outcome.

The telephone call came from Dr. Mary Rowell, librarian at a local church school. She too was moving. Her library was to be recarpeted and she had to move all of the books out, then back a week or so later. She was seeking advice. She reported that she had found a small room down the hall where the books could be stored, stacked on the floor, and she had forty-eight volunteers lined up to help with the move. As we talked, she kept mentioning different ideas for storing and marking the books, ways to organize the workers, and all kinds of other options.

I eventually realized that she was under a lot of pressure—unsure of herself, quite distressed at the responsibility that had been thrust upon her—and that she was waiting for me to tell her that one of her options would indeed be the right way to go.

For myself, I was focused on those forty-eight volunteers. That's enough to move half a million books. Once we both got into the same frame of reference, I asked her to describe her collection and then to count the shelves. The collection turned out to be about 2,500 volumes. With that information, she and I worked out a move plan.

I sent her ten of our large move carts. With two helpers she loaded the books on the carts and rolled them down the hall to the storeroom, then rolled them back two weeks later. It took fewer than four hours each way.

That call got me thinking about other people for whom I had planned and carried out library moves. They were competent librarians; respected managers with complex administrative duties; professionals experienced at a wide variety of planning, organizing, and management tasks. But faced with a move, they turned to outside help. They were willing to pay very large amounts of money to someone else to do the move for them. In some cases they had been willing to pay me what I considered to be a lot of money to do the work. The problem, of course, is that most of us move a library maybe once in a career. We learn a lot in the process, but we rarely get a second chance to apply what we learn.

I have had the opportunity to move many libraries. The first was pure happenstance; I was available when my director needed someone to assign to the task. Neither of us had any idea what was involved or how to go about it. Because my director considered that first move a success, he assigned me to do another one. After that, the word got around, and I was asked to do other moves. (For the record, that first move was a disaster; it took too long, used too many people, and had way too many mistakes.)

What Dr. Rowell needed, what my first director needed, what most of the people for whom I have moved libraries needed, and what I needed those first times was an instruction book. We needed a practical how-to-do-it manual to give an overview of the process, step-by-step instructions, and the value of the experience of someone who had been through it already. More than that, we needed something or someone to teach us how to prepare for the task and to give us the confidence that we could conduct a move effectively.

Like Dr. Rowell, most librarians are not in a position to pay someone to plan and carry out their move. They have no choice but to do it themselves, and they have to get it right the first time.

A move is a daunting task, but the individual pieces are not that difficult:

- The way we measure collections is simple; we usually assign pages to do it.
- Calculating growth rates is just a matter of plugging numbers into a spreadsheet until the number of shelves you need equals the number of shelves you have available.
- Deciding the best way to move a lot of books at one time is a bit involved, but there are a finite number of options, and it is not hard to pick one that will work for you.
- Organizing a large move is complex, but there are specific things that have to be done. We can list those things and cross them off when they are done.

With a clear set of instructions, and the benefit of a little experience from someone who has done it before, almost anyone can move a library collection. More specifically, with clear instructions, with a few tips from someone who has already made most of the mistakes, and with a little confidence of your own, you can move your library collection safely, accurately, and quite efficiently.

Part 1

PLANNING

" Adventures happen only to those incapable of planning. "

Richard Evans Schultes, ethnobotanist

Overview of a Move

Here's how you move a library collection. Pick up the first book. Walk it over to the new building. Put it on the shelf. Go back and pick up the next book. Walk it over and put it next to the first one. Do this enough times and you'll look around and find you're almost half done.

That's how you do it. That's the basic plan. You could stop reading right now. The rest of this book is all about how to make the process a little more efficient.

Consider: You could cut your total trips in half if you picked up one book in each hand. Of course, you'd have to remember which one you picked up first. You might, for instance, put a piece of BLACK tape on your LEFT hand as a reminder.

You could move even faster if you put a lot of books in a box or on a cart and took 20 or 50 or 250 at a time. Of course, now you have to remember which end of the cart you loaded first. You might put a piece of BLACK tape on the TOP of the LEFT end of the cart.

You could save a lot of walking time if you could take more than one cart or box at a time, so you might rent a truck and fill it up each trip. Of course, you'd have to remember which cart was first, so you might number them.

Now you could really speed things up if you got some people to help you. Of course, then you would have to assign each of them a job, keep their work separate from yours, and make sure they kept all of the books in order. So, you'd solve those problems: you might divide the collection so each work crew had a separate area of responsibility, color-code the carts of each crew so they didn't get mixed up, and mark waypoints on the shelves so crews could check their accuracy.

And so it goes.

A wise person told me there are two ways to eat an elephant. The common wisdom is that you just take one bite at a time. That's a metaphor for breaking a problem into little pieces and dealing with each one separately. But sometimes the pieces are so intertwined, each one dependent on all the others, that you can't break them apart. Then you just take the whole thing in one big bite and keep chewing away until it is gone. That's the other way to eat the elephant. That's a metaphor for what it feels like when you are the move coordinator.

I have worked to make this book as practical as possible. I've tried to identify all of the pieces of a collection move, explain how each affects the others, and make specific recommendations based on actual experience. If I make a recommendation, it is something I have used myself on a real move. On those few occasions where I offer a suggestion I have not tried myself, I identify it as such.

I have moved well over ten million books, ranging from tiny branches to the four-million-item collection of the Allen County Public Library. On one move, the entire crew consisted of me and one other person. Three times I supervised moves with crews of more than one hundred. I have moved public, college, and school libraries. I have worked with many bright, energetic, and creative people and have adopted solutions they developed. The information and advice in this book is based on those experiences. The techniques, tips, forms, and spreadsheets are the ones I use. Master copies of most of the electronic and printed matter you will need are included in the appendixes. Refer to them from time to time.

There are some intangibles in every move. They are not something you can plan, acquire, or staff for; they just happen. When they do, those intangibles are a great asset to you.

Your move will be a major event in your community. "Your community" may be your school, church, or university, or it may be your entire town. Use this to your advantage. News media will be interested in the process; take advantage of the publicity. People will want to be associated with the move. Give them the opportunity to sponsor or contribute supplies, boxes, food, prizes, a truck, or other equipment.

Your staff will *want* to help—not necessarily all of them, but enough to provide crew leaders, supervisors, and at least some knowledgeable, motivated workers. Staff may fear the magnitude of the task, but they won't want to be left out, especially if they see outsiders handling "their" books. Engage staff early and make sure they know no one will be asked to do something beyond their abilities.

People will get caught up in the process. Competitions arise. Crews become proud of their speed. It actually becomes exhilarating. People start out thinking the task is impossible, then find out they can do it, and most find out it is actually fun. The move coordinator's task is to support, encourage, and help them find efficiencies. When they do, the books will just melt off the shelves.

Throughout the text I use the term *books* whenever I am referring to generic library materials. The processes and techniques I describe work equally well with books, videocassettes, CDs, DVDs, laser discs, slides, 16 mm and 8 mm films, scores, LPs, 45s, 78s, cassettes, eight-tracks, government documents, talking books, stereoscope cards, papyrus scrolls, and clay tablets, all of which I have moved. I do discuss microforms and periodicals and a few other formats separately, primarily because of differences in the way we measure the collections.

The book is divided into two parts, which parallel the process of the move: first you plan, then you move.

Nearly all of the work of the move team takes place long before the move starts. This is when you develop your plan and assemble equipment, supplies, and workers.

The first task is to put together your planning team (chapter 2). In a small library that may be just you; in a large library there may be seven or eight of you. With this group you make some basic decisions:

- When is the move?
- Who is to move the books?
- What is the budget?
- Should you hire a move professional or a consultant?
- How should your own staff be involved?

Early in your planning you have to decide how you will move the books and other materials (chapter 3). In all but the smallest moves, the choices are carts or boxes. This choice must be made early in the process because it affects nearly all later decisions.

You measure your collection, calculate how much growth space you have available, and establish waypoints to divide the collection into manageable portions that help you catch and correct any problems before they get out of control. In chapter 4, I provide a simple way to take these measurements and build your collection map along with forms, templates, and a set of spreadsheets to make the calculations for you.

You may combine collections from several locations into one shelving order (chapter 5). Less frequently you may have to divide a collection because there is not enough room for all of it on the main shelving run.

A library move requires the help of many people, your staff, and perhaps others. You may recruit helpers, and you will need to train them in their duties (chapter 6).

You accumulate quite a lot of specialized equipment and supplies to support your move (chapter 7). If you plan ahead and use a little creativity, you may be able to get the necessary items at little cost. Start early to make certain everything is ready for move day.

You must pick a convenient route to move books through your buildings (chapter 8). You may find it necessary to protect walls, floors, elevators, and other surfaces.

Often, at the same time you are moving the collection, someone is moving furniture, equipment, and staff effects. I recommend you hire a professional office mover to do that job, and chapter 9 includes advice on integrating and managing this other move.

In part 2, I discuss the move itself.

Chapter 10 is a checklist of things you should do in the last few days before move day. To take advantage of the crew's initial enthusiasm for the new task, it is important to get off to a smooth, efficient start. This chapter tells you how to get the crew started on their first tasks. It also offers an agenda of topics to be covered in a first-day, all-staff meeting.

Chapters 11 and 12 are parallel descriptions of the move process, step by step. Chapter 11 covers a move with library or book carts. Chapter 12 is about moving with boxes transported on hand trucks, dollies, or pallets. In each case the steps are the same, but the process at each point is slightly different.

No matter which method you use, you need to maintain control of the move to provide a smooth flow of materials and ensure the books stay in order at every stage in the process. You also need to know what to do when something starts to go wrong or when a bottleneck develops. This part of the move is more art than science, but in chapter 13 I show you some ways to achieve accuracy and balanced efficiency at all stages. I also describe how to diagnose and correct reshelving errors.

Microforms are a special case, enough different from books that the subject warrants its own chapter. Chapter 14 describes several methods to measure, calculate and allocate growth, mark, pack, move, and reshelve microfilm. The set of options you choose is determined by the size and nature of your collection.

Some moves involve special conditions such as card files, very large books, valuable or delicate items, loose magazines, and other materials that cannot be moved as books or microfilms. In some situations you may have to conduct an interrupted move with time out to move, build, or paint shelving. If you are moving a very small library, or a large one over a very long distance, you may modify some of the methods described in other chapters. Chapter 15 includes some suggestions on how to manage those moves.

Finally, when you are "done" with the move, you still have work ahead of you cleaning up, reading the shelves, making signs, and getting ready to open (chapter 16). You also get to celebrate your success.

Let's start at the beginning . . .

Chapter 2

Planning the Process

Picture this: four people, sitting around a small office they have grandly dubbed "Galactic Central." They are surrounded by maps, charts, and schedules. Color-coded floor plans cover the walls. Three land lines and a plethora of cell phones provide instant communication to all parts of their empire. They are tense, excited, and ready to jump at the slightest hint of need. It's 9:30, on the first day of a multimillion-item move.

There was a brief flurry an hour ago when the office movers showed up unexpectedly to start taking furniture, and we had to activate a work team a day earlier than planned. Now we wait, expectant. It is quiet in the command post. No telephone rings. No head peeks around the door frame. From outside there are a low hum of activity and the steady rumble of carts passing by.

We look at each other. Eyebrows rise. Shoulders shrug. Stillness reigns. Eventually Sandy, who is morale officer, leaves to order twenty-five large pizzas for lunch. Lynn, who is responsible for moving staff and their effects, decides to check progress of the office movers. I wander down to watch the dock crew load trucks. Kay remains poised over the silent switchboard.

Is this what your move will be like? Sorry, but no. That was a one-off; never happened before, won't happen again.

What will your move look like? In a word, chaos. But if you plan carefully, involve the right people, don't get seduced by untested assumptions, and concentrate on the things you *can* influence, it will be controlled chaos—and that's good enough.

What makes a move start and run smoothly? A good plan. Well, that and about a hundred other things, most of which you can't control. The move plan covers those things you can influence.

THE MOVE TEAM

The move team is the planning group. In a small library it may consist of one person. In a large move there are duties enough to occupy seven or eight people. Anything more than that is a debating society. More exactly, as the size of the committee grows past seven or eight, the responsibilities begin to overlap and that chaos thing starts to happen. Below is a list of the areas of responsibility. You may not have the luxury to assign one person to each, but all of them need to be done.

In most of the moves I have been associated with, there has been a fairly loose planning group representing many points of view. In some smaller libraries, all of the staff have attended the meetings. Within that, however, has been a much smaller group of core planners who knew they would have the primary responsibility to carry out the actual move.

Move Coordinator

This person may be in charge of nothing but is overall in charge of everything. Directs the move. Coordinates other members of the move team. The final decision maker. This person must be intimately familiar with the collection layout, the move plan and timetable, and the process of the move. He or she should also be familiar, not necessarily to the same degree, with all other aspects of the move. This is the person who has to have the confidence to take on this huge task and direct it to a successful conclusion.

The person selected as move coordinator must be in a position to devote a significant amount of time to the planning process, possibly over many months. Even with the support of an excellent move team, this is an incredibly time-consuming job. It is not possible for me to overstate the amount of checking and rechecking; telephone calls; versions of the floor plan, timetable, or work schedule; counts of shelving; meetings; walk-throughs; and just plain thinking that is required to complete even a moderate move. The move coordinator must be able to be relieved from or to delegate to subordinates enough regular responsibilities to free up the time required.

The move coordinator also must have, or be vested with, considerable authority. In many cases the coordinator is in a position of giving instructions and directives to staff throughout your organization, possibly including staff who are equal or higher in the normal organizational structure. The library director must support this level of authority, and the move coordinator must not abuse it. The director should make clear to all staff the extent, and the limitations, of the move coordinator's authority.

The move coordinator must be able to work from floor plans and extrapolate from them to the reality of a building that may not yet be built. Conversely, the coordinator must be able to extrapolate from the reality of books on shelves and furniture on the floor to lists, spreadsheets, and other representations and must be able to manipulate those representations confidently.

It is possible, I think, to plan and conduct a move "by the book"—literally to put together a plan gleaned from the existing literature or from the experience of someone who has done a previous move, follow the steps one after the other, and conduct a successful move. It may not be pretty; it won't be elegant; it may take too long and cost too much. But in the end the books will be moved and back in order, the library will be open, and everyone involved will receive well-deserved congratulations.

If your move coordinator is a person who can maintain a vision of the entire move; who can keep track of all of the pieces of what has been done, what is being done, and what has to be done next; who can adapt the plan on the spot to respond to problems or opportunities; who can gain and maintain the move under control, then your move will be efficient, elegant, and a source of pride for your staff for many years to come.

FFE Coordinator

Usually at about the same time the collection is being moved, a parallel move of furniture, office furnishings, and staff personal effects takes place. This can be an event as major as the move of the books. Many support staff whose duties do not involve direct public service are much more concerned with the office move and may see the move of the collections as having little impact on them.

UNDER CONTROL

That point in a move where

- everyone is working productively but not necessarily yet at highest efficiency.
- there is a smooth flow of loaded carts or boxes toward the destination and a flow of empties back to the origin.
- unshelving crews have an adequate supply of empty carts or boxes, reshelvers have a constant flow of material to shelve, and there is little or no backlog.
- whatever carts or boxes are on the origin loading dock are sorted into some recognizable order.
- you, as the move coordinator, know what work is going on and what will be addressed next.

The move will *not* be under control at the start. People will be unsure of themselves, crews will be working out efficiencies, and you will be reacting to problems, not fine-tuning a well-oiled machine. You may find that the move is not under control for a time at the start of each day. Don't despair. You *will* achieve control, and it *will* be faster each time.

Your goal is first to bring the move under control and then to bring it to maximum efficiency.

Someone should have this part of the move as a primary responsibility. I include this person as a member of the move team. The two moves are intertwined in both time and space and absolutely must be coordinated. In my universe, the FFE (furniture, fixtures, and equipment) coordinator is subordinate to the move coordinator.

This job should be assigned to a detail-oriented person, a good planner, but most of all a person who can work effectively and sympathetically with your staff. A move is a traumatic time for everyone; old habits and work environments are being disrupted and replaced with unknowns. The person to whom this responsibility is entrusted must be able to elicit from each person their real needs for space, furnishings, equipment, and environment; to reassure staff that their wants are being duly considered without acceding to every personal quirk and demand; and to communicate the wants and needs of staff and the ability of the library to provide for those wants and needs in all directions. Previous experience as a tightrope walker is a definite qualification for this job.

I recommend most strongly that you hire an experienced mover to move equipment, furnishings, and personal effects. The office move coordinator is responsible for organizing that move and is the liaison between the movers and the library. If it is necessary to bid the move, the office move coordinator prepares and conducts the bids.

Personnel and Morale Officer

You organize and schedule many people during your move. You may move entirely with your staff, entirely with people hired for the purpose, or any combination thereof. Even if you use all your own staff, the normal reporting relationships are almost certainly lost—and I argue that they should be. There is a unique opportunity to organize staff for the move without regard to department lines and to ignore normal reporting relationships. Think of the possibilities for communication, camaraderie, and improved relationships if a move crew consists of the finance clerk and the head of the art department working under the leadership of a page from the reshelving department.

The personnel officer recruits the staff, prepares lists of job assignments, and makes sure there are enough people to do the job. This is the person you call if you can't make it in to work today and the person who tells you not to come in tomorrow if you didn't perform up to expectations.

The other face of this position is morale officer. In this capacity the person is responsible for whatever amenities and incentives you may provide for your crew, usually food and "prizes." Previous experience as a mother is a useful qualification for this position. This person needs to be involved in the planning from the start. He or she must understand what work is required and what workers are needed to get it done. This person is also in charge of soliciting and collecting prizes and giveaways and arranging for other amenities if you plan to provide such, and these take time to collect.

Optional, but Useful, Team Members

The move coordinator, FFE coordinator, and personnel and morale officer tend to be the core planning team. You may also include several other persons:

Buildings and grounds representative. It is extremely useful to include on the move team a person from your maintenance or housekeeping department. In planning, you need information such as floor loads, elevator capacities, and other technical details. You want someone who understands the move plan and is familiar with the elevator repair company, fire alarms, and locations of circuit breakers. During the move, it is essential to have ready access to someone who can fix a cart, cut a new dock plate, build wall and floor protections, or just turn on the lights. This person may not need to be part of the core planning team, but the participation of a buildings and grounds staffer is invaluable.

Secretary. You generate a lot of paperwork in a move. It is good to have a record of decisions and a list of things to be done. The secretary may be responsible for a newsletter, minutes, and other communications.

Contractor's representative. If your building is under construction or remodeling, you must coordinate your move with the completion of your building. Maintain communication with the builders so you can keep up to date on progress, potential delays in completion, and changes from the building plans and so you can communicate your needs to the builders.

Computer technician. If you are moving a significant number of computers, you should coordinate with that move as well.

Shelving expert. I like to include the head of the paging or reshelving department. These staff will be the backbone of your move if you move with your own staff. They are also the people who know the quirks of your collection arrangement.

Maintenance of service. If you plan to maintain some level of public service during the move, it is useful to have someone on the move team who has this as their primary responsibility.

Director

Unless the director is the move coordinator or holds one of the specific portfolios above, he or she should not be a member of the move team. The director can and should sit in on some meetings, and the team must report regularly and thoroughly to the director, but there must be no doubt that the move coordinator is fully in charge of the move.

Even though the move into new spaces may be one of the most significant events in the history of the library, the planning and execution of the move are often made the responsibility of subordinate staff. Usually the director has a full-time job as director. Especially in the last stages of a building or remodeling project, the director is busy with additional and unfamiliar tasks—finalizing the building, dealing with last minute construction issues, and planning a grand opening. The director does not have time to plan and execute a move in this same time frame. For this reason and except in the smallest libraries, the task of move coordinator is often delegated.

During the move, the move coordinator should have final authority over anything pertaining to the move or affecting its completion. The coordinator who has been planning the move for months or years is in the best position to judge what is needed and to make decisions quickly.

What then is the role of the director? In a word, cheerleader. It is important for the director to be visibly involved in the move. At least once, and preferably once every couple of days in a longer move, the director should be seen, dressed in grungy clothes, unshelving, reshelving, or pushing carts. When possible, I like to assign the director and one or two administrators or board members responsibility to move some specific and very visible small collection. Not only does this demonstrate leadership on the part of the administrators, but it also gives them bragging rights and a good appreciation of the work and effort that goes into sustaining a move.

At least once a day the director should make the rounds, encouraging and supporting the staff. This has much greater impact after the director has actually worked a shift on the project. The director should lend a hand and encourage other administrative staff to do the same: stack a box or push a cart occasionally, and show an interest in the work.

The director should reinforce the decisions and instructions of the move coordinator. If there are any disagreements between the two, they should be resolved in private and the move coordinator should announce the results. Everything possible should be done to maintain the authority of the move coordinator. A move with multiple coordinators is a major disaster with no recovery plan.

PLANNING

The first point I would make is "Don't overplan." Yes, you need a plan that is complete, covers all possibilities, has backups for the backups, and includes every important detail and most of the unimportant ones. Just don't overplan.

Overplan. I see in the literature all kinds of techniques designed to keep track of exactly where every book is at all points in the moving process. One library went so far as to put a patron bar code on every box, check out each book to the box, and then check it in when it reached the new shelves. Others create elaborate logging systems that take as much time and as many staff hours to operate as to do the actual move. This is an unnecessary expenditure of time. Make sure your plan keeps all the materials in order and minimizes the time they are off the shelf. For that rare occasion you do have to hunt down something in transit, it will take you much less time to look for that one item than it will to track all of them.

Overplan. There are many and varied systems to estimate how long it takes to move X number of books Y distance under Z conditions. The problem is, every situation is different. There is no chart published that can take into account the thickness of the pad under your carpet (thick carpet slows the carts and makes them harder to push), the coefficient of friction of your book jackets (slippery covers limit how many books you can

> ## MAJOR DISASTERS
>
> Not a problem if you plan for them.
>
> Mistakes happen, no matter how carefully you plan. But when something happens that disrupts your entire plan, that's a *major disaster*. If the move coordinator has a clear understanding of the plan, even a major disaster can be taken in stride. I usually tell clients that I will budget "seven mistakes and two major disasters" into their move plan.
>
> Here are a few recent major disasters and what we did about them.
>
> - The only elevator broke down on the second load of the move. Solution: We had the repair person on premises for the first day of the move. He fixed the problem within minutes.
> - Two days before the move started, the city building department refused an occupancy permit because construction workers were still in the building. This meant that nonconstruction staff (my move crew) could not work in the building. Solution: Limited the people in the building to essential personnel. Got OSHA-compliant hard hats and shoes for those working in the building. Time lost: none.
> - The library borrowed thirty move carts and had thirty more built locally. The local builder delivered them the morning of the move. He used cheap wheels, and when we loaded the carts we couldn't even move them; the weight caused the wheels to bind on the frame. We had people for five crews, carts for only three. Solution: Called my cart builder, ordered 120 wheels ASAP, and started a courier to drive 500 miles round-trip to get them. This library had a large periodical collection on a mezzanine with no elevator. We changed the order of the move and used the three extra crews to form a human chain to hand the periodicals down the stairs using one crew worth of carts. Time lost: less than an hour.
>
> The point is that on none of these moves did we lose as much as an hour of productive time because we were able to shift rapidly to a backup plan.
>
> The moral: Make a plan, as good as you can get it. Then make a backup plan for everything. Then evaluate. If you think there is even the slightest possibility that you will have to use the backup plan, then make a backup to that.
>
> Confidence is the most important characteristic for a move coordinator. Anybody can oversee a move when everything is going well. The move coordinator has to have the confidence to handle a major disaster.

grab in one handful), or the upsurge in late-day output when your morale officer brings around a plate of warm cookies about 3:30 (people work harder when you show you appreciate them). A truck parked on a 3-degree rising grade can take twice as long to load as one parked 3 degrees nose down. I have never once seen the slope of the loading dock apron mentioned in any time-and-motion study.

Overplan. Some people—and many of the major move companies are particular adherents to this one—try to map exactly where every book will rest on the new shelves. They measure extensively and create elaborate charts showing the inclusive call numbers for every shelf, with calculations to account for items absent when the count is taken and a labeling system that maps every box to the exact shelf. The reshelvers are supposed to check every book against these charts. The problem, of course, is that a library collection is dynamic. Between the time you measure and the day you move, circulation, weeding, and acquisitions can change the content of a particular shelf quite dramatically. With every book earmarked to a specific shelf, one little shift causes a ripple effect through the whole collection. Of course, we hope you will have more shelving in your new building, so there is little correlation between the books crammed onto your shelves now and the spacious new arrangement. So why would anyone use this system? Well, we librarians have this finely developed sense of order and it plays to our fears that we will lose track of our collections. As for why the professional library movers like the process, just consider the billable hours. On one bid for a large library move, the costs to prepare the inventories and shelving plan appeared to be almost 45 percent of the total, or over $100,000. That level of detail is costly indeed. (In chapter 4, I show you a quick, easy method to make sure you have plenty of room for all your books, regardless of the ebb and flow of the collection.)

Overplan. Create a detailed, day-by-day timetable weeks or months in advance. There are many examples for you to copy. They are very comforting and give a great sense of security. But what will you do when the box company delivers only half your order and the timetable is irretrievably blown by noon the first day? What will you do when your crews work much faster than you planned and outstrip the supply of resources you have scheduled for them? It is much better to build a plan that is flexible, that lets us improvise, adapt, and overcome problems and opportunities as and when they present themselves. You'll have to do that anyway.

Overplan. Buy a commercial planning program and fit your move into it. If you're comfortable with PERT, PLAN, or GANTT, fine. They are wonderful tools. The point is, go with what you know; use the tools that are familiar to you. If that is nothing more than a shelving layout and task list, and you're confident with it, that's a perfectly good way to record and represent your move plan.

So, what should go into the plan? Let's consider some of the issues:

When Will the Move Take Place?

There are more constraints here than you might think. First and most obvious, the building has to be finished, or nearly so. I don't think I've ever moved into a building that was totally finished, but most of the work must be done. Construction delays can upset the most carefully drafted timetable.

You may not be able to start moving in until the building is "done" to some predetermined point. Your insurance company or the contractor's may have a provision in its policy that denies coverage to nonconstruction persons working in a construction zone. Check with your insurer and get a letter from the contractor stating specifically whether your workers can be in the building, where they can go, and what they can do. This is a job for the contractor's liaison person on your planning team.

On the Allen County Public Library moves, our insurance company sent a "loss control consultant" who attended a move team meeting. We explained our planning, demonstrated what the various workers would be doing, showed him the safety training we do before the move, and toured him through the buildings. He gave us a letter saying that we would be covered if we did those things and offered one or two suggestions we had not thought of. Your insurance agency has a vested interest in helping you complete a safe move. Use whatever services they are willing to provide.

A related issue could have a major financial impact. In every building contract there is defined a point at which the "Owner," that's you, is deemed to have "accepted" the building. Often when you have moved in some portion of your people and property, you have met the definition and "accepted" the building. "Accepted" means that you are willing to take the building in the condition it is in then and there. If something major is left undone, you just absolved the contractor from having to complete or fix it under the original contract. This is a negotiable point and there are ways to work around it, including punch lists and other written agreements, but you need to have a resolution in place before you set the time for your move. If a dispute should arise later with the contractor, a premature "acceptance" of the building could have incredibly costly consequences.

Schools and universities often try to move during summer or semester break to minimize the impact on students. A semester break may be a very small window if there are any construction delays.

The final timing of a surprising number of moves is determined because someone set a date for the grand opening, and it just has to be done by then. I got my first moving job and my first big promotion because my director promised the board that a branch would be open by a certain date, and the first person assigned to the task could not get it completed.

Weather may also affect your timing. A moderate amount of snow is not an impediment, nor is a brief summer afternoon shower, even an intense one. Extreme cold, though, is hard on the dock crew and slows their work significantly. Dark, misty, humid days with a persistent drizzle may force you to postpone a move. The humidity and rain can damage the books even if you cover them. Workers and cart wheels track in an incredible amount of mud and dirt from around a construction site.

Construction delays, bad weather, and all sorts of things beyond your control affect the timing of your move. Try to stay flexible and concentrate on the things you can control:

- Make sure the workers know that the start date could slip. Keep in touch with them and identify extra workers in case some have to drop out.
- Get supplies in stock early, ready whenever you can start.
- Talk with the proper authorities well in advance to be certain you can close streets, cover parking

meters, or make other official arrangements. Find out their deadlines and explain to them that you may have last minute changes.

- If you rent a truck, forklift, or other equipment, make sure the supplier can get what you need on short notice.

- Try to build in a time between the expected end of the move and the opening event. Your staff need time to unpack and get settled in their new spaces, find their way around, train on new equipment, and get themselves prepared to meet the public, all polished up and professional. If something does slip, you have a bit of a cushion. Workers naturally want to get their personal effects unpacked, make sure everything survived the move, and set up their own space. Schedule time for each worker to do these tasks, and you'll find that they pay more attention to their move duties knowing they will have time to do the other things too.

- Consider a "soft" opening. A hard opening is the one where you invite the dignitaries, make speeches, cut the ribbon, and open for service to the huge opening day crowd. It is an incredibly satisfying closure to all your work. It also puts an absolute premium on having everything done by a specific date, no matter what problems have to be overcome. We moved an entire 50,000-volume university library on a Sunday because the dean planned the grand opening for Monday. The kicker was that the shelving was not delivered until Friday afternoon. The activity that weekend was best described as "intense." A soft opening is the opposite. When you're ready, you open the doors. A few people come in, the word gets around, and you're in business. Some time after you open, you schedule the official grand opening. If the construction timetable seems to slip repeatedly, a soft opening may be a reasonable option. The delayed "official" opening can be timed for good weather, a significant anniversary date, or the availability of a notable speaker.

- Consider also the possibility that you have to move much earlier than expected. This happened to me once. After the first meeting of the move team, the director suddenly announced that he wanted to advance the move date by eight months to take advantage of an opportunity to save substantial lease costs. That library had a large storage collection that had to be moved and interfiled—a long, slow linear job. In less than two weeks we had a crew started on that move. The move team planned the rest of the move even as this crew worked.

- Get involved in the planning of the building, as early as possible. I have had several projects for which the entire space was designed without input from, and in some cases even without the knowledge of, the library staff. These have included notable operational disasters: reference desk on the second floor, reference books on the first floor with periodicals because the architect thought all the wide shelves looked better together; an "artistic" shelving layout that followed the architecture but precluded any possible logical collection flow; enough periodical shelves to hold the collection three times over but the allocation for nonfiction too small to hold the collection even packed tight (librarians were told to weed nonfiction until it fit). Get a seat at the table and do your best to make yourself heard.

- Determine how long you want the move to last. To some extent this is a linear equation. Double the number of people and resources, cut the time in half. There are practical limits, of course, but using the waypoints system (see chapter 4) and planning the routes carefully, you can operate a large number of crews simultaneously. This is a good backup plan if you think you may have a last minute slippage in the building completion and still have to complete the move in time for a hard opening. As soon as you see the delay coming, recruit more staff and contact your suppliers to get more boxes, carts, trucks, and other supplies. Alternatively, you can use the same resources and run a double crew over two shifts to get the job done faster without adding to the equipment and supply costs.

How Much Will It Cost?

As part of the plan, you almost certainly have to prepare a budget. I can't begin to predict your costs or even what items your budget should include. Instead I offer two actual expense sheets from previous moves, primarily to serve as examples of the kinds of expenses you might encounter.

Figure 2.1 is a list of actual expenses for a university move in 2004. The move required extensive planning, then last minute replanning because of a building completion issue. We moved some 300,000 books over five days with a crew of about eighteen students and some paid temporary workers. Library staff supervised and participated. A small move of staff effects and some library furniture occurred simultaneously. The library purchased thirty move carts and borrowed thirty more from me. (Note: This library had taken formal bids from move contractors before they contacted me. The turnkey bids ranged from $80,000 to $120,000; the do-it-yourself cost was $41,997.87, including my consulting fees.)

Figure 2.2 is the expense list from the move of Allen County Public Library into temporary quarters in 2001/2. We moved about 1.5 million storage items slowly over a period of several months with a single crew, storing these books in boxes in the basement. We moved about 300,000 books and 150,000 microfilms in eight days with a crew of about twenty staff and twenty temporary employees. Then we moved the last two million items in nine days using a crew of about one hundred at a time, twenty of whom were outside temporary workers. Also included are expenses for remodeling the building; tearing down, moving, and rebuilding shelves; and moving staff effects and a small amount of library furniture and equipment. (Note: This budget does not contain any cost for consultant or planning. Before we decided to do this move ourselves, we had a quote from a move consultant for $224,508 to plan, but not carry out, the move.)

Another move, 60,000–70,000 books over four days with a crew of about ten paid temporary workers and another ten unpaid conscripted students using borrowed move carts cost just over $7,000, more than half of which went to the company that moved the furniture.

As you develop your plan, you begin to get an idea of how many staff you need and for how long. Chapter 6 gives you some rule-of-thumb estimates of how many staff you need for a move. Difficult situations such as tight aisles, stairs that require a human chain, or major interfiling operations increase that number.

In general, your overhead—truck, forklift, rented carts, drivers and dock crews, dispatchers, and supervisors—costs the same whether it is used sparingly or at full capacity. The least expensive move is one that is balanced so there are enough move crews working simultaneously to keep the rest of the staff and equipment working at full capacity.

In addition to equipment and supplies mentioned throughout the book, you may incur miscellaneous costs such as these:

- printing floor plans
- copying—a move plan generates a lot of paper
- supplies such as tape, tie-down straps, or shrink-wrap that are not part of your usual stock, especially in the quantities you will need
- colored paper for flags, waypoints, and sequence cards
- temporary telephone, electric power, or HVAC costs
- dust cloths, lots of them
- costs to move copiers and other specialized equipment—owners of leased equipment often require you to use their moving services
- insurance to cover temporary employees

Who Will Plan and Carry Out Your Move?

Two of your earliest and most basic decisions concern who plans the move and who does the actual moving. Your options are to plan and carry out the move yourself; hire a professional mover for a turnkey job; or hire a consultant to help you plan and oversee the move. Because you are reading this book, I assume that you are at least considering the do-it-yourself option. Let's look briefly at the other two:

Professional Library Mover

About ten companies nationwide are in the business of moving libraries, and at least twenty more operate on a regional basis. Most, perhaps all, of these companies offer a turnkey moving service. For a fee they will

- measure your collection
- develop a detailed shelving plan, usually *very* detailed
- provide equipment, boxes, carts, and supplies for the move
- provide trucks and loading equipment
- bring in their own supervisors and hire local temporary employees to conduct the move
- provide book cleaning, shelf reading, interfiling, bar coding, stripping, shifting, and other specialized services as needed

300,000-VOLUME UNIVERSITY MOVE
ACTUAL COSTS

PAID TO	DESCRIPTION	COST
Materials and Supplies		
ACE Hardware	Straps, plywood, general materials	$165.59
Home Depot	Materials	$94.90
Home Depot	Masonite floor protection	$353.45
Walmart	Tape	$12.21
		$626.15
Book Truck Construction/Loan		
Gymtex	Move cart construction	$4,348.22
Home Depot	Tie-down straps	$253.92
Econolodge	Hank's hotel stay	$45.29
Thrifty Car Rental	Truck to Fort Wayne to borrow carts	$315.93
Gas	Gas for Thrifty truck	$45.00
		$5,008.36
Consultant		
Fortriede	Consulting	$18,655.00
Fortriede	Hotel room, 7 nights	$800.80
		$19,455.80
Temporary Labor		
NBC Personnel	Labor pool	**$8,807.61**
Office Mover		
Meyers Relocation Services	Office and staff effects move	**$7,007.00**
Other Expenses		
Thrifty Car Rental	Truck during move	$440.50
Young's Corner Market	Gas for Thrifty truck	$48.84
Owens, reimbursement	Food expenses for work crew	$109.60
Totten, reimbursement	Food expenses for work crew	$480.01
	Propane for forklift	$14.00
		$1,092.95
TOTAL MOVE COST		**$41,997.87**

Figure 2.1 Sample expense list, university library.

ACPL MOVE EXPENSES, 2002		
VENDOR	**DESCRIPTION**	**COST**
3M	Base plate units for security gates	$1,643.98
Beers, Mallers Backs & Salin	Legal fees for lease	$782.17
Binding, Inc.	Carpet evaluation Ren Sq	$100.00
Frank Brook	Signs for Ren Sq	$3,866.00
Contract Furniture Maintenance	Install office landscape panels	$48,175.45
Contract Furniture Maintenance	Book stack relocation	$53,000.00
Current Mechanical	Steel dock plates	$248.00
Duffy's	Box sealing tape	$586.33
Duffy's	Box sealing tape	$383.04
Duffy's	Hand tape dispensers	$119.94
Duffy's	Box sealing tape	$574.56
Exponents of Indiana	Move phone system to Ren Sq	$19,485.00
FCS Groups	In-wall book return	$1,048.00
H P Products	Cleaning supplies	$804.38
Hollander Storage & Moving	Move staff effects & furniture	$59,128.50
Instant Copy	Copies of building plan Ren Sq	$24.00
Irmscher	Brace book shelves	$6,804.00
Kelly Box & Packaging Corp	40,000 boxes for long-term storage	$56,341.22
Koehlinger Security	Rekey exterior locks at Ren Sq	$689.70
C. H. Kraus, LLC	Cut down uprights for shelving	$4,972.00
Martin	Dumpster rental	$2,623.51
Microfix	Move all equipment (copiers)	$479.00
Micro Warehouse	HP Jet directs move Sirsi printer	$595.53
Midwest United Companies	Pallets	$2,175.00
MSKTD & Associates, Inc.	Architectural design for Ren Sq	$13,155.00
Otis Elevator Co.	Survey of elevator Ren Sq	$1,500.00
Peters Woodworking	Book moving carts	$28,119.76
Ris Paper Company	Pallet stretch wrap & dispenser	$376.36
Ris Paper Company	Stretch wrap	$93.69
U-Haul	Rental of truck, 7 months	$10,418.70
Verizon Wireless	Cell phones	$94.00
Wages for temporary workers		$77,474.88
TOTAL		**$395,881.70**

Figure 2.2 Sample expense list, large public library.

- coordinate, do themselves, or write bid specifications for moves of furniture, personal effects, shelves, and so forth
- clean up after themselves and leave you ready to open

If you have the money, or if you don't have the time, staff, and confidence to do the move yourself, the professional library mover may be your best option. Don't, however, assume that you and your staff can escape all involvement. You will be involved in the work of measuring your collection. At the least you will provide someone to guide the movers through your collection to make sure they measure everything and in the correct order, including remote collections to be interfiled. You will be very involved in the collection layout. You and your staff must work with whatever arrangement is settled upon; it is much better for you to involve yourself in the planning than to shift the collection after everyone else has taken their money and gone home.

Even if you use a professional mover, you will probably appoint a move coordinator from your staff to act as liaison. During the move, you should at least plan to have someone on site to monitor that everything is being done carefully, accurately, and according to your expectations.

If you engage a library mover, be careful to determine whether the company you select has actual experience moving a library. Many office and general moving companies advertise that they can move libraries. These companies may have considerable experience and all the right equipment to move your furniture and personal effects but lack either equipment or expertise to move large quantities of books, keeping them all in strict order. Check thoroughly and make sure.

If you hire a mover, you solicit prices and other information about the company through a formal document—a quote, a request for proposals, a bid, or some other form. State or local law may limit which processes you can use and what level of detail is required. Check with your attorney to determine which method is appropriate for you.

In addition to the usual "boilerplate," make certain that the following items are covered in the proposal or contract documents:

- What items are to be moved and how many of each kind. Include books, other library materials, furniture, equipment, and anything else you expect to be moved. Typically when I write such specifications, I give the best possible estimate for the size of the move but write a stipulation that, if the actual number falls within X percent larger or smaller than the estimate, the contractor will be paid exactly the bid or quoted price. If the actual number falls outside that range, the price is adjusted up or down according to some agreed-upon formula. This construct reduces the points of conflict over small variances.

- The timetable, and what costs are incurred if the timetable has to be adjusted by the library. If the contractor has to work double shifts because the building was not done on time, you should expect to pay overtime or shift differentials. The mover will have other jobs pending. If your schedule slips into one of these, the mover may have to hire additional crew, lease an extra truck, or incur other costs. The contract should state how these costs will be passed on to you. Also include a penalty to be paid to you if the contractor does not complete the move within the specified time frame.

- Who is responsible for preparing and protecting the buildings, what level of protection is required, and what damages must be compensated. Also specify who is to remove the protections after the move is done. Typically these provisions cover buildings and people. You may want to specify what protections are required for the books and what damages are to be paid if books are damaged. A mover might, for instance, skip the step of shrinkwrapping carts to save time. If the books rattle off the cart, or if the cart upsets, books can be damaged. Make sure the document clearly assigns responsibility for your materials, and you may want to go even further to specify special handling for rare or valuable materials.

- Insurance and indemnities to protect your building, people, and materials and to protect the library from acts of negligence by the mover.

- What labor will be used, who will supply and administer them, and what minimum qualifications the workers must have. Require a criminal background check. If any part of the move will take place while the library is open to the public, request a sex offender check as well.

- Some movers request, require, or base their price on uninterrupted access to a loading dock. If they must share dock space or use some other entrance, make sure that is noted in your original request for a price and that it is specified in the contract.
- Include wording that describes the type and size of your collection, furnishings, shelves, or whatever is being moved. Require evidence that the company has moved other libraries the same size or larger. I have seen advertisements from commercial movers who have moved one or two small libraries and therefore believe they are qualified as library movers. There is an enormous difference between moving a 10,000-volume library and moving a 100,000- or 1,000,000-volume collection. The difference is one of quality even more than quantity.
- If you have collections that require special handling, describe them thoroughly and specify exactly what handling is acceptable.
- Require that every contractor tour both the origin and destination buildings with a library representative. Require them to sign a statement that they have had the opportunity to see the collections and conditions of the move.

Do not just sign whatever contract is offered, no matter how "standard" it is said to be. Make sure you are satisfied that it fits your needs and your collection.

Move Consultant

Several of the national moving firms provide a consulting service. For a fee they help you with any part of the move you cannot do yourself. My contract work for the past few years has been of this nature.

Most of the real work of a move is simple and straightforward. You pick up a book, box it or put it on a cart, move it, and reshelve it in its new location. We all do collection shifts and small moves. However, as the move becomes larger and more complex, other skills are required. Measuring the collection, planning the new layout, calculating growth, devising a move plan, and overseeing the move itself are skills that most of us use only once or twice in a career. We never get much experience with them and we have little opportunity to learn from our mistakes. In this case a move consultant can save you both time and money.

It is important to hire the consultant early in the process, before you commit to a particular move method and certainly before you move any books. Several times I have interviewed for consultant jobs only to find out that the library had already moved some books, usually into storage. Never once did the library measure the books first. One library had the books moved by their maintenance department and made no attempt even to keep the books in order. The experience of the move consultant would temper the early decisions and can save much unnecessary expenditure of time and money.

Hiring a move consultant may be a less formal process than hiring a firm to do a turnkey move for you, if for no other reason than that the cost is likely to be less. The degree of formality of the process is often triggered by the expected cost of the project. The agreement with the consultant should spell out exactly which duties and responsibilities fall to the consultant and which remain with the library. Typically a consultant's fee covers personal services only, but even then you should specify what travel, communication, and other expenses are to be reimbursed and how they are to be documented. Occasionally the consultant is made responsible for supplying move carts or boxes or for paying the workers, with the costs to be included in the consultant's fee. If so, these items must be carefully specified.

Many of the specifications included in a bid request or contract with a turnkey mover are not part of the initial agreement with a consultant. To prepare a bid or a request for proposals, you need to measure your collection, establish a rough timetable, and specify enough conditions of the move that potential movers can base their price on a common understanding of the work to be done. In contrast, it is usually part of the consultant's

TIP

Generally it is more cost-effective for the library to pay costs directly. When consultants are responsible, they have to pay the same amounts as would the library, but they also mark up the cost to cover overhead, insurance, and other costs. Additionally, a consultant is working in a new community and does not have local contacts and sources for needed materials and supplies and thus may incur higher costs, plus travel expenses, that offset any advantage to the library.

job to take the measurements, help you establish the timetable, and decide the best way to conduct the move. For that reason, many consultants are paid at an hourly rate for the actual time spent.

There is a middle ground. You may find it worthwhile to hire a consultant just to help plan your move, measure and lay out the collections, and hire a moving company to do the actual book move. The consultant works for you and has every incentive to keep your costs low.

Do You Stay Open during the Move?

This is another basic decision. If at all possible, you should try to keep patrons out of your buildings during the move, for their safety as well as for the efficiency of the move operations. If you decide to maintain some level of service during your move, you must consider the implications throughout your planning. Even a small point such as the best route from a block of shelves to the loading dock may have to be changed if the preferred route crosses a pathway that might be used by an unwary patron.

A move is more efficient and entails less risk to everyone if you can keep all nonessential personnel, staff as well as patrons, out of the building and out of the way. Do not underestimate the potential danger of having patrons in the same area as the move crews. You can train movers to be safety conscious, but you cannot do that effectively with the public.

Another potential problem during a move is theft, not only of books but of computers and other equipment. During the move, there are many strangers in the building, some in nonpublic areas. Books, equipment, and furnishings disappear from view as they are packed and moved. An unauthorized disappearance that would be immediately noted at any other time may be ignored in the disruption of the move.

Sometimes you do not have the option to close completely. If a university library cannot move during a semester break, students still need access to resources. Public library patrons sometimes expect service throughout the move.

The best way to provide service is to complete the move as quickly and accurately as possible and get the library back to full service with minimum downtime. Sometimes even that is not enough, and you may need to plan for some or all services to remain available through the move.

Full Service

If you provide full service during the move, your plan needs more detail about which collections move when. You need a tight timetable and you have less flexibility about how you assign work crews. Even such things as elevator use and travel routes must be included in the plan. Here are some things you can try:

- Consolidate all services at one desk, close to an entrance. The space is likely to be crowded, but it may help to keep patrons concentrated away from the move workers. You can assign staff, trained in the safety precautions, as runners to fetch books for patrons.
- Confine your move to one specific department or area at a time. Rope off a safety zone around the space. Mark off a safe travel path to the loading dock. If necessary, post traffic wardens at places where the public might cross the path.
- An ever-increasing percentage of your materials will be located in the new building. At any given moment your patrons will not know where to find a specific item. You could create a monitoring system to track the progress of the move crews and keep staff and patrons up to date about which materials have already been transported. You still have to decide whether to set up a system to retrieve books from the new building, operate service points in both buildings, or just consider the books in the new building unavailable at the moment.
- Once a majority of the materials have been moved, you might shift the service point to the new building. The same problems of access, safety, and availability of materials apply.
- Move the least essential materials first, or last, to keep the bulk of the most needed items intact as long as possible.
- You can move at night when the library is normally closed, probably paying a higher cost for workers. You would also have to assume that whatever staff worked on the move at night would not be available for public service the next day.

Minimal Service

It is much easier, safer, and less disruptive to maintain a lower level of service during the move. There are some services you really must provide and others you can provide with little effort and cost.

Service desk. Find a place where you can set up a service point away from the bustle of the move. Mark off the safe area around it with caution tape. A space near your front door is ideal, unless you are using that door as your loading dock. Install a computer for check-in or checkout, telephones, and whatever other equipment you might need. The service point can be in either building. People seem to find it more easily in the old building. Also, the telephone and computer systems may not be fully installed and tested in the new building, so it may be better to stay in the old one. It may be difficult to keep people from wandering around to get a sneak preview of the beautiful new building.

Returns. Set up an area where patrons can return material. No matter how widely you publicize your move, some people don't get the word and show up at your door expecting service. At the very least they expect to return books that are due. Plan to set up an area where you can receive and store returned materials. Ideally you will check them in and store them on shelves where they can be kept in order, ready to be boxed or put on carts as the last step in the move. Find an area of shelving close to your service point and arrange to move those books first, opening the shelves for storage and interfiling of returns. You can use staff who are not able to be actively involved in the move to receive materials, check them in, and arrange them in order on the shelves. Make an effort to keep these staff up to date on the progress of the move. They will get a lot of questions.

> **LOADING DOCK**
>
> This is the area where you load and unload carts to and from a truck for transport between buildings. It may or may not be an area designed as a loading dock. It may well be the hallway to the staff door opening into your parking lot. Wherever it is located, we'll call it the loading dock.
>
> The best circumstance is a flat dock, perfectly matched to the height of your truck, with plenty of climate-controlled, covered space to stage and prepare carts, an adjacent elevator, and easy access to all parts of the building. If you are really out of luck, it is the front door of your Carnegie building with twelve steps down to the street and no place to park the truck.

> **TIP**
>
> When you check out books in the last weeks before your move, adjust the loan period so no books are due during the time you expect to be closed. This reduces the number of people who need to come to your building while you are moving and the number of books you have to handle twice. Make up a bookmark or flyer explaining that the loan period is extended this one time only. Invite patrons to return the books at your beautiful new building. Give the date when they can begin to return books and provide a map to your new location. Make this a positive PR piece and an invitation to the new building.

Reserves pickup. Use book carts or spare shelves to put holds or reserve materials close to the service point. Many patrons depend heavily on holds for their reading and are distressed, or worse, if a book they have waited for for weeks is held up even longer because of the move. In a university, student access to course reserve material may be crucial. Some of the material being returned is likely to have holds on it, especially in a public library. Decide whether to process these holds on the spot or wait until the move is complete before you make them available to the next user. Staff accordingly and provide the necessary equipment.

Renewals. If books are due during the time you are closed, you should provide a way for patrons to renew them. The easiest way to resolve this problem is to adjust the due date so that no materials are due until you reopen. This eliminates any need for a patron to renew books during the closed period. If you cannot or do not adjust the loan period, it is relatively easy to set up a circulation terminal and renew materials at the service point. Alternatively, you can just forgive any fines on materials that came due during the move. This may be a preferred alternative if you cannot predict how long you will be closed.

Reference service. It is relatively easy to set up a telephone reference service in some room away from the activity of the move. You can serve walk-in reference patrons from a back-room location by installing a telephone at the service point. We approached this service by challenging the librarians to select the one hundred most critical books they needed in the room with them, along with their computers, knowing they would not have access to any other books during the move. After

TIP

If you forgive fines or extend the due date for materials due during the move, be precise in explaining which fees will not be charged for which days and explain why. An exact statement helps your staff deal with other patrons who may argue that they too should be included in the general amnesty.

several meetings, the librarians demanded two hundred books. After two weeks, they were quite surprised to find they had used only forty-five of them.

Computer room. Access to computers has become one of the most essential library services. Some patrons depend on library computers to keep in touch with friends, seek employment, pay bills, and do other critical tasks. If your library will be closed for an extended time, you may want to plan some accommodation for these patrons.

Study area. School or university libraries may need to provide a study area for students. For safety and quiet, try to locate this room away from the move area, perhaps in a classroom or other space that can be repurposed for the duration of the move. This room should not open onto the routes being used to move books.

Will You Clean, Strip, Bar Code, or Inventory Books during the Move?

Planners are often asked to include other tasks in the overall move. The argument is made that "since the books are off the shelf anyway," the other tasks can be done more efficiently. Okay, let's think this through:

Moving your collection, your staff, your furniture, and your equipment and rebuilding your services in a new location is one of the most complex tasks you will do in your professional life. It calls on all your planning, management, and interpersonal skills. It requires the utmost of vision and dedication. It taxes your strength and will, physically, mentally, and emotionally. Do you really want to make it harder?

I prefer to handle processing tasks as a project separated in time from the book move. Ideally any book-by-book tasks take place prior to the move. This identifies any out-of-place books and gets them properly filed before the move starts. The extra handling of each book individually during the move greatly increases the chance that something will get out of order. The overhead costs for dock crew, drivers, truck rental, and forklift are carried over a longer period. You have to acquire additional carts or boxes, since you will have more of them tied up in transit or at the processing station. The total cost of your move is very likely to increase rather than produce a savings.

If you must clean books, do it in the weeks prior to the move. Test-clean a few hundred books to see if cleaning makes enough difference to justify the cost. Even the dirtiest books may need to be cleaned only on their top edge. Books with fragile pages and desiccated leather bindings should be treated as a conservation project. Seal them in plastic bags to move them.

What Will You Do with Staff Not Involved in the Move?

You may have staff who are not actively involved in the move, because

- you selected a turnkey vendor
- you have a union that forbids work outside contractually specified duties
- you have staff who are fully engaged in their regular duties; after all, someone has to do the payroll
- you have staff who are physically unable to do the work of the move
- you have staff who are able but unwilling to do the work of the move

In the last case, able but unwilling, you have a decision to make. Do you allow your staff the option not to participate? I prefer to move with willing helpers. A move is a team-building experience without peer, and, at the end, those who have been through it together tend to be extremely proud of their contribution. My experience is that even people who choose to sit out the move become swept up in it and eventually decide to participate. On the other hand, even one unwilling worker who complains, malingers, ignores the process designed to keep materials in order, or otherwise subverts the move is a real detriment.

You must make your decision based on the dynamics of your own staff situation. If you have staff who are unable to push carts or lift boxes but who do want to help, there are many jobs available that do not require physical labor. On a large move, you might have some or all of these jobs available:

- solicit prizes and giveaways
- bake cookies or make chili
- plan and organize lunches and snacks
- operate the dispatch desks
- prepare way-finding and stack signs
- clean up and recycle cardboard
- organize supplies, keep the master list of what sequence cards are assigned to which collections, and update the drawings to show what has been moved
- direct furniture and office movers to the proper rooms
- staff a service point or telephone reference desk to provide minimal services
- check in returned materials and sort them onto the return shelves
- measure the collections—shoot the shelves and strings (see chapter 4)
- edit a newsletter for staff

On one move, we had to assign a crew to scour the building and identify all of the missing or burned-out lightbulbs. On another we stationed a person to direct traffic at a busy blind intersection to prevent cart crashes. You can find worthwhile odd jobs for any of your staff who are willing to help.

You still have to decide what to do with the staff who are not working on the move. First, you need to determine what options are open to you. You may be constrained by legal or contractual requirements. In many jurisdictions you cannot move people and their effects into a building until a government agency or building department has issued a certificate of occupancy (contractors call it a "C of O") or other approval. This process is the government's control to make certain the building has been constructed according to code and that any other requirements were complied with. If the building is not fully or very nearly completed, or is not in compliance, you can't get the certificate. If you don't have the certificate, you can't move in.

At times we have been able to get a temporary certificate of occupancy to allow us to move in books but not people. In other cases we have argued successfully that the books are part of the furnishings and thus not subject to the certificate. Your contractor and architect can tell you what requirements are in force in your jurisdiction. Keep in close touch with them as you get close to the move day. A delay in the certificate process could upset your entire move schedule.

While we are on the subject, make certain your elevators have been inspected before your move date. In many states the elevator inspection is done by a state agency, separate from the local agency that issues the certificate of occupancy. You cannot use your elevators if they have not been certified.

You may find that your construction contracts prevent you from moving in until the building has reached a certain degree of completion. Construction areas have their own dangers, and construction crews have standards of safety that are trained and ingrained into them. They have safety officers to enforce their rules. As librarians, we are as untrained and inexperienced in that environment as one of the builders would be interfiling government documents. The contractors may not want you in the building until they have completed their work and cleaned up the area. They certainly do not want you in areas where they are working overhead, painting, finishing drywall, or doing electrical work. In fact, you do not want to put books, let alone people, into that environment either.

On a large move, you may have to start moving books while substantial construction is still in progress. Conditions of your access should have been included in the construction contracts. If not, or if the terms prove unfavorable, you should be able to negotiate access to parts of the building that are finished or nearly so. Negotiate for a safe route to the area and ask that you be informed before any further construction is done in the area where you have placed your books. If drywall finishing or sanding is being done anywhere in the building, ask that the contractor place additional filter material in the ductwork leading to the areas in which you are working. Drywall dust, in particular, gets everywhere. When it gets on books, it is difficult to remove.

Talk to the contractor's safety officer about your plans and ask the safety officer to do an orientation or training program for your workers.

It is usually not difficult to place those staff members who have jobs that continue during the move. As much as possible, leave them in their usual workspaces until they can move to the new building. Make sure they are warned about possible move traffic in their immediate area. If the workspace fronts on a hallway or other area being used for move traffic, post a sign on the inside of the door reminding anyone who exits the room to look both ways before stepping outside.

Staff whose regular jobs have been preempted by the move but who are not participating in the actual move may be more of a problem. Keep nonworking personnel out of the spaces where people are moving books. Aside from the danger of accident or injury, nonworking spectators can be a real morale killer. It is bad when a spectator offers advice or instructions to the move crews. Worst of all is when the spectators heckle the workers. Those persons must be removed from the area immediately and very visibly. This is one of those times when the director needs to be seen loading boxes or pushing a cart.

One of the worst major disasters I ever got involved with happened when a strong-willed but nonparticipating department manager took it upon herself to rearrange her whole department, including the shelving layout, after the move started.

You can find other options for nonparticipants:

- encourage them to take vacation or other time off
- put them on leave, paid or unpaid
- plan intensive in-service training and staff development opportunities
- send staff to branches or to nearby libraries as a training or staff-exchange program
- catch up on collection development, processing, and other long-term projects

MOVE TEAM OPERATIONS

Most of the move team's work is done before the move ever starts. The major responsibilities are as follows:

- plan the move and prepare the budget and timetable
- identify and acquire the necessary equipment and supplies
- determine who is to do the physical work of the move and hire or assign those persons
- carry out the move, possibly including moves of people and their effects, furnishings and equipment, shelving, and computers and communications equipment

All of these responsibilities are described in detail throughout this book. Other considerations are addressed below.

Communication

Recognize from the outset that a move is a traumatic event for all concerned. Your staff will be worried about the move, unsure of their ability to do whatever work is asked of them, concerned about their new workspace, and uncertain of their ability to work effectively in a space that they have not yet seen. Over time, people develop work habits with which they are comfortable. It may be so small a thing as a file cabinet placed to the right, not the left, or a place to set a favorite plant. Often seemingly insignificant details take on an unwarranted importance.

Expect your entire staff to be intensely curious about all aspects of the move. They will look to the move team as the source of all information, very likely for things that go well beyond the scope of the move team. It is to your benefit to be open about the process:

Publish minutes. Publish minutes of move team meetings.

Post the schedule. As soon as you have even a tentative schedule, post it. Make sure everyone knows it is *tentative,* and promise, and deliver, updates as soon as they are available.

Hold frequent Q&A meetings open to all staff. Answer all questions as directly as possible. "I don't know" and "We haven't started that part of the plan" are direct answers but only if you follow up when you do have more information.

When possible, offer tours of the new building. Wait until it is finished enough that you can point out where furniture will go and where each person's workspace will be located. You may have to arrange a special time with the contractor, but it is well worth the effort. Once staff have seen the space and can begin to visualize themselves at work, the anxiety level goes down and enthusiasm increases.

Listen to people. Really listen. Most of the concerns are nothing more than general expressions of anxiety. Once in a while, you find out something really important. On one of my jobs, the early planning had been done by the buildings and grounds staff. At my first meeting, the planners warned me about a librarian who was becoming a "nuisance." Sure enough, at the end of the day she accosted me on my way to dinner. Her space was too small, she wouldn't be able to provide services, she didn't have enough room. She was so frantic I went back to her office to go over the plans with her. Everything looked fine on paper, but she was insistent. Finally,

I got her to help me measure the collection. Oops! She had told the planners she had 152,000 books. Someone transposed numbers and entered 125,000. Her planned shelving was one hundred sections too small. The next day we presented our evidence to the planners and found room to fit in some extra shelving. Had that librarian not made a "nuisance" of herself, we would have encountered a major disaster with few options to correct it.

Publish a newsletter. This is a great way to communicate. Think up a catchy title. Find some fun graphics. Keep it short, to the point, colorful, and publish it regularly (figure 2.3). Include information about the move, updates to the schedule, exhortations to clean up workspaces, instructions on how to pack and label, safety, and the like. We have found it useful to include a Q&A column. If you get legitimate questions, answer them. If not, you can make up your own questions and provide the answers. It is a great format for rumor control.

Use technology. The vast array of electronic communication tools can help you keep everyone informed. Homemade videos are an excellent way to demonstrate packing and labeling techniques. Make certain you match the medium to the message. Much of your information is for internal use only and should not be placed where it can be accessed by the public. Other communications are addressed specifically to the public.

Slimming Down

If you don't have it, you don't have to move it.

Librarians are notorious pack rats. It is in our nature to collect, organize, and preserve. Sometimes we're not so picky about the organize part. One task of the move team is to encourage, entice, cajole, inveigle, beguile, exhort, or otherwise motivate people to throw away things they do not need.

Weed the book collection. It makes no sense whatsoever to move a book you're going to throw away. Empty out files. Keep what you really need but get rid of the rest. Go through the supply cabinets. Do you really need typewriter ribbons? Forms that are yellowed with age? Lightbulbs for the movie projector that died in 19whatever?

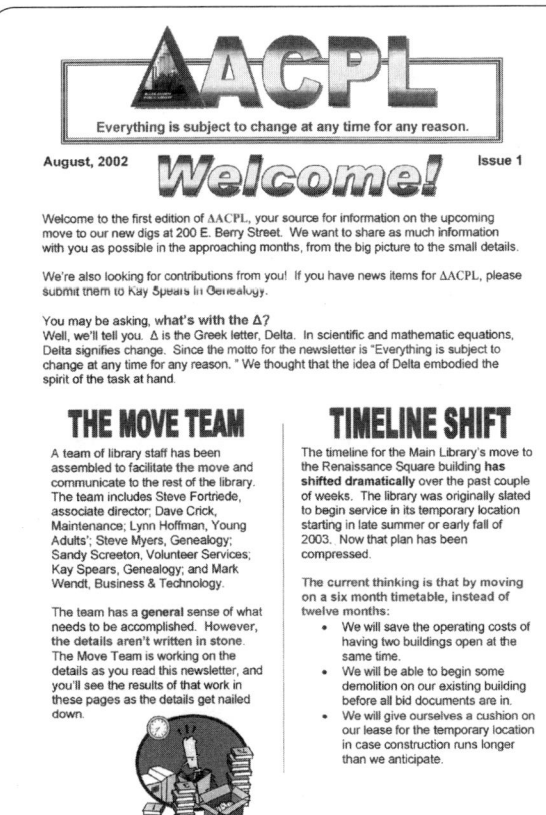
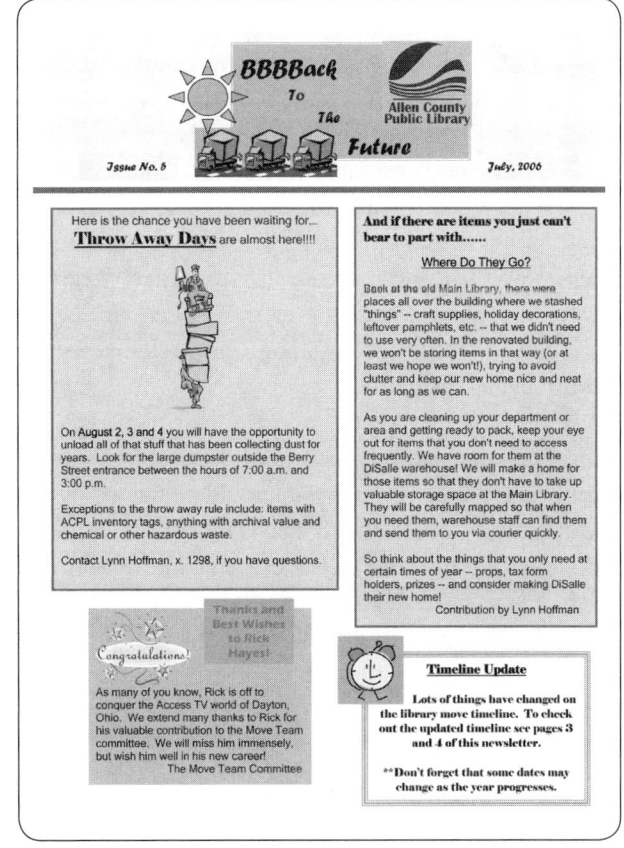

Figure 2.3 A newsletter is a great communication tool. Publish frequently and regularly.

Form a team of department managers and administrators and walk through the entire building. Identify all the items you no longer need: pieces of shelving; broken equipment you have kept for parts; boxes you kept to return equipment long out of warranty; packing material; old chairs. Recycle what you can and throw away the rest.

One technique is to hold one or more "Dumpster days." Rent a large Dumpster for a few days and encourage staff to dispose of everything they no longer need. Limit the period the Dumpster is available to reduce procrastination. Try to have a roving team of two or three people to help with moving large or heavy objects. At one library we had to station a guard at the Dumpster to keep staff from hauling things right back into the building.

Packing

Another task you may have is to make sure all staff have packed their personal effects properly and on time. If you use a professional mover for your furniture and staff effects, the mover has boxes sized to their dollies and a labeling system to which their staff is accustomed. They show your staff how to pack and label, but they do not stay on site to ensure that it is done. The move team may have the responsibility to monitor the progress of packing and labeling. It is natural to keep essential tools and working files available until the last minute, but some people have very different interpretations of what is essential. What is really essential is that everything be packed, labeled, and ready to go when the movers appear. Their move plan, and the price they quoted, depends on having immediate access to everything in an area at the same time. If they have to wait, or come back for the "last minute" items, they charge you extra.

Some staff may prefer to move their own personal items. It is reasonable to discourage, but not forbid, this. If an item is library property, it should be moved by the library's hired contractor. It may make sense to allow individuals to move their own personal mementos, pictures, plants, and other items of personal property if they so desire. It may help give some people a feeling that they have at least a little control over their part of the move.

Layout Planning

In some moves, the move team is tasked to determine shelving layouts or even to assign offices and workspaces, but I consider this inappropriate. Certainly the individuals on the move team are likely to have the most complete knowledge of the new building, the latest information on the size of the various collections, and possibly the clearest view of how it will all come together. They have the resources to do the planning accurately.

However, the move team has authority outside of the normal organizational structure and may not include many of the people who have a stake in the ongoing operation of the library after the move. For that reason, the assignment of offices and workspaces and the placement and general flow of collections should be decided by department managers and administrators. The planners on the move team should be assigned to work as support staff to those decision makers during this phase of the planning process.

The Move Team during the Move

Some move team members have specific tasks to perform during the move. A team member tasked to the FFE move is likely unavailable for other tasks. Team members who hold specific portfolios may find themselves fully occupied. Other members may be designated to supervise move crews. We usually station the personnel/morale officer at the dispatch desk in the origin building at the start of the move and shift that person's base of operations to the destination at about the halfway point. The move coordinator, of course, is expected to be everywhere, all of the time.

A useful way to track the move is to keep a whiteboard or other chart at the origin dispatch desk. The dispatcher records the starting waypoint for each crew assigned and the color of the sequence cards assigned to that crew. When the crew finishes a task, the dispatcher lines out or erases that record. If the crew has not finished at the end of the day, the dispatcher records the last sequence card used. This method tracks progress and makes it easy to plan the next day's starting assignments.

The move team should plan to meet as a body at least once every day of the move to review progress, problems, personnel, and morale issues and to fine-tune the work plan for the next day. It seems to work best to schedule a meeting an hour or so before quitting time; this keeps the meetings short and leaves time to implement any decisions made. The meetings should be brief and focus on upcoming tasks and opportunities. These are not planning meetings. If you have supervisors who were not part of the move team, include them in these meetings. It works well to hold these meetings in the origin, within sight of the dispatcher's whiteboard.

You may want to schedule brief "check-in" sessions at lunchtime with the people most responsible for carrying out the move.

Schedule a meeting for the first day of the move with all staff and workers to introduce everyone to the project, discuss safety, talk about work schedules and other details, and make the initial job assignments. This meeting is described in detail in chapter 10. It is best to hold one meeting for all staff and to hold it at the origin building. Yes, some of the crew will have to travel to the destination building before they can start work, but it is worth the time to make certain everyone hears the introduction at the same time in the same way. In chapter 10, I offer ways to begin the move to minimize the lost travel time.

If your buildings are any distance apart, you may have to duplicate any subsequent meetings, one in each location. If you provide a lunch, you may want to offer it in both locations to cut travel time.

You need a brief start-up meeting each day, just to cover any changes made the day before and to assign the work for the day. The move coordinator can conduct the morning briefing at one building, and the personnel officer or a supervisor can handle the other. These are informal meetings. Often we just tell each group its assignment and any other information they may need as they arrive and send them on their way. If you have contests running or a special lunch that day, this is the time to remind people.

The End

By the time the move nears completion, the move coordinator and the supervisors have become good at setting up "skipaheads" (see chapter 4) to clear backlogs, at assigning crews and resources to clear up leftover collections and finish the small tasks, and at moving workers around so that everyone is working at maximum efficiency. The result is that most moves do not just trickle out; they end, not with a whimper, but with a sudden crash. One minute everyone is working at full speed, and the next the job is done—there is nothing more to do. The feeling of anticlimax can be almost overwhelming. I have known people to shed tears.

At the end of the move, you may be surprised to find that people don't want to quit. There is an incredible feeling of accomplishment that accompanies the completion of a successful move. Describe it as you will—pride, teamwork, camaraderie, doing the impossible, endorphin rush, the thrill of victory—whatever it is, people don't want to give it up.

Plan some event or activity to mark the end of the move. The grand opening won't do it. That will be a celebration for the whole community. Plan an event specifically for the people who participated in the move. Don't even invite the staff who did not participate lest you cheapen the reward for those who did the work. Schedule this meeting closely after the move is completed but not necessarily on the last day. Because you may not know much in advance when the move will be finished, you need to plan something that can be flexible with regard to timing. Here are a few ideas:

Conduct tours of the new facility for the workers and their families. Few of the workers will have seen the whole building. Those working at the origin building may not even have seen it. They will welcome the sneak preview and the chance to show off to family the great work of which they were a part. Whenever possible, a tour, even an informal one, should be part of the closure.

A pizza party is always popular.

On one move we gathered on the last evening for a carry-in picnic and a ceremonial burning of the boxes.

If you used book carts or if you built move carts, ask all of the workers to sign one cart. Display that at the grand opening. If you don't have something iconic to sign, pick a section of shelving and ask the workers to sign the underside of the shelves. Great artists always sign their work.

Hold the Move Olympics. Let people show off the skills they have developed. Award prizes to the winners. Don't play games with the forklift. Don't ride the carts and dollies. Events could include

- *Speed loading.* Teams of two load one side of a cart or four boxes. Side-by-side competition. Fastest team advances.
- *Box drag.* Stack up empty boxes and drag them a short distance. Tallest stack with no spills wins. The pro course includes stairs.
- *Spilled book re-sort.* Two contestants, two tables, twenty books spilled randomly on each table. Put

them in order. Timed event. Five seconds penalty for every book out of order.
- *Cart/dolly obstacle course.* Best run in and around the empty stacks at your origin building.
- *Eagle eye.* Two sections of books in perfect order. Referee randomly misfiles five books per section. Head-to-head competition. First contestant to find and fix all five advances. Contestant who misfiles a book is disqualified. This is an Olympic-level event.

I've never done it, but a talented person could put together an awards program/celebrity roast. Mix legitimate awards or certificates of appreciation with less serious awards that recognize memorable events or personalities from the move. Have somebody vet the script in advance to maintain a modicum of good taste.

I get my greatest satisfaction from walking through the now-emptied origin building after everyone else is gone. It feels somewhat like walking over the field after a victorious battle.

Selecting a Method

Early in the planning process, you must decide how you are going to transport your books. Detailed instructions for each method are included in later chapters. Here I provide a general overview to help you make your initial decisions.

At various times I have used five different methods to move library materials: stack movers, human chains, boxes, book carts, and move carts. The first two have specific, limited uses.

STACK MOVERS

Stack movers can be used to move an entire range of stack, without removing the books. Each mover consists of a vertical arm with a clamp at the top and wheels on the bottom. A stack mover clamps to each upright. A jack on each mover lifts the entire range just enough to clear the floor. The range can be moved, carefully, and jacked back down to allow the stack movers to be reused on another range. Stack movers are incredibly efficient but are limited to moves on a flat floor, with no doorways shorter than the stacks and no corners tight enough that the stack cannot be turned. They are most often used in recarpeting operations where the stacks are all moved out of the way, then returned once the new carpet is down.

Several companies can supply stack movers for rent. Some also supply an operator or foreman.

HUMAN CHAINS

For small, short moves, consider using a human chain. Line up a group of volunteers and pass the books down the line one handful at a time. I know of a church library (approximately 3,000 volumes) that moved into a new room about 200 feet away using this method. It took about forty volunteers and less than two hours.

I have used the method several times to get books up or down stairs where no elevator was available. We looked at all sorts of conveyors, sleds, temporary lifts, and many other "labor-saving" ideas. In the end, the human chain has always been the easiest and most reliable solution. By the time you buy or rent the equipment, pay someone to set it up and sometimes to run it, modify the building as necessary, get the books to the starting point, provide power or fuel, and deal with mechanical breakdowns or just unfamiliar equipment, the time, expense, and uncertainty can exceed any savings.

Turn on some music. Get up a pool and give a prize to the person who comes closest to guessing the fastest time the crew can move enough books to fill one cart or a stack of boxes. Encourage chatter. Call out when a book is extra heavy or slippery. Make it as much fun as you can, so it isn't boring beyond belief. I did one job bringing 50,000 books two flights down a circular staircase in a Victorian mansion. It took two and a half days, in August, with no air-conditioning. The camaraderie was incredible! At the end, the crew was begging for more.

The problem, of course, is that a chain, even the human kind, is only as strong as the weakest member. There is also the problem that the chain cannot operate at all if any one member is not present.

If the move is a large one and there is no elevator, you may have to use a lift, conveyor, or slide. The larger the move, the more cost-effective such assists can be. The cost of acquiring and setting up the equipment and any building modifications is spread over a larger number of books. If you use a lift, get someone familiar with its operation to set it up, certify its load-bearing capacity, and make any necessary building modifications.

A conveyor is more expensive than a simple slide, but it is a preferred option. A conveyor controls the speed of descent and can be run in reverse in case you have to move empty boxes back to an upper level. A conveyor can be used to move single books to be loaded onto a cart. Doing this with a slide is much slower; you cannot start one book down the slide until the previous book has been removed. To send boxes of books down a slide, you need a long, flat runout area at the bottom, or you can place a piece of carpet or other high-friction material at the bottom of the slide to slow the boxes. I have never tried a slide, but I have seen others do it.

BOXES

Simple, right? Just box up the books and move them. Let me try to talk you out of it:

- Carts are heavy to push, but boxes are heavy to lift. Over the course of a day, I can push much more than I can lift.
- You need to take extra care in planning the move to reduce the number of times you have to stack and restack boxes. Every restacking introduces the possibility that they will get out of order.
- Boxes are hard to come by, unless you need only enough for a small collection. If they are too big, they are hard to lift; if not all the same size, they won't stack well; if not strong and well made, they fall apart. If you buy good, strong boxes, they are relatively expensive.
- Boxes require hand trucks, dollies, pallet jacks, or some other conveyance to move them. It may be more difficult and expensive to assemble these items in sufficient quantity than to buy or rent carts.
- If you try to pack boxes full, the books get out of order; if you pack them with the books standing up, as they would be on the shelf, you have a lot of wasted space in each box.
- If you use volunteers or nonlibrarians to pack, it is relatively difficult to monitor how well they keep the books in order in the boxes.

This is not to say that boxes don't work. They do, and for collections up to 10,000 volumes or so, that may be the way to go. I have moved many libraries with boxes, most of them much larger than 10,000 volumes.

There is one circumstance where I do recommend boxes: if you need to store books for a length of time, boxes, properly constructed and stacked, work effectively. See chapter 12 for suggestions for storage of books in boxes, including the specifications for a professionally engineered cardboard box storage system.

If you do decide to move with boxes, there are several things to think about:

Box Types

Boxes for moving books must be strong; easy to lift and carry; have a closed top; and, above all, be all the same size. The strength of a box comes from the cardboard material itself as well as the method of construction. The strength of cardboard is measured by its "crush weight." A box for moving books should have a crush weight of at least 230 lbs—enough to hold the weight of the books and allow the boxes to be stacked.

The method of construction also affects the strength. A box that is folded up and simply glued is least strong (figure 3.1, left). The flap can tear loose under stress. The figure shows the most common type. A box with the end panels glued and reinforced with heavy-duty staples is much stronger (figure 3.1, right).

Figure 3.1 (left) Glued edge can be a weak point. (right) Stapled boxes are very strong.

Most boxes are made with either two or four hinged flaps for the top or bottom. Once you have formed the box, you fold in the bottom flaps and tape them to hold the shape of the box and provide strength. Use a good-quality plastic or thread-reinforced strapping tape for the purpose. Masking tape is not strong enough. Duct tape is expensive and tends to pull loose and roll at the ends.

The strongest boxes are simply folded, made with no tape or glue at all. These boxes have a double or triple end panel that takes the weight when they are lifted. The long side panels of these boxes can pull apart slightly, but they slip back into position when you add weight. The downside is that these boxes require a separate lid. The time you save folding the box is consumed by making the lid. The lids can be designed so that they can be folded together without tape. If you are borrowing boxes or having them donated, you must take what you can get. If you are having them made to order, this triple-wall, no-tape box is the one I recommend. Drawings are included in appendix A.

Boxes must be easy to lift and carry. Several things work together to make handy boxes. Size is one. You must be able to grasp the box comfortably at the ends. A box 16–20 inches long is about right. You get the most lifting power when your arms are shoulder-width apart. If you have to spread your arms to lift a longer box, you have to work harder to make the lift. If you are trying boxes on for size, remember, it's not the first one you need to consider, it's the five hundredth. Yes, you can lift a bigger box, but can you do it all day?

One dimension of the box should be at least 11½ inches, inside capacity; 12 inches would be better. The normal maximum height for books not considered oversize is around 11¼–11½ inches. You want the box that can enclose that size comfortably. The other dimension can be as little as 9½–10 inches. If you have a choice, make the 11½-inch dimension the height of the box so that the books can stand on end.

If you do have a lot of oversize books, you may want to get some larger boxes. Keep the 16- to 20-inch length limit, but make the boxes up to 17 inches tall by 13 inches wide. You may have some books even larger than this, but we have other ways to move those.

Resist the temptation to use a larger box. When we load the boxes, we want one row of books, standing on end just as they are on the shelf. We don't fill up the rest of the space with loose books, because it takes far too long, and too much library knowledge, to sort them back into order.

A handle is another requirement. You can pick up a solid box under the bottom, but a handhold cut into each end makes the job much easier. You can also use the handhold to drag the boxes without lifting them. When the manufacturer cuts the handholds on single-wall boxes, the cutout piece is usually left attached, hinged at the top. You fold this piece back into the box as an extra layer of protection for your fingers. Die-cut cardboard is sharp. It can give you a paper cut that will make a slice from bond paper seem like a mere nick. This is why I recommend you buy leather gloves for the box makers.

Another advantage of the triple-wall, folded box style is that the additional thickness of the end panels provides a much stronger and less sharp handhold than a single-wall box.

Third requirement is the top. A good integral top requires four hinged panels, one from each side. The two end panels fold down first and provide some support for the side panels. If you have only the two side panels, they slide down inside the box and provide no support at the top. You do not need to tape the top of a four-panel box. It provides sufficient support with the tops just folded into place. For additional support you can interlock the top. Fold down one side panel—always start with a long side—then an end and the other side (figure 3.2). Then lift up the open end of the first side panel, fold down the last end panel, and tuck it underneath. This top may not be flat and may cause a stack of boxes to lean or topple.

Separate lids can be strong and are flat. They also have the advantage that, if a book sticks up slightly above the top of the box, the lid can ride up with it and still stay flat and provide support. On the other hand, the lids have to be made up separately, and every time

Figure 3.2 A box top folded like this is not flat. A stack of them may topple.

you reuse a box you have to return the lid as well as the box to the original building, effectively doubling the workload.

The fourth requirement is that all of the boxes must be the same size so that they stack and move easily and the stacks don't topple. Note, though, that for a very small library—7,000–10,000 volumes or less—you could just use whatever boxes you can find. The effort to collect identical boxes is not worth the return, and, if something gets out of order, it is not that much trouble to fix it.

Box Sources

Plastic milk crates work. They are a bit small, but they are enormously strong, have great handholds, and stack solidly if you do not overfill them. You might have to use some creativity to figure out how to put a card pocket on one. I've never used them, so I can't help you there.

You could save up the boxes from your book supplier. These are strong boxes, but they do not have handles and you have to do a lot of sorting to get enough boxes all the same size.

You might ask your book jobber to give you enough boxes for the move. Mention that your move is bound to attract publicity; newspapers and television love to show pictures of books being moved, and, of course, all of the boxes will have the jobber's name on them.

Think about local manufacturing and shipping companies. Most packing boxes are not heavy enough, so try to think about a company that manufactures something or receives components that are fairly heavy for their size. Mention the publicity thing.

Several companies rent a form of plastic crate that is advertised for moving books (figure 3.3). I find these less than ideal. They work best in a situation where you are packing them full, without trying to keep the books in order. They leave too much empty space when you are packing books in a single row. The crates have sloping sides, so they stack easily, and molded-in braces add strength, but these features reduce the amount of space for books inside. The crates are much heavier than a box, even empty, so it takes extra effort just to recycle them for another load. They are also fairly expensive to rent or buy, at least compared to boxes.

Box-Moving Equipment

You have several options for moving the boxes. Two-wheel hand trucks work well and minimize stacking and restacking, but they are limited to four or five boxes per trip. Flat four-wheel dollies also work well, as do pallets moved with pallet jacks. They can carry many more boxes per trip, but they require more lifting and restacking of boxes and put a real premium on having a fool-resistant numbering system.

BOOK CARTS

Common library book carts work well, especially for moves within one building. They don't hold many books, so you need a lot of carts. On the other hand,

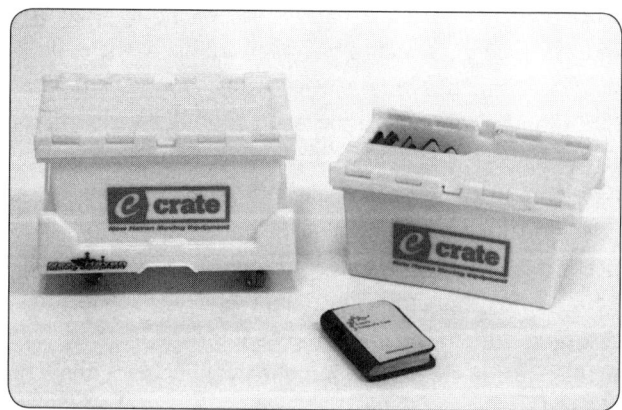

Figure 3.3 Several companies rent plastic move crates. I do not recommend them.

most libraries already have them, and it may be easy to borrow extras from neighboring libraries.

A major drawback with book carts is that they are difficult to transport between buildings. Many styles of cart cannot be forklifted in and out of a truck, forcing you to use ramps. Ramps work, but the heavier the carts are loaded, the more difficult and potentially dangerous it is to use them. Also, it is difficult to keep books from jarring loose during transport in a truck or over rough flooring. One way to keep books on the cart is to shrink-wrap each cart; this is effective, but it takes time to wrap and unwrap, and it is not cheap. If you have a choice, get carts that have slanted shelves to help hold the books in place.

If you do use book carts, you can attach a card pocket to one end of each cart and use the sequence card numbering system.

The number of book carts you need for each move crew depends on several different factors:

Capacity. Carts vary widely in size and number of shelves. The more books a cart holds, the fewer you need to keep a crew busy.

Distance to the new shelves. The quicker you can get empty carts back to the unshelvers, the fewer carts you need. If you are moving within one building, you need fewer than if you are transporting them between buildings, where you may have a backlog at the loading dock, carts tied up on the transport truck, and so forth.

Schedule. The more time there is to do the move, the fewer carts you need. You can afford some inefficiency. Fewer crews can be used simultaneously, which allows you to control the flow of materials more closely.

For a move within a single building, with limited time to do the work, I would have a minimum of eight to ten carts for each crew for most efficient use. If it is necessary to transport the carts between buildings, that number increases to at least fifteen per crew. It may be possible to have too many carts, but it is much, much better to have too many than too few.

I have done quite a few moves using book carts, including moves between buildings. In the largest of these, we moved about 600,000 books over a weekend, all within one building. We had thirteen crews working simultaneously and 150 3-foot, two-shelf book carts. It was not too many carts.

One decision to be made is how to load the carts. There are two options:

1. Treat each cart like a mobile shelf. Load one side top to bottom and left to right. Then spin the cart and load the other side. With this option, you need to identify the side you loaded first. I put a piece of easily visible tape over the top of one end of the cart and always start loading or unloading from the taped end. I prefer black tape. I also always put the card pocket on the taped end, for no good reason other than consistency.

2. Load the entire cart from one side. Most carts hold two rows of books. In this method you load one row on the top shelf; and then put another in front of, or behind, it; then do the same on the other shelves, working top to bottom. This method is fast to load, but not as fast for the reshelvers who have to keep reaching through to get the first row of books before the second row. Alternatively, the loaders can put the first row of books closest to the unshelver and reach through to load the second row. This speeds up the reshelving process at the expense of the loaders.

Whichever method you use, pick one and *stick to it*. If the reshelvers have to check the call number on each row of books, their speed suffers and they make more mistakes. Don't get halfway through and let someone decide they have found "a better way."

MOVE CARTS

Quite frankly I believe move carts (figure 3.4) are the best way to move a lot of books in a hurry with minimum (although still a lot of) effort and maximum efficiency. They are specially designed and constructed to hold a large quantity of books, to be moved over many kinds of surfaces, and to be forklifted on and off of trucks for transport.

There are several national companies that rent move carts at a—sort of—reasonable rate. You can build or have someone build carts for you at a—sort of—reasonable price. Appendix B includes complete plans for my version of a move cart. My version includes several custom modifications I have not yet seen on the commercially available carts, including color-coded ends for

32 Selecting a Method

Figure 3.4 Move carts are designed for efficient library moves.

easy orientation, card pockets and numbering systems to keep them in order, and detachable side panels to keep the books from shifting in transit. I also have a packaging and transport system to move microfiche and film on the same carts.

These carts are typically built of plain plywood and are rugged rather than pretty. They have three or four shelves a side and may be from 30 inches to 4 feet long. A 32-inch cart holds about 250 books; a 4-footer holds close to 400. A loaded cart may weigh from 700 lbs to nearly a ton. With the proper wheels under them, they are easy to push on a flat surface.

My carts are designed so that one end is identified with black tape. All loading starts from the TOP with the BLACK end to the LEFT so that unshelvers and reshelvers always know where to start.

These carts all have a central keel, which means they must be loaded one side at a time, then spun around and the other side loaded. For this reason, the length of the cart should be sized to the width of your aisles. This is an important point if you rent carts. You want to be able, at least, to roll the cart down the aisle perpendicular to the stacks so that you can load or unload it easily. Ideally you would be able to spin the cart in the aisle. This is where you may have to compromise a bit. If your aisles are the ADA minimum of 36 inches clear, the cart can be only about 32 inches long if it is to be spun in the aisle (yes, a 32-by-24-inch rectangle will not spin in a 36-inch aisle, but the cart spins on the wheelbase, which is smaller).

The major drawback with move carts is that you cannot use ramps to load them on or off a transport truck; you have to forklift them. You *can* push them up or down a ramp that is no steeper than an ADA handicap ramp, but you must be careful. The problem is that the carts are designed to roll easily. Going downhill, they can get away from you. Going uphill, they are just heavy and hard to push. It is absolutely *not* safe to roll a loaded cart up or down a ramp from a U-Haul-type truck. On the other hand, forklifting them is quick and easy and much safer.

If you are moving within one building, you need six or seven move carts per crew to keep a constant flow going. If you are moving between buildings and may have a backlog at the loading dock, carts held up in the transport truck, or other delays, you need ten to twelve carts per move crew for smooth workflow. It may be possible to have too many carts, but it is much, much better to have too many than too few.

To sum up:

- Use stack movers if you are recarpeting or just rearranging the stacks without rearranging the books on the shelves.
- Use a human chain to move books short distances and up or down stairs if there is no elevator. In a cart move, you may also use this method to get books from the shelf to the cart if you cannot get the cart down the aisle to the books.
- Use boxes for small moves or for storage.
- Use book carts for smaller moves or moves within one building if you can assemble enough carts to do the job efficiently.
- Use move carts for most moves between buildings.

Time is the most important consideration in the choice of method. If you have more time to make the move, you can use boxes or book carts. If time is short, you should give greater consideration to move carts. Time is money, and move carts may save you more in staff cost than they add in rental or construction cost.

The key to efficiency is size. It takes much less time and fewer people to move a whole range, still fully loaded, with a stack lifter than to move the same number of books with a human chain. Move carts require fewer people and resources than book carts, and book carts are more resource-penurious than boxes. The cost of efficiency is planning and preparation time. The smaller the move, the more the cost-benefit curve tilts toward the less efficient, but less costly, methods.

TWO OTHER WAYS TO MOVE

At least two other move methods are often referred to in the literature and in casual accounts of moves. I do not recommend either of them:

Checkout-and-Return Method

This is a simple concept. Get your patrons to check out all of the books at the old building and return them at the new. Problem solved. Not really.

Rarely can you get people to take all of the books; you still have to move most of them. Then, some people check out books and return them late, return only part of them, or not return them at all. And you still have a reshelving problem when people do return the books. You have spread the reshelving over the period of a few days, but you have added a major interfiling problem and probably lost any advantage you might have gained by using waypoints to avoid shifting.

Walk-in-Line Method

In this move, you recruit some volunteers, staff, and other workers. Someone directs the move at the origin building with another supervisor at the destination. The first worker takes a handful of books, walks to the destination, and puts them on the shelf. The second worker follows behind with the second handful, and so on. If you have more books than workers, everyone cycles back to the origin for another load.

There are variations where every worker carries a box of books or pushes a cart. In another variation, the library builds trays similar to those I recommend for sorting and two workers carry each tray, in line, to the new building.

An advantage of this system is that it is incredibly simple. I have never used it, but it could work for a very small library moving over a very short distance.

The potential problems are legion: The load of books I accepted was fine at first, but it is unacceptably heavy two blocks and two flights of stairs later. If I drop a load of books, do I put them back in the right order or just pick them up and go on so I don't lose my place in line? If I step out of line to walk with my friend who is a few spots ahead of me, will I remember to step back into place, or will I follow the instructions of the reshelving supervisor who doesn't know I jumped the line and just put my books next to my friend's? The problems are just multiplied when the loads are larger in trays or boxes.

I can think of one good use for the walk-in-line method. Recruit community volunteers. Invite the mayor, local dignitaries, your board of trustees, kids pulling little red wagons, mothers with strollers. The media, of course. Get a fire truck up front with sirens going and a police escort. Load up a few hundred books and parade them over to the new building. Make it a major media event. Talk to the reporters. Pose for pictures. Tell all about your new building, your great collections, your fabulous staff. Thank all the construction workers, your great contractors, your fabulous architects. Mention all of the people who will help with the move, your great move team, your fabulous move coordinator. Then, when everyone goes home, go move the library with carts.

I had this all set up one time. Human chain for five blocks. Two streets and a bridge closed, 450 volunteers. Everybody who was anybody. For two glorious weeks *Good Morning America* was scheduled to broadcast on site. Then *GMA* bailed and we chucked the whole idea. Only reason to do it was the publicity.

Measuring the Collection and Designing the Shelving Layout

In most of the moves I have done for other people, measuring the collection is the task that causes the most uncertainty and even fear among first-time move planners. The published literature does not make the task seem any easier. In a quick survey you can find the following tools and methods:

- tables of average width of books, by subject, to be used in estimating the length of shelving necessary to hold the collection
- formulas to determine what percentage of books are lost or missing
- formulas to determine how many books are in circulation and how many shelves you would need if they all came back
- methods to predict the growth rate for various subjects; the ones used to predict periodicals are particularly complex
- time and motion studies for every part of the move including how long it takes to do the time and motion study
- weeding formulas and methods
- tools and methods to estimate collection length from shelflist cards, statistically significant shelf samplings, catalog dumps, and other sources

There are many more, some conflicting. Let's look at just the first of these, the table of average widths. Assume you have a modest collection of 100,000 books. Now assume that each of your books is only four pages longer than the books used to calculate the published average. Go with the published average, and at the end of your move you would have to shift enough to find room for an extra twenty-eight shelves of books.

The problem is, case studies are exactly that, reports of what happened in a particular case, under a particular set of circumstances that may or may not apply to any other situation.

Don't worry. In this chapter I show you a fairly simple and very practical way to measure your collection quickly and directly. It gives an accurate measurement and allows us to control the direction of any error to ensure us a little extra wiggle room when we reshelve the books.

MEASURE YOUR COLLECTIONS

When you designed your building, you probably used general estimates for the sizes of the various parts of your collection. Now we need a much more detailed measurement. The purpose is to get an accurate measure of the total length of your collections, as if they were packed tight. We use that length to calculate how much growth space you have and to distribute that growth appropriately throughout the collection.

Waypoints

A waypoint is a defined spot in a collection designated by the call number of the book to be filed immediately after the waypoint. You assign waypoints wherever they are useful, depending on the nature of your collections.

Calculating waypoints is a lot of work, but it pays off during your move. The basic concept is that you break up your collections into small segments and calculate where each segment will fall on the shelves. There are many advantages:

- Calculating waypoints forces you to look, in detail, at your collection and how it will fit on the shelves.
- It allows you to program more, or less, growth into specific parts of the collection.
- During the move, it gives you frequent checks to make certain everything will fit on the shelves. If a collection runs over, you know in time to make adjustments before you have to shift the entire collection.
- It gives you great flexibility as you assign crews during the move. You can start a crew at any waypoint with confidence that they will not overrun preceding or following groups.
- If a reshelving crew gets seriously backed up, you can break into their backlog at the next waypoint and assign a relief crew to do a skipahead to help them catch up.

If you have fragmented collections, overflow areas, or other materials that are out of order but are to be shelved together in the new building, interfile all of them you possibly can before you start counting. Even if you have to cram materials into the existing shelves, it is far easier to calculate growth, and to execute the move, if you interfile as much as possible now. If possible, you should also read the shelves before you start counting. The entire move is based on keeping the books in the same order as they were before the move. If books were misfiled in the old building, they will be out of order in the new arrangement as well. Also, if you happen to select a badly misshelved book as a waypoint,

> **THE SKIPAHEAD**
>
> Using several waypoints in each collection allows you to start a moving team at any waypoint. You do not have to move each collection from beginning to end, and you can have many crews working in one collection at the same time. At times a reshelving crew may get behind, with many carts loaded and ready to be reshelved. If that happens, you can relieve the backlog and restore the workflow with a skipahead. Look through the waiting carts until you find the next collection flag. Match that flag to its waypoint marker and assign a team of shelvers to begin at that point. We call this a "skipahead."
>
> Note: Almost never does the collection flag happen to fall at the start of a cart. No problem. Have the skipahead crew start at the flag and empty the rest of the cart, starting their shelving at the waypoint. Then the skipahead crew goes on to the next higher-numbered cart, leaving the partially empty cart as the last cart the regular crew shelves short of the waypoint.

you might end up having to shift a significant number of books.

Start by making a list of all of the separate collections. A collection is separate if it will be shelved together in one order, separate from other materials. Reference is usually a separate collection. Ready reference or course reference may be separate from that. If you shelve children's books in their own space, they are a separate collection. Children's reference may be separate from that. Fiction is usually separated from nonfiction. Don't forget the nonbook collections.

The Layout Spreadsheet

Appendix C is a spreadsheet that can help you measure your collection and design the shelving layout. It also has instructions for modifying the spreadsheets to interfile more than three collections and for printing out waypoint markers and collection flags. Before you start, familiarize yourself with the detailed description and cell-by-cell instructions for use in appendix C. The same material is available for download in electronic format from the American Library Association at www.ala.org/editions/extras/fortriede09942. **WEB**

The Layout spreadsheet contains tabs for four separate kinds of Excel spreadsheets:

The Data tab (figure 4.1) is a form you can print out and use to record the measurements of the shelves using the shelves-and-strings process (see below). You do not enter any data in the electronic version of this worksheet. The instructions on the sheet are set up for a relatively large Dewey-classified collection. You may need to modify the specific instructions to match your own collection.

There is one Master tab and fifteen copies, marked Sheet 1, Sheet 2, etc. You use one copy for each of your collections. Rename the Sheet tabs to identify each of your collections. In a large library with many collections, you will need to download additional copies. Each download provides another fifteen Sheet tabs. Enter the information you have recorded on the Data sheet into the appropriate tab, which you use to calculate growth, waypoints, and shelving layouts. Each tab also contains a section where you can calculate an exact count of the shelving you have assigned to each collection.

There is a tab customized to calculate Periodicals layouts.

There is a tab customized for Microforms.

In some instances you use one of the Sheet tabs for periodicals or microforms, depending on how you measured those collections.

The Layout spreadsheet set is a powerful tool that saves you much time, effort, and calculation. Use it to

- calculate the total length of each collection
- calculate how many feet of shelving you need in the new building
- calculate the average growth space available for each collection and distribute the growth over the collection
- assign additional space to fast-growing collections and less to areas that grow more slowly
- calculate the cumulative number of shelves to the end of every range in your collection
- identify waypoints and calculate the starting shelf number for each one

> **SECTION AND RANGE**
>
> A section is a unit of shelving one shelf long and one or more shelves high. A standard section is 3 feet long (actually 35.5 inches of shelving space). A section is either single-faced or double-faced. A double-faced section has books on both sides. A section may be described by the depth of the shelf and the type of shelf. A 7-inch section has shelves with a flat top area 7 inches front to back, plus an additional 1 inch (if double-faced) or 2 inches (single-faced) of room behind the shelf. Some shelves are provided with a backstop that limits the depth of the shelf. Any section that is not 3 feet wide is described by its width. The height of the section is important. It may be given in inches, or in the number of shelves, or both. The base is considered a shelf unless you are talking to a shelving manufacturer or installer, in which case a "7 hi section" is described as "a base and 6 shelves." The type of shelf is also described. Flat, sloped, periodical lift-up, and x-ray are most common. A full description of a section might be "30-inch single-faced, five hi, 9-inch flat."
>
> A range is some number of sections installed together as one unit. A range may be single- or double-faced. It is described by height, shelf width if not 36 inches, depth of shelves, type of shelves, length in number of sections, and whether single- or double-faced. A full description might be "double-faced range of 10, 60 inches high, 4-shelf, lift-up." The length of a range is always the number of sections in it, unless you are talking to the shelving manufacturer or installer, in which case it is "a starter and X adders." A range of 10 is "a starter and 9 adders" in Installerese.

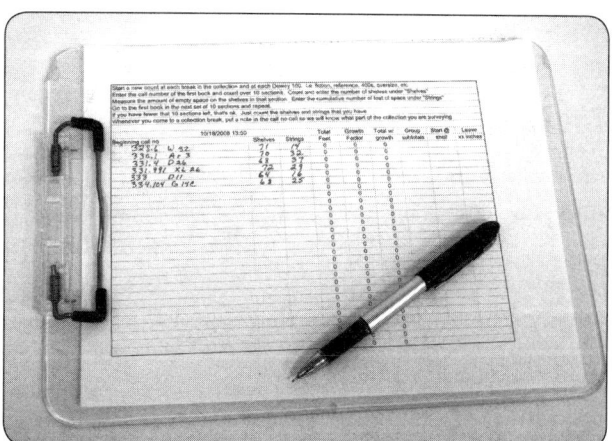

Figure 4.1 Data tab worksheet records your measurement of the collections.

- virtually interfile up to three collections and calculate the total space required for the integrated collection
- calculate how many inches of growth space you must leave on every shelf
- provide all of the information to print collection flags and waypoint markers

Appendix C includes a copy of the Data sheet you can use as a printing master. Use this sheet to record data as you measure the collection. Enter information from the paper Data sheet directly into the Layout spreadsheets.

You need one page of the Data sheet for each separate collection. Print off enough copies for all of your collections and a few spares.

Shooting Shelves and Strings

The process is called "shooting shelves and strings." I don't know why. We picked it up somewhere. It's an easy phrase to remember and adds cachet to a somewhat tedious process. Make a tape measure 10 feet long. The best I have found is a piece of that woven nylon tape used for tie-downs or luggage straps. Whatever you use should be durable and supple and must not stretch. Mark it in 1-foot increments with a magic marker and number them 1 through 10 (figure 4.2).

Book Collections

Work in teams of two people. One person counts and measures and calls out the numbers. The other enters the information on the Data sheet and double-checks the measurements.

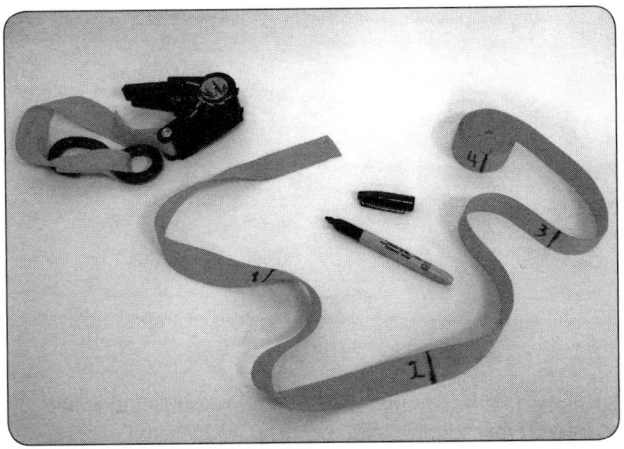

Figure 4.2 Nylon strap makes an excellent tape measure.

Pick a collection to start. Write the name of the collection on the Data sheet. On the first line of the sheet, record the call number of the first book on the top shelf of the first section of shelving. This is your starting point or first waypoint. Count over enough sections to include between forty and seventy shelves and tip the first book on the top shelf of the *next* section. Count a larger number of shelves, up to seventy, if you have plenty of growth room in your new shelving arrangement; use fewer if your new shelving will be more tightly packed. If another collection is to be interfiled with the one you are measuring, count fewer sections.

Now count the actual number of shelves in the area you just counted off. Usually you can just multiply the number of sections by the number of shelves per section. Make sure that some individual sections do not have more or fewer shelves; if some do, add or subtract as needed. Also subtract for any shelves that are completely empty. This gives you the number of shelves. Enter this number in the Shelves column, next to the call number.

Next shoot the strings (figure 4.3). The "string" is that tape measure you made. Now you are measuring the empty spaces at the end of a shelf. Start with the 0 end of the tape in your left hand and the rest of it loosely held through your right. Measure the empty space, if any, on the first shelf, sliding the tape through the fingers of your right hand. Then move your left hand over to capture the tape you have already used and measure the next shelf. With each shelf you are using a bit more of the tape and you are getting a cumulative measure of the unused shelf spaces.

When you reach the end of the tape, call out "One" and start over. Each time you call out a number, the second person on the team makes a tick mark on the Data sheet to keep track of the progress. It's easy to lose count. If the tape runs out in the middle of a shelf, start the new tape at that point. When you get to the end of the tape a second time, call out "Two," and so forth. Continue to the end of the section you counted off. Do not go past that book you tipped. At the end of the section, look at the 1-foot markings on the tape and read off the last number that you used.

Let's say, for instance, that you counted three times through the tape and then to the 7-foot mark. That is 37 feet of empty shelf. Enter the total feet of empty shelf in the Strings column, next to the call number.

The process is much easier to do than it is to describe. After a few minutes of practice, a team can shoot two hundred or more sections in an hour.

Figure 4.3 Shooting the strings: (A) Write down the call number of the first waypoint. (B) Count over several sections and tip the next book. (C) Subtract any empty shelves from the shelf count. (D) Measure the total empty space at the ends of each shelf. (E, F) If the tape runs out in the middle of a shelf, start measuring from that point with a new string. (G) When you reach the tipped book, write down its call number and measure to the next waypoint.

Occasionally you encounter shelves that are a non-standard length. When you do, count them as a full shelf in the shelves count. Adjust the strings accordingly. If the shelves are short, measure the empty space as if they were full length. If, for instance, a standard shelf is 36 inches and the short shelf is 30 inches with 4 inches open, measure the 4 inches of open space with the tape, then slide over another 6 inches on the tape to account for the short shelf. Or consider a 4-foot shelf with 7 inches open. This shelf contains 5 inches more books than a standard 3-foot shelf (4 feet − 7 inches = 41 inches, or 5 inches more books than a 36-inch shelf can hold). In this case subtract the extra amount from the cumulative measure on the tape.

Do not concern yourself too much with a few odd-size shelves. They will not make much difference in the total collection layout.

The strings measurement does not have to be precise, but if you are going to err, measure less, not more. Normally I do not measure any shelf with less than 2 inches of open space, and I always round the last tape down, not up. The strings measurement is subtracted from the length of the shelves. We want the final measurement to be accurate, but we would rather show too many books than too few. The rounding ensures that we have slightly more growth room than we expect, not less. When we get to reshelving, we may be happy to have just a bit more wiggle room.

Now write down the call number of the first book in the next uncounted section (the book you tipped). This is your next waypoint. Count off the same number of sections you used before, tip the next book, and shoot the shelves and strings. Enter this information on the worksheet. Continue in this fashion until you have finished the collection.

Periodical Collections

The shelves-and-strings method is designed to distribute the materials on the destination shelves evenly between waypoints. Periodicals don't work that way. We need room for growth at the end of a title, not evenly over the shelves. I use one of two methods, depending on the situation.

Use Method One if you want the new shelving space to be very forgiving with plenty of space for growth. I just use a lot of waypoints—one every two or three sections or every fifteen to twenty shelves. Instead of starting a waypoint at the top shelf of a section, I put

TIP

I like to start each waypoint with the first book on the top shelf of the section. It makes it easier to find the book again later when it is time to flag the collection.

it where a title breaks. For long runs of a title the waypoints may be more than two or three sections apart.

Write down the title of the journal, or call number if you classify periodicals. Then shoot shelves and strings to the next waypoint just like you did for the books. You will have many and frequent waypoints and less total growth between waypoints. This makes it much easier for the reshelvers to organize the shelves title by title, for they are working with much smaller increments.

I try to put the most experienced periodicals librarians in charge of the reshelving and let them use their judgment in how to arrange the volumes, how to handle ceased titles, and where to leave the growth. With frequent waypoints they rarely go wrong, and shifting is minimal. This method is quick, simple, and relies on a great asset—the librarians' knowledge of their collection—for its success.

Method Two is more time-consuming but much more precise. I have used it a couple of times when the destination shelving had to be very tight. Start with a list of every title, in shelf order. Enter the titles on a copy of the Data sheet.

Measure each title separately. Don't bother to count the shelves. Instead use the strings tape measure and measure the volumes, *not* the empty spaces. You can use the Data sheet, but modify the directions: put the length of the existing run in the Shelves column and the growth under Strings. Measure the run in feet and the growth in inches.

Next calculate the growth of each title. The easiest way to do this is to decide how many years of growth to allow. For an example, let's say you want to leave room for ten years of growth. Use a ruler or tape to measure the space required for the latest ten years of the title and enter that number, in inches, in the Strings column on the Data sheet. If the title is closed or ceased, enter 0. Yes, some titles grow, cease, or condense over time, but we can't predict this. This method gets you as close as possible based on the state of your collection today and allows you to make adjustments gradually over the years.

This method assumes a gradual, slow growth in your bound periodical collection, which is typical in the current environment. If you expect major growth in your periodicals, use Method One and plan for plenty of growth space.

If you measured in shelves and strings under Method One, use one of the Sheet tabs to calculate growth and waypoints, just as you do for books. The Periodicals tab used to lay out the collection for Method Two is designed to calculate the total length of shelving needed for each title. In effect, it calculates a waypoint for each title. Assign an experienced periodicals librarian in charge of the reshelving crew. When you reshelve, you work directly from the spreadsheet. You fit each title into the allotted space. You can pack ceased or closed titles tight, and you can fill up a shelf in the middle of a long run to leave all of the growth space at the end of each open title. Detailed instructions for data entry and for calculating the space allocated to each title are included with the Periodicals sheet in appendix C.

In some collections, periodicals are classified and shelved with the book collection. You can use the same shelves-and-strings process we use for books. Assign a higher growth factor to those waypoints where you expect extra growth in a periodical run.

Combining Collections

You may need to combine collections in your new shelving arrangement. Perhaps you had to put books in storage or into an overflow area, or perhaps you had to fragment your collection to fit the architecture of an old building. The spreadsheets can be used to consolidate up to three collections, and you can modify them to do more.

With Books on Shelves

Here's the process if all your collections are on accessible shelves:

Decide which collection is the "main run." This should be the largest single collection if possible, but it must be one that is on shelves where you can measure it—not in boxes.

Print enough copies of the Data sheet to record measurements for all of the collections.

Shoot shelves and strings on the main run. Set waypoints more frequently than you would for a single collection, maybe forty to forty-two shelves apart.

Now start a new set of Data sheets. What you are going to do is measure how many books in the second collection have to be shelved between every set of waypoints you established when you shot the main run.

The first book on the top shelf of the first section in the secondary run is the starting point for that run. Locate the point where the second waypoint you established for the main run would fall in the secondary run. Tip the next book.

Note: When you shot the main run, you counted off the same number of sections between waypoints. In this second collection, the number of sections varies from waypoint to waypoint.

Now go back and shoot shelves and strings between the starting point and the book you just tipped. Enter the shelves and strings in the appropriate columns next to the call number of the first book. What you have done is determine how much space must to be added between the first set of waypoints on the main run to allow you to shelve all of the books to be interfiled from the second run. At this point, you have not considered any growth space. The spreadsheet adds both runs and calculates the total, with growth.

Now write down the call number of the tipped book and locate the point where the next waypoint you established for the main run would fall. Tip the next book, shoot the shelves and strings, and record the numbers. Continue throughout the second collection. You can straighten the tipped books as you complete each waypoint. We only tip them to help us keep track of our place.

If you have a third collection to interfile, start with a new set of Data sheets and do it all again, keying everything to the waypoints you established in the main run. Remember my suggestion to interfile everything you can before you start counting? This is why. Every little subcollection that is to be interfiled after the move would have to be considered a separate run. By interfiling first, you save a lot of time and effort in the move, even if the origin shelves are overfilled before the move.

With Books Stored in Boxes or Otherwise Inaccessible

If the books are in order in boxes, and the boxes are in order, *and* the contents are marked on the boxes or in a record somewhere, it is not difficult to calculate the amount of space they take between the waypoints.

Use another set of Data sheets. Use the same waypoints you established for the main run. Write those call numbers—the same ones you used on the main run—on the Data sheets. Count the number of boxes that would fall between each set of waypoints. It is certain that most of the waypoints will fall in the middle of a box, but that's all right. You can take a best guess as to where the waypoint falls in the middle of a box, or you can round each count up to a full box. Then multiply the number of boxes by the length of each box in inches and divide by twelve to get feet. Enter this total as a *negative* number in the Strings column; the spreadsheet interprets this as the space needed to interfile these materials.

If your boxes and the books in them are in good order, you should be able to get a fairly accurate measurement. If the stored books are not in order, it is more difficult. I have three suggestions:

1. Put them in order. If you have time and some free shelving space, you can unbox the books, put them in order on temporary shelves, and do your counts from these shelves. Even if you have to rebox the books to get enough room to complete the sorting process, this approach gives an accurate count and saves reshelving time. This is my preferred method.

2. If you can generate a list in shelf order of all of the stored books, you could count the number of books between each of the waypoints and calculate an average width per book by measuring the books that are on open shelves. Average widths vary widely with the subject. When you measure to get the average width, try to measure a whole shelf of books together, then count how many books are on that shelf and divide to get the average. This gives a more accurate number than trying to measure each book individually. I used this method one time and it worked fairly well.

3. If nothing else, you can guess at the total length of books to be interfiled into each collection. We treat this as an addition to the whole collection; we do not have any way to distribute the additional length accurately for each waypoint. The spreadsheet allocates the measured materials over the total length of shelving, leaving extra growth room on each shelf for you to interfile the remaining materials.

This growth space is evenly divided; you will likely have to do some shifting to fit the actual materials onto the shelves. I have had to do this several times. It is more accurate and forgiving than it might seem.

Guess the total length of the books that are not in order. Enter the amount, in feet, in cell C17 on the spreadsheet. When you allocate shelves to the various collections in your new arrangement, make sure you assign enough shelves to handle all of the measured runs, plus the estimated length of the unmeasured books, plus growth. This makes it seem that you have a lot of growth space when you complete the spreadsheet. Don't worry; you'll use it when you begin to interfile the stored books. Be sure to enter this estimate only on the particular spreadsheet tab you use to calculate the collection into which you will interfile the books.

The streamlined shelves-and-strings method described here is a quick, inexpensive, flexible, yet very accurate way to measure a collection. Several of the national library moving companies go much further than this. They generate a virtual "collection map" that shows the position and contents of every shelf in the library. Basically they calculate a waypoint for every shelf. I have never used this method, and I think it is unnecessary to be so specific, for several reasons:

- It takes longer to reshelve. Shelvers have to check the call number on nearly every book, certainly every shelf.

- The plan is too specific. If you buy books after the count, or if your patrons return books just before you move, the shelving map *will* be incorrect.

- It is next to impossible to create the map if you have to interfile collections.

- It is incredibly costly. The work is so detailed that the move consultant has to bring in contract workers. It takes many hours to map a collection, and you are charged the full hourly rate.

- It is unnecessary. We planned a move of one nonfiction collection interfiled from three separate locations that allocated 600,000 books over more than 14,000 shelves. At the end of the move we had exactly three shelves left over. The waypoints method provides excellent accuracy and spreads any inaccuracies evenly throughout the collection.

> **TIP**
>
> You can download the spreadsheets, tab by tab, to a laptop, skip the Data sheet, and enter the data directly onto the computer. Don't miss a waypoint.

The counting part of the work is tedious, but it is neither hard nor especially complicated. Anyone familiar with the collection, including shelvers, can do it. Attention to detail and accuracy are the most important things to remember.

When you have finished counting, transfer the data to the spreadsheet. Detailed instructions are included in appendix C. There is a separate tab for each of the collections you measure. Click on the tab you renamed for the collection you want to calculate. The Data sheet is just a printed version of the first three columns of each of those sheets. Copy the call numbers, shelves, and strings into the spreadsheet tab. The spreadsheet adds up all of your shelves, subtracts the strings, adds back any corrections you have made, and gives you the minimum number of shelves you need to allocate for that collection, *packed tight*.

Double-check to make certain that all the waypoints were recorded and then check again to make certain all of them got transferred to the spreadsheet tab. If you forget a waypoint and don't catch it until you reshelve the books, you will have a major disaster on your hands, and the recovery plan can be quite draconian. You will have to find a way to fit an extra 150 or 300 feet of books onto the remaining shelves. On the other hand, you can fix it with a few keystrokes if you catch it now.

DESIGN THE SHELVING LAYOUT

Long before you start moving, you need to make a detailed map of your new shelving spaces showing what materials are shelved in each area and specifically the shelf where each of the waypoints falls.

Calculate How Much Shelving Will Be Available

It is easiest to work from an architect's floor plan, the bigger the better. Make sure the shelving arrangement it shows is, in fact, the one that was built. Let me say that again: *Make sure* the drawing shows exactly what shelves are available. If possible, take the drawing to the work site and verify each section. Make sure the range lengths match. Make sure every range shown on the drawing is built on the floor. Check the height of the ranges and the number of shelves in each section. I don't think I have ever completed a move with the same shelving plan I was given when we started laying out the collections. With the spreadsheets it is not difficult to correct for minor changes, but if someone decides that each range needs to be shortened by one section to make a wider aisle or someone ordered 42-inch shelving where you planned to put 90-inch shelves, you may have to redo the entire layout. It helps to make friends with the shelving installers. They know what is really going to be built.

We do a rough count first. Most libraries have shelving in multiple locations. Rarely is it installed in one block. The first step is to make certain you have enough shelves in each area for the material you intend to put there. This is an interactive process between you and the architects—one that should have been considered from the earliest stages of design.

Let's start at the point where the design is done, the building is nearing completion, shelving and furniture layouts are set, and you are ready to plan the move. Your first count is just to be sure you have enough shelving in each area to hold the books you plan to put there.

First, count the shelves in each area. The best way I have found to count shelves works like this: From the blueprint pick the longest range in a block of shelving and count the number of sections. Write down that number. If the range is single-faced, write "× 1"; if it is double-faced, write "× 2." Next determine how many shelves there are on one side of a single-faced section. Make sure to include the base shelf. Write down an "×" and that number. Now go through the block of shelving and count how many ranges have exactly that configuration of length, width, and number and type of shelves. Write down an "×" and that number. You should end up with something that looks like "8 × 2 × 7 × 5," which indicates ranges of eight sections long, double-faced, seven shelves high, quantity of five.

Go to the next-longest range and do the same until you have counted all of the shelves. Make sure you have counted each range once and none of them twice. If you miss one, you'll have a lot of space left over; count one twice and you'll run out of shelves. It helps to put a tick mark on the drawing by each range as you count it. Also make certain that you count only ranges with the same types and numbers of shelves. You have to count each type of shelf separately. Even though they are the same length, a range 42 inches high has less capacity than one at 90 inches. A range of periodical lift-up shelving does not help you shelve bound periodicals.

A full count of a shelving block might look like this:

$$8 \times 2 \times 7 \times 5 = 560$$
$$8 \times 1 \times 7 \times 1 = 56$$
$$7 \times 2 \times 7 \times 12 = 1{,}176$$
$$6 \times 2 \times 2 \times 4 = 96$$
$$5 \times 1 \times 7 \times 3 = 105$$
$$5 \times 1 \times 3 \times 3 = 45$$
$$2 \times 2 \times 7 \times 2 = 56$$
$$= 2{,}094$$

Multiply all of these numbers out and add up the results to get the total shelves in the block. This example has 2,094 shelves. Do this for all the shelving in your layout. I pencil in the total capacity of each area right on the prints for easy reference.

Allocate Shelving for Each Collection

Compare the areas of available shelving to the size of each of your collections and allocate each to an area of shelving. If possible, allocate extra space for growth and easy reshelving: 10 percent growth is a bare minimum; 20 percent is adequate; 50 percent is none too much. (Ten percent gives about 3 inches of growth space per shelf; 20 percent leaves about 7 inches; 50 percent leaves only about 12 inches free space per shelf.)

If the spreadsheet says you need 1,000 shelves packed tight and you allocate 1,100, you have allowed 10 percent growth. If you allocate 1,223, you have allowed 22.3 percent growth.

The process of fitting the collections into the available shelving is a nonscientific one. You need to consider workflow, collection flow, departmental boundaries, architectural issues, lighting, and many other factors. You may do several layouts to get the best fit. I have never yet drafted a layout that did not benefit from some tweaking—or a major rewrite. Make sure you have plenty of copies of the floor plan when you start.

As you assign shelves, keep in mind the type of shelving and the number of shelves per section. These factors directly affect capacity and what kinds of materi-

> **TIP**
>
> Here's a tip from someone who's been through it. If you have 90-inch shelves with canopy tops, you can plan to get only five shelves plus the base in each section if you are shelving nonfiction or most children's books. You lose about 3 inches for the toe kick at the bottom, another 2 inches at the canopy, and almost 1 inch for each of the shelves. That leaves only 79 inches, which means that five of your shelves can have only 11 inches clear between the shelves. A common height for tall books is 11¼–11½ inches. Without the canopy tops, you can use six shelves plus the base for all but oversize books.

als you can put where. You may be able to relocate some shelving units for the best fit. That's another reason to make friends with the shelving installers.

You cannot expect to make major shelving changes at this point. The direction of light runs, carpet borders, pillars, and other architectural issues may preclude some changes you might like to make. In many cases the shelving package may already be contracted, and the most you may be able to do is switch one type of shelf for another. Also be aware that double-faced ranges may be 20, 24, or 30 inches deep, depending on the type of shelving they hold. If you exchange a 20-inch base (used for 7-inch or 9-inch flat shelves) for a 30-inch range (periodical lift-up or x-ray shelving), you may narrow an aisle below ADA minimums.

Rough Layout

When I do layouts, I first work in pencil—it's easier to erase outdated and confusing notations. As I get to a layout I'm ready to present for evaluation, I code the various collections graphically so people can see at a glance what goes where. This is also a convenient way to catch any shelves I may have missed. Figure 4.4 is a sample.

Let's work through an example. Say the shelving block you assigned to fiction looks like that in figure 4.5. You counted the shelves as

$$6 \times 2 \times 6 \times 5 = 360$$
$$3 \times 2 \times 6 \times 5 = 180$$
$$= 540$$

The spreadsheet says you need 363 shelves, packed tight.

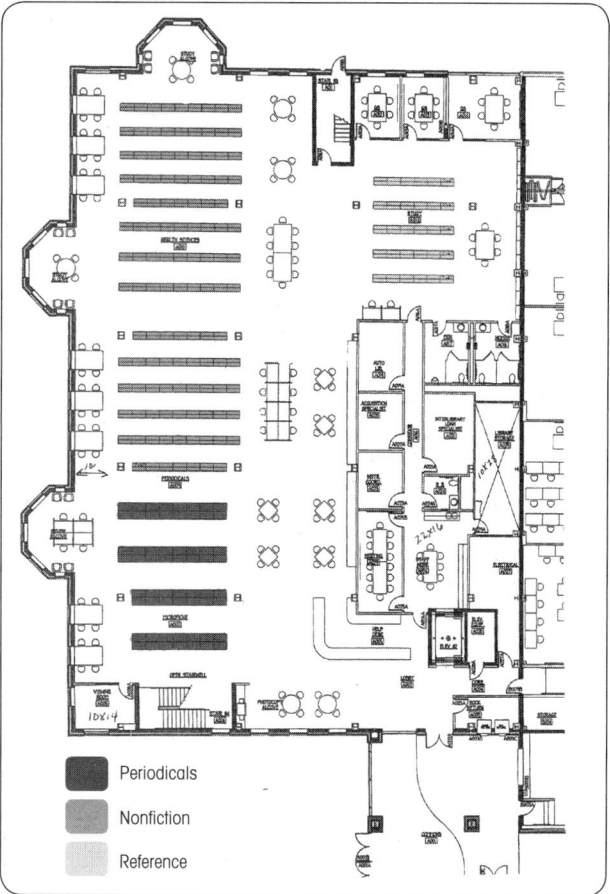

Figure 4.4 Part of a collection layout plan, ready for staff approval.

You could put the first book at B or Q. Let's choose B for the example. Your shelving plan runs from B to C. Now you have a choice. You can jump the aisle to D or turn back to H and shelve the long ranges down to O, then start over at Q and come back to E. Either plan works. Let's choose the jump to D option. When we get to E, we turn back and shelve along F through I, then turn again and shelve J through M, and so on, ending at N.

Finished Layout

On each worksheet tab there is a place to calculate precisely the shelving for that particular collection. For this exact count, we treat everything as a single-faced range and we count each side of each range separately and in the exact sequence in which the books will be shelved. The count for our sample block is as in figure 4.6.

Notice that the spreadsheet gives the cumulative number of shelves at the end of every range. This is helpful when you lay out the waypoints on your drawings and is well worth the effort. Be accurate. The total number of shelves you counted in the rough count has to equal the number calculated by the worksheet. If it doesn't, someone goofed. That would be you!

The left side of figure 4.6 shows the shelf count exactly as it appears in our sample layout. Each side of each range is counted separately and in order, following the flow of the shelving arrangement.

Now let's adjust the layout. You have plenty of room for growth, about 12 inches per shelf. You decide to put a range of face-out new book display from B to C. This range is no longer available for shelving. Change the length of range 1 to 0. Note on the right side of figure 4.6 that the cumulative number of shelves changes from that point on.

Now you decide to leave single empty shelves where patrons can put books they have used, one at K and another at R. In the Adjusted section for range 5 and range 17, enter "–1" in the Adjust column. Note that the cumulative shelves count adjusts again from these points on. The right side of figure 4.6 shows the revised shelf count and the cumulative total of shelves at the end of each range.

Later, when you are ready to make the final collection map showing all of the waypoints, you will use the cumulative shelving counts to make the process of locating the waypoints relatively easy.

Calculate Growth for Each Collection

You have two choices: calculate an average growth for an entire collection, or customize the calculation to reflect faster or slower growth in some subject areas. The spreadsheet is set up to calculate for five different growth rates within a single collection—average growth, growth 10 percent faster or slower than average, and growth 25 percent faster or slower. A single average growth rate for the entire collection may be sufficient for smaller, homogenous collections, for fiction, and for collections where the new shelving will be loose. If you have a large nonfiction collection—40,000 volumes or so with a substantial portion of older volumes—it may be worth calculating differential growth rates. You may find you are buying more books on computers and technology and fewer in literary criticism, or perhaps you will be building resources to support the university's new engineering curriculum.

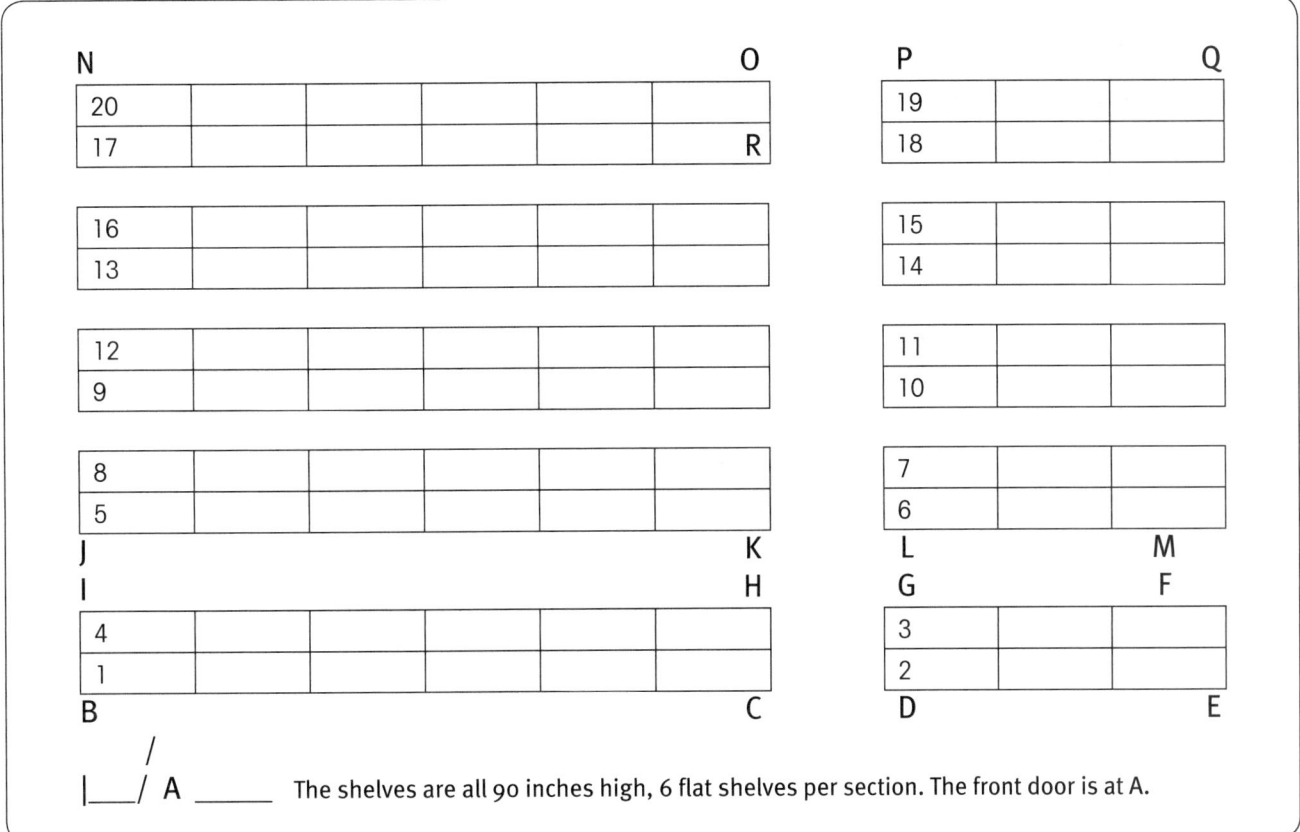

Figure 4.5 Sample layout.

The process is simple. You get five categories, numbered 1 to 5. Go through the spreadsheet tab for each collection and assign a category to every waypoint. Involve staff in this process. The category should reflect the expected growth for most of the books that fall between the two adjacent waypoints. Slowest growth is 1; fastest is 5. Most should fall in 3, average growth. You do not have to balance every 5 with a 1 or every 4 with a 2. The spreadsheet adjusts to your inputs. Enter the category number in the Growth Factor column on the worksheet. The default growth is 3. If you want average growth throughout the collection, do not change this column.

Now comes the fun part. Pick a collection to start and open that worksheet tab (figure 4.7). Cell O19 (in the Excel application, this is designed with green numbers on blue fill) shows the number of shelves you need to hold all of your books. At this point, with no growth yet calculated, this is the length of your current collection, packed tight, which you established in the shelves-and-strings exercise. Cell O20 (blue number on yellow fill) shows the number of shelves you allocated to this collection. It is pulled automatically from the shelf counting portion of the spreadsheet where you numbered and counted each side of every range.

The shelves available number should be larger than the shelves needed number. If it is not, your collection will not fit, even packed tight—in which case you need to go back and allocate more shelves for this collection or redo your entire layout to relocate this collection to a larger block of shelving.

Cell C23 (red numbers on blue fill) is where you enter the growth rate for the collection. The default is 1.0, no growth. You enter numbers in this cell, in decimals greater than 1.0, until you find the magic number that makes the shelves needed equal the shelves available. As you enter trial numbers, the spreadsheet applies that growth to every individual waypoint and distributes the growth as evenly as possible, then calculates the total shelves needed at that rate of growth.

As an example, go back to the sample layout we used to illustrate the shelving layout process. The shelves needed were 363, packed tight. By the time we subtracted the display section and the two returns shelves, the shelves available were 502. Having 502 shelves when

FIRST COUNT					ADJUSTED				
Range	Length	Shelves	Adjust	Total	Range	Length	Shelves	Adjust	Total
1	6	6		36	1	0	6		0
2	3	6		54	2	3	6		18
3	3	6		72	3	3	6		36
4	6	6		108	4	6	6		72
5	6	6		144	5	6	6	−1	107
6	3	6		162	6	3	6		125
7	3	6		180	7	3	6		143
8	6	6		216	8	6	6		179
9	6	6		252	9	6	6		215
10	3	6		270	10	3	6		233
11	3	6		288	11	3	6		251
12	6	6		324	12	6	6		287
13	6	6		360	13	6	6		323
14	3	6		378	14	3	6		341
15	3	6		396	15	3	6		359
16	6	6		432	16	6	6		395
17	6	6		468	17	6	6	−1	430
18	3	6		486	18	3	6		448
19	3	6		504	19	3	6		466
20	6	6		540	20	6	6		502

Figure 4.6 Counting shelves and adjusting the count.

363 are needed leaves a lot of room for growth, at least 25 percent. For a starting point, we enter 25 percent (in the form 1.25) in cell C23. The spreadsheet expands the shelves needed for every waypoint by 25 percent, rounds to whole shelves, and calculates the total needed as 454. Not enough. There are many unassigned shelves, so we try again.

25% (1.25)		454 shelves needed, 502 available
Try 35% (1.35)	Much closer	490 shelves needed, 502 available
Try 39% (1.39)	Too much	505 needed, 502 available
Try 37% (1.37)	Very close	501 needed, 502 available
Try 37.3% (1.373)	Good	502 needed, 502 available

In a large collection it is not uncommon to run this to five or six decimals to get an exact match of shelves needed to shelves available. With the spreadsheet this takes only minutes.

If you assigned growth factors to some parts of your collection, the process is exactly the same. You plug numbers only into cell C23. The spreadsheet does all the work. It expands the areas you identified for faster growth by a larger percentage, the slow-growth areas by less. The actual percentages are shown in cells D25–D29.

Do this process for every collection, even the small ones, each on its own spreadsheet tab.

Now that you've done all of the above, here's what you have:

- your collections, divided into handy subcollections, with frequent waypoints where you can check your progress against the plan and make corrections without having to shift the entire collection

Layout Spreadsheet

INSTRUCTIONS: Use this spreadsheet to calculate growth rates and waypoints.

There are 15 copies of this spreadsheet. Use a different spreadsheet for each collection. Use the worksheet labeled "Layout Spreadsheet" as a master copy to make additional spreadsheets if you need them. RENAME each worksheet for the collection it represents.

There are enough rows on each spreadsheet to calculate 200 waypoints. If your collection requires more than 200 waypoints, put any extras on a separate worksheet.

There are enough columns to calculate waypoints for a main run and two interfiled collections. If you do not need to interfile, you can HIDE columns E&F and G&H. If you must interfile more than three collections, see the instructions to learn how to modify the spreadsheet to accommodate the additional collections.

If you have a collection to interfile and you were not able to measure shelves and strings, enter your estimate of the total length in cell C17. (See chap. 12.) Enter the length of a single shelf in cell C19.

Row	B	C	D	I	J	L	M	N	O
17	What is the estimated total length in feet of any collections you were unable to measure?								
19	What is the length in inches of most of your shelves?	35.5			Total number of shelves you need				502
20					Total number of shelves you have				502
23	Enter growth rate options in cell C23 (red number) until the number in cell O19 equals the number in cell O20 to spread growth over your entire collection.	1.373			Enter trial growth numbers here.				
25		1	1.0298						
26		2	1.2357						
27		3	1.373						
28		4	1.5103						
29		5	1.7163						
30					Enter Growth Factor (1 - 5)	Total Shelves/w Growth	Start @ Shelf	Leave xx Inches	Natural Growth
32		Main Run Shelves	Strings	Total in Feet					
33	Beginning call no. of waypoint								
34	328.6 W32	71	14	196	3	91	1	9	9.64
35	330.1 Ar3	70	32	175	3	81	92	9	9.64
36	331.4 D26	68	37	164	3	76	173	9	9.64
37	331.991 Xl 26	72	29	184	3	85	249	9	9.64
38	333 D11	64	16	173	3	80	335	9	9.64
39	334.104 G14e	68	25	176	3	82	415	9	9.64
40	Etc.	5	2	13	3	6	497	9	9.64

Callout: The top number changes as you adjust the growth rate; the bottom one stays constant. When they are equal, you have distributed the growth evenly.

Figure 4.7 Spreadsheet calculates waypoints, growth space, and available shelving.

> **FROM FULL SHELVES TO EMPTY SHELVES**
>
> Too much growth space can become a public relations problem along the lines of "You spent all this money on a new building, and now the shelves are empty!" Growth rates of 50 or 60 percent leave shelves reasonably full, but as the growth reaches or exceeds 100 percent you may want to take steps to change the appearance of the shelves. Here are some things you can do:
>
> - Do not install one or more ranges. Fill the remaining shelves a little more fully. You can always store and install the rest of the shelves later as your collection grows.
> - Install fewer shelves per section; put the rest of the shelves in storage. A 90-inch section with only six shelves (including the base) subtly reduces unused growth space and gives you 13 or 14 inches between the shelves. Again, you can install the remaining shelves later as your collection grows.
> - Turn some sections of shelves into face-out displays.
> - Leave the top or bottom shelves unused, filling the middle shelves more fully. For some reason, casual observers tend to pay more attention to the condition of the shelves at eye level and don't notice the top and bottom.
>
> If you remove shelves from use, go back to the shelf counting portion of the spreadsheet and recount the shelves. Then recalculate growth to spread the collection over the remaining shelves.

- the number of the shelf where each waypoint starts
- the number of inches of growth space to leave on each shelf
- a running count of the empty shelves in the order in which your collection will flow to use when you map the waypoints

Map the New Shelves

Build a Shelving Map

Next step is to put the waypoints onto a drawing of the shelving plan. Get an unused floor plan. If the plan does not accurately reflect the shelving the way it was built, cross off, white out, or draw in the shelves to make the drawing accurate. Verify your drawing with the shelf counting list. Make sure the list is accurate.

Now go to the end of range number 1. From the worksheet, get the cumulative number of shelves and pencil it in at the end of the range. Do the same for each range, in the order the collection will flow (figure 4.8). The spreadsheet gives you the cumulative total of shelves at the end of each range, so you don't have to count them.

Transfer Waypoints to the Map

From the appropriate tab, print the waypoints for each collection. See the instructions in appendix C. Start at the beginning of that collection on your drawing. Figure 4.9 shows the collection map for our sample shelving section with the waypoints marked.

The first waypoint is easy: it is the top shelf of the first section. In the example, we put a 1—for the top or first shelf—in the space of the first section and write the call number in the aisle adjacent. You do not need to write the whole call number, just enough that you can distinguish it from all the other waypoints.

Look at the second waypoint. Assume the spreadsheet tells us this waypoint falls on shelf 45. Count down that number of shelves. Shelves, not sections. Pay attention to the number of shelves in each section and to any unused shelves, like the two you left empty for returns. The easiest way is to count by sections—"6, 12, 18, 24, 30, 36, 42"—until you get to the last full section, then count the shelves—"43, 44, 45." Shelf 45 is seven sections (six shelves each) plus three shelves of the next section. Put a 3 in the space for the eighth section and write the second waypoint call number in the aisle.

Assume the third waypoint is at shelf 95. You could start from the beginning to count ninety-five shelves. Instead, look at the number penciled in by point I, "72." There are seventy-two shelves, ending at point I. You can start counting down cumulative numbers of shelves at each section in the next row at 78, 84, 90, and you will need five more shelves of the next section. Put the number 5 on that section and the call number in the aisle.

After you have counted out fifty, or five hundred, waypoints, the time you spent counting shelves, putting data into the spreadsheet, and penciling all the shelf counts onto the drawing will have been well worthwhile.

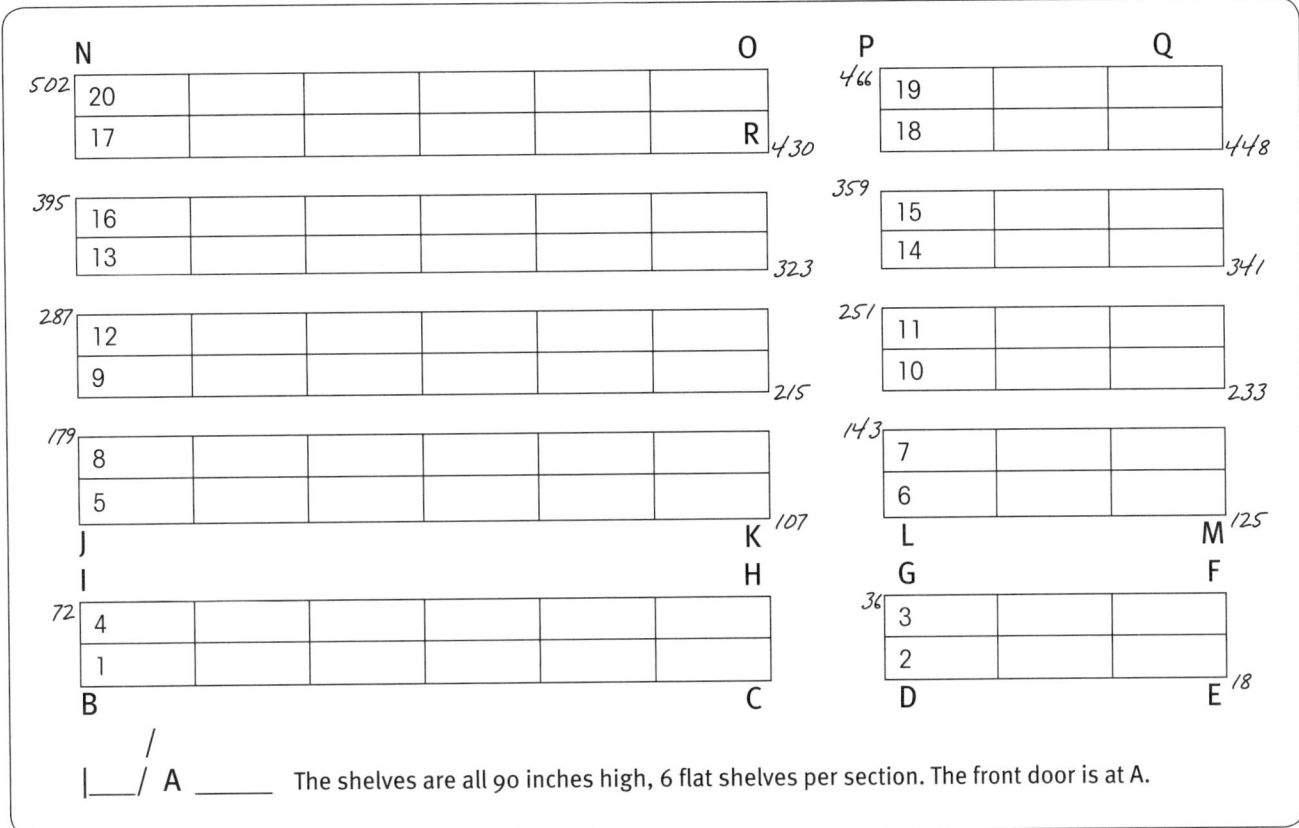

Figure 4.8 Pencil in the cumulative shelf counts at the end of each range.

Flag the Collection

Print a master copy of the collection flag found in appendix D or download an electronic copy from www.ala.org/editions/extras/fortriede09942. [WEB] It is the page headed "Insert this flag immediately ahead of _____." Make enough copies for all of your waypoints in all your collections, including small collections and any overflow or storage areas. I like to use bright-colored paper so the flags are easy to see. If you are interfiling, all of the waypoints for each collection are identical even if a book with that call number is not present in the collection. Just insert the flag where it would be shelved.

Pick a collection to start. Using the waypoints list you printed to make the collection map, write the call number of each waypoint on a collection flag.

Keep the flags in order if possible. It also helps to clip together all flags for one collection as you finish them and to write the name of the collection on the first flag. Make a flag even for the small collections that have only the starting waypoint; this helps identify the collections during the move. Continue until you have flags for all your collections, including any to be interfiled.

A few days before the move, insert the flags into your collections. The easiest way to do this is to treat the flags as books you are shelving. Slip them into the collection by call number. If you took my suggestion and selected the first book on the top shelf of a section as the waypoint, they are easy to find. If the actual book you picked as the waypoint has been checked out or is otherwise missing, just shelve the flag in its place.

 TIP

You can use mail merge software to print the collection flags and waypoint markers. Make sure to print the call numbers large enough to read easily.

50 Measuring the Collection and Designing the Shelving Layout

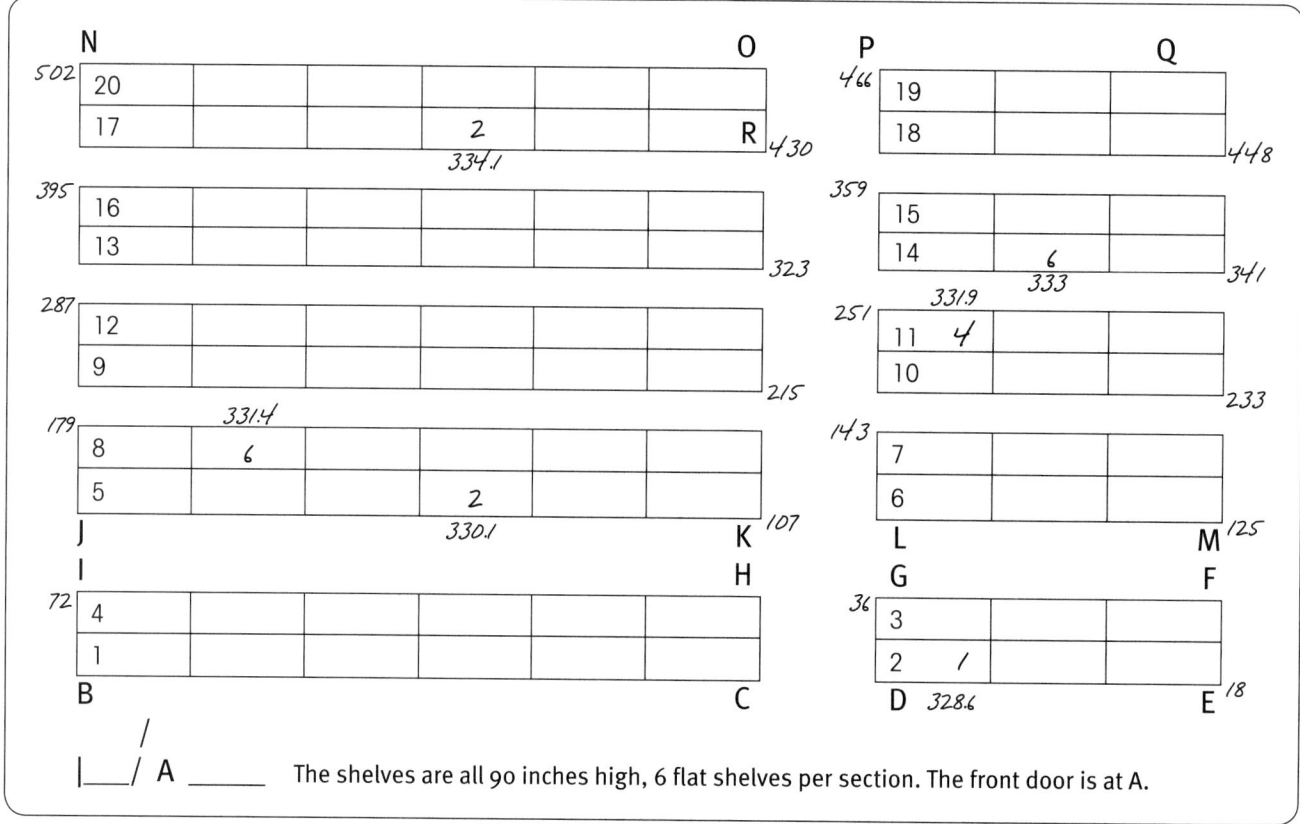

Figure 4.9 Add waypoints. Number shows on which shelf the waypoint starts. Call number segment in aisle identifies the waypoint.

Put Waypoints on the Shelves

Print a master copy of the waypoint marker found in appendix D or download an electronic copy from www.ala.org/editions/extras/fortriede09942. [WEB] It is the page headed "Start _____ Here." Make enough copies for all of your waypoints in all your collections, including small collections and any overflow or storage areas.

Pick a collection to start. Using the waypoints list you printed to make the collection map, write the call number of each waypoint on a waypoint marker. Also fill in the blank with the amount of growth space to leave on each shelf following this waypoint. If you assigned different growth rates to some portions of your collection, the growth space will vary from waypoint to waypoint. If you are moving with boxes, mark the stacking order "1-up" or "1-down" on each waypoint marker.

Keep the markers in order if possible. It also helps to clip together all markers for one collection as you finish them and to write the name of the collection on the first marker. Make a waypoint marker even for the small collections that have only the starting waypoint; this helps the shelvers know where to put these small collections. Continue until you have markers for all your collections, including any that you have to interfile.

A few days before you move, put the waypoint markers on the new shelves. Have ready your drawings with the waypoints marked, the stacks of waypoint markers, and some painter's tape. It helps—a lot—if you also have an assistant.

You may need to clean the shelves before you mark them. This can be a big job in itself and you may need to plan for enough staff, supplies, and time to do this job (see chapter 8). Any new construction, especially drywall work, guarantees dirty, dusty shelves. Check with your contractor and shelving installer. It may be that the cleaning of the shelves was included in one of their contracts. If so, work with them to time the cleaning just before your move starts, but make certain they understand that the work must be completed by the time you are ready to start moving.

Tape the waypoint markers to the shelves in the positions you calculated on the drawing. Match up the sections and then tape the marker on the shelf you indicated, counting down from the top. Yes, you do need to tape the marker down. You absolutely do not want someone accidentally or otherwise moving the markers after you have them set.

If you have a small collection and only a few ranges of shelves, it is fairly easy to keep track of where you are. The more shelves you have, the more you can use someone to help you. It works well to have one person hold the drawings and keep track of which range you are working on while the other works up and down the aisles taping the markers in place.

If you reserved some shelves for display, returns, or other special functions, it is a good idea to mark them now. Otherwise the reshelvers may not notice they are supposed to leave them empty. Plastic caution tape, available at most home improvement stores, is cheap and works well. You can also just tape a note to the shelf.

Check your work. This is the last chance to make corrections on paper. From now on, you make all adjustments the hard way, by moving books.

STACKING TERMINOLOGY

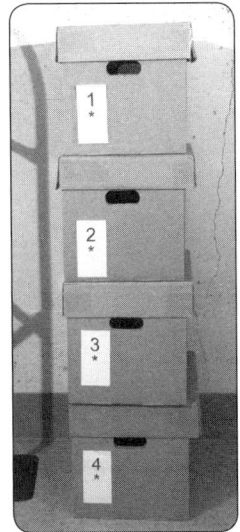

1-up is a method of stacking boxes so that the lowest-numbered box is on top of the stack, ready to reshelve. This method requires unshelvers to load all of the boxes for a single stack, then build the stack with the highest number on the bottom. Boxes are stacked 1-up if they will be moved without being restacked or if they have to be restacked an even number of times.

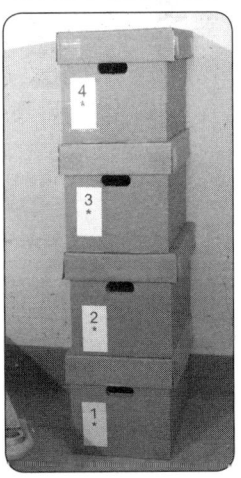

1-down is a method of stacking boxes so that the lowest-numbered box is on the bottom of the stack. This method allows unshelvers to build the stack, one box at a time, as each is filled. Boxes are stacked 1-down if they will be restacked once or an odd number of times. A single, or any other odd-numbered, restacking brings the low-numbered box to the top of the stack, ready to reshelve.

Chapter 5

Interfiling and Dividing Collections

Sometimes you have to combine collections from two or more locations into one order on your new shelves. This can be a time-consuming task that slows your workflow to a crawl, but it may be unavoidable. Whenever possible, I encourage you to interfile collections prior to the move and before you measure the collection. Even if interfiling means that your shelves are impossibly overcrowded for a bit, it saves time, staff, morale, and money during the move; in a well-planned move, the books just seem to melt off the shelves. That constant reminder of progress is what heartens the crew and helps them work harder and faster. When you have to slow down the process at an interfiling choke point, it seems to sap energy from the entire project.

In this chapter I discuss six very different ways to interfile during the move as well as a way to divide a collection should you find it necessary to shelve fewer books in your new location.

NEW COLLECTION, BOOKS IN NO USEFUL ORDER

The first move I ever did was this type. We opened a new branch. My library had been buying and saving books for several years. There were about 70,000 books in the opening day collection. When the books came to the branch, they were in boxes marked "Adult" and "Juv." They were in no other order. I was a brand-new librarian with a few months' experience. A veteran branch manager had tried to get the books on shelves ready for opening day but was unable to make much progress. I was sent to "make it happen" and given a twenty-day deadline. I was promised a significant promotion if I succeeded.

After a couple of false starts, the method that worked was as follows:

1. Open a box, pull out the nonfiction.
2. Leave the fiction.
3. Throw, literally, the books into ten piles in an arc around the stack of boxes, one pile to each Dewey hundred. With a collection in another classification scheme such as SuDocs or LC, adjust the subdivisions accordingly.
4. When all the boxes are emptied, go to the 000 pile. Throw, literally, these books into ten more piles: 00X, 01X, 02X, . . .
5. Go to the 00X pile. Throw, literally, these books into ten piles: 001, 002, 003, . . . Keep going until the piles are small enough that you can put the books into strict order in a reasonable amount of time. Put them on carts and move them to the shelves.

6. Then, back up to the next pile, subdivide it, and work through the entire collection. Then go back and start the fiction. Another crew works on the juvenile books.

This was time-consuming with a lot of floor work, but it was the fastest method we found, given that the books were not in any order at all to start. "Throwing" books carefully, flat, sort of like a Frisbee, we did not damage any of them.

Under the circumstances, it was not possible to calculate any waypoints. We started each collection at the beginning of the shelves designated for it and simply worked through to the end. We did a lot of shifting. It took four people fifteen working days to sort 70,000 books with an untrained and incredibly inexperienced crew. Three weeks later we did it again at another branch, this time with a crew that was now experienced. It still took fifteen working days. I conclude that there is an irreducible minimum effort required with this method.

I would not recommend this method unless you are starting from scratch with books that are not in any usable order.

INTERFILING TWO OR MORE COLLECTIONS

This situation commonly arises when two or more branches are combined or when an open-shelf and a storage collection are interfiled on the shelves of a new and larger building. The essence of this method is to interfile the collections two at a time. This is usually done at the destination building, but you can do the work wherever there is sufficient space. If you can, locate the interfiling point near the largest of the collections to minimize the extra packing and moving steps.

First, build trays that hold the books spine up at an angle where the call number can be read easily, as in figure 5.1. Plans for the trays are included in appendix B.

Two trays are used to interfile two collections. For each additional collection, you need two more trays. If you have two or more crews working simultaneously on different parts of the collection, you need a duplicate set of trays for each crew.

If you have two collections to interfile, the process works like this:

Figure 5.1 Sorting trays hold books at an angle to ease reading the call numbers.

Figure 5.2 Interfiling station for two collections.

1. Set up an interfiling station with two trays on a table, or on the floor if you like to work that way (figure 5.2). Choose a location with good lighting and easy access to and from. You cannot do this work for long in a poorly lighted or cramped location.

2. From the calculations on the Layout spreadsheet tabs, create one set of flags for each collection. Insert the flags in each collection just before you start moving. Each spreadsheet tab calculates for up to three interfiled collections, and you can modify the spreadsheet to calculate a single arrangement for as many collections as you have to interfile. A general description of the process is given in chapter 4, and the detailed instructions are in appendix C.

3. Load the books onto carts, each collection on a separate set of carts. Use the same process I described for moving books; that is, load from the BLACK end and use the numbered card system to keep the carts in order. Bring the carts to the interfiling station, keeping the collections separate.

4. Use a team of two people at each interfiling station. Depending on time and distance, you may need one or two people to load the carts and bring them to the station and one more person to take the carts of interfiled books to the reshelving location. It works the same way if one or both of the collections are in boxes. Either unbox the books onto carts at the storage location and move them on carts, or move the boxes to the interfiling station and unbox them directly onto the trays.

5. Load the trays from the right, pushing the books to the left as they are interfiled and removed to a cart or box for transport to the shelves.

6. One interfiler loads the trays from the carts. Each tray is used for one collection. This same person is responsible for pushing the books toward the left of the tray so the other interfiler can concentrate on reading and interfiling call numbers (figure 5.3). The books go onto the trays in order, which assumes that you kept them in order when you loaded the carts or boxes.

7. The second person on the team interfiles the books and puts them onto a cart, loading, of course, from the TOP, BLACK, LEFT. You can, if necessary, put the books back into boxes to move them, but carts are much easier, even book carts, if you are already in the destination building.

Figure 5.3 One person loads the trays, the other sorts books and loads them onto the cart.

 TIP

Put the largest collection on the tray closest to the interfiler to reduce the number of times that person has to reach across the first tray.

8. When you come to the flags, just leave them in place between the books. For each waypoint there is an identical flag in each collection. As you work, all of these matched flags fall in the same place in the interfiled collection.

9. As soon as a cart is loaded, a pusher can take it away to the reshelving area. Use the numbered card system to keep the carts in order. There may be a temptation to reuse one deck of the cards that you used when you brought the books to the interfiling station. Resist this temptation. For one thing, the interfiled collection is larger than either of the collections you brought to the station, so you would run out of recycled cards quickly. For another, reusing cards of the same color and series in close physical proximity can lead to confusion and may result in a cart bypassing the interfiling process and getting directly to the shelves. The technical term for this event is "Oops!"

The process is slow compared to a straight shelf-to-shelf move. The books have to be handled at least four times, compared to two for the shelf-to-shelf move. The person doing the interfiling often gets tired, mentally and visually, after a short while and may start making errors, just from the overload of numbers and letters going through the brain. You may find it helpful to rotate the crew among the various jobs every two hours or so to provide a rest for the interfiler. Occasionally I have found individuals who thrive on interfiling and can do it efficiently all day. If you find such persons, cherish them.

Typically we find that one individual can unshelve, load, and push enough carts from two collections in the same building to keep a single interfiling crew busy, unless the pushing distance is long. At the reshelving end, one crew of reshelvers with one pusher can usually keep up with four or five interfiling crews. The reshelving crew rotates among the reshelving areas each time one or two carts have accumulated there.

As a rule of thumb, a move interfiling two collections takes about five times as long as a straight shelf-to-shelf move using the same number of people. Each additional collection interfiled lengthens the move, but by a smaller increment. You can shorten the total time by increasing the number of interfilers and interfiling stations. Increasing the number of interfilers saves money overall because the one set of drivers, dock crew, trucks, and other overheads can service many interfiling crews.

If you have three or more collections to interfile, the process is similar, but you begin to build a tree with one branch for each collection. You interfile the collections two at a time, always interfiling the smaller into the larger. You interfile the first two, then load that combined collection onto the next set of trays, until you reach the trunk. If you have three collections, you need four trays, three interfilers, and two sorting stations. Four collections require six trays and three stations. If possible, set up your interfiling area so the combined collection from the first interfiling can be moved directly onto one of the trays at the next interfiling station, only a step away.

I did one library of seven interfiled collections (figure 5.4). We were combining two branches into a larger building. One of the branches had an extensive storage collection. The librarian for the new branch was buying new books to supplement the opening day collections, and both branches had been pulling from the main library collection. We had to combine all of these. The tree stretched almost fifty feet.

NO TIME TO INTERFILE

Interfiling during a move slows progress tremendously and requires more highly skilled personnel. Reading and comparing call numbers, hour after hour, takes far more time, skill, and willingness than simply loading and unloading a cart or box.

What if you don't have time for a long move? Perhaps you are up against a tight opening deadline. Perhaps the move has to be completed during the semester break. Perhaps you simply can't be closed to the public for as long as it would take to interfile all of the books. What then?

Well, first, interfile everything possible before the move. Start as early as possible and do all you can. Although interfiling and shifting take time and effort,

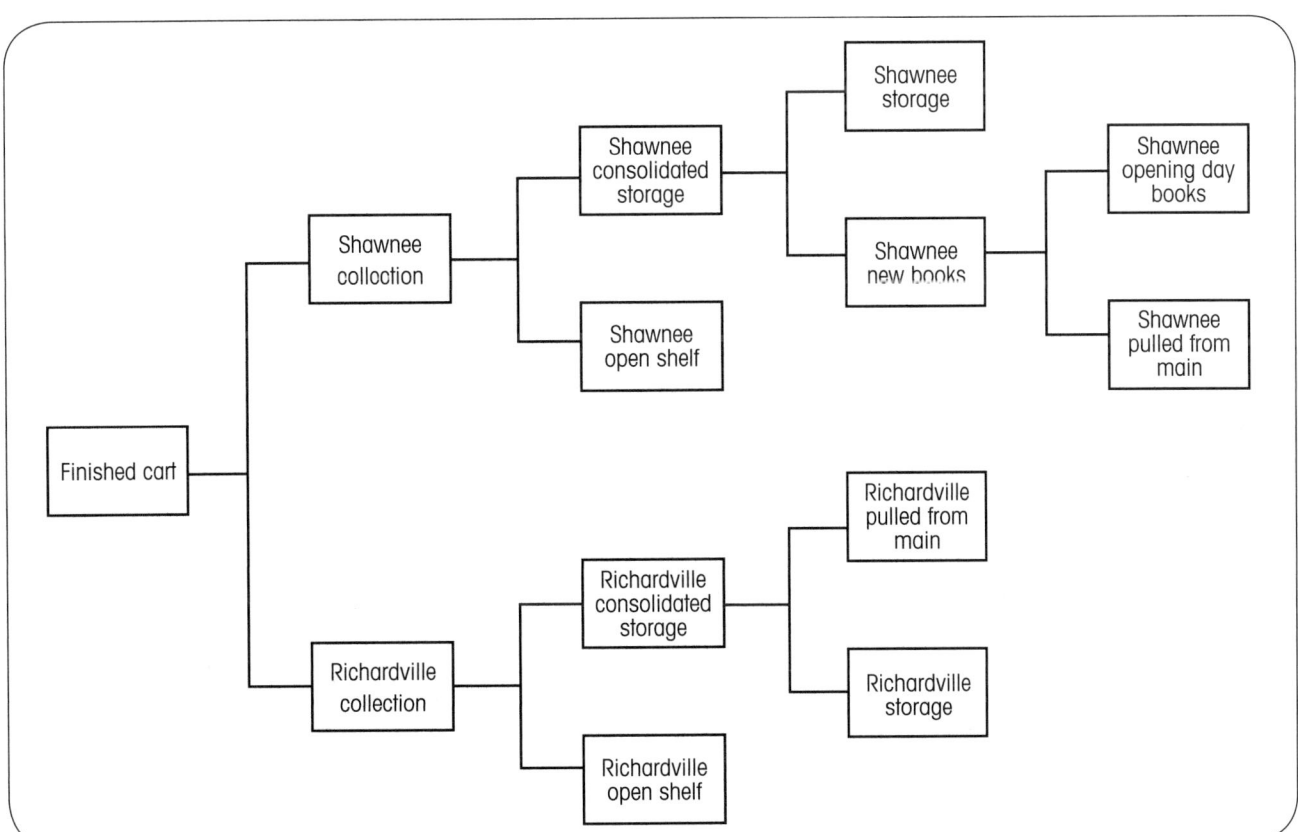

Figure 5.4 "Tree" layout for interfiling seven collections.

you can spread the work over a longer time, and it is nothing compared to the effort required to maintain efficiency and morale and still interfile during the move.

What if you simply do not have enough shelving to interfile everything even if you had the time? If you have only two collections to interfile and you have plenty of growth room on the new shelves, there is a method you can use. It takes a lot of planning, but it gets your books on the shelves quickly, with similar books close together, though not interfiled. You still have to do that task, and likely some shifting, but you can operate and people can find books.

This approach is more acceptable in a closed or storage collection where only staff are looking for materials. You end up with two collections stacked on top of each other, as in figure 5.5. The same call numbers from each collection are on the same section of shelving or very near it. Later you can go back through the collection and interfile, section by section. In the meantime, similar books are close enough that, if you find one call number, you can usually find other books with the same number without moving your feet.

I have used this method several times with two collections. I tried it once with three: two collections about equal in size and one much smaller. It worked, but only because it was in a nonpublic area, and the people who planned and carried out the move and subsequent interfiling had a lot of experience. I do not recommend this method if you have more than two collections to interfile.

Here's what you do:

1a. Decide which collection is the largest overall. Measure it using the shelves-and-strings method and establish waypoints. Use more frequent waypoints than you would in a shelf-to-shelf move. This is the main run; label it A.

1b. Measure the other collection—the second run; label it B.

1c. Add the two to get the total number of shelves needed to hold the combined collection, packed tight. Label this C.

2a. Count the number of shelves in the new shelving arrangement; detailed instructions are included in chapter 4. Double-check. Don't make any mistakes. Call this D.

2b. Subtract the number of shelves you need (C) from the number you will have (D). Divide the result by the number you need (C): (D − C) / C. If the result is

Figure 5.5 Interfiling two collections into temporary stacks more or less on top of one another.

less than 0.20 (meaning 20 percent growth), your new shelves are not sufficiently loose and this method will not work well. You should consider some other method. If the result is less than 0.15, this method will not work at all. If you have at least 20 percent growth, continue the process.

3a. Decide how many shelves you will have on each section. For 90-inch shelving this would be seven shelves, six if there are top canopies or other close overhead obstructions. Call this E.

3b. Calculate how many shelves you can afford to use for the main run: Multiply the number of shelves in the main run (A) by the number of shelves in one section (E) and divide the result by the total number of shelves you need (C): A × E / C. Round this to the nearest whole number; label this F. (Aren't you glad you paid attention in algebra class?)

3c. If E is 7 or 8 and the number you just calculated (F) does not round to at least 4, or if E is 6 and F is not at least 3, you did something wrong. What you are trying to do is determine, for every section, what proportion of the shelves will be used for books from the main run. Because the main run is the larger of the two collections, that proportion is always something more than half.

3d. Go to www.ala.org/editions/extras/fortriede09942 for a spreadsheet that does this calculation for you. **WEB** Use the 5.1 tab (figure 5.6). Enter the length of the main run and second run and the number of shelves in the destination. Also enter the number of shelves in each single-faced section. The spreadsheet tells you whether you have enough shelves to use this method. If you have enough shelves to use the method, but not efficiently, the spreadsheet suggests that you consider another method and tells you what percentage of growth you can expect.

4. Make up a collection layout map for the main run. Review the general process in chapter 4. Here we create a collection map for the space, but we pretend we have only F shelves in each section. Also, we leave the first section in every seven empty and pretend those do not exist either. We may have additional empty shelves just ahead of each waypoint. We load the books fairly tight on the remaining shelves. When we interfile, we move the first interfiled books onto the empty section and add in growth on every shelf. Follow the directions in chapter 4, except:

- Before you count the available shelves, cross off the first section and every seventh section thereafter (sections 1, 8, 15, 22, . . .).
- When you put the number of shelves per section into the Layout spreadsheet, use the number you calculated (F) instead of the actual number of shelves in the section.
- When you count out the shelves for the waypoints, do not count the shelves in the sections you marked off. The spreadsheet lists for you the correct shelf number on which each waypoint will fall.
- Do not enter any growth factor unless you have a lot of growth room in the new shelving arrangement. You already used 15 percent of your growth when you left every seventh section open. If the growth you calculated using (D – C) / C is more than 30 percent, you can make the interfiling a bit easier if you put a growth factor of 1.1 into the appropriate spreadsheet tab at cell C23. If you calculated growth at 40 percent or more, do yourself a favor and put 1.25 in cell C23, which leaves extra working room on each shelf as well as every seven sections.

Interfiling and dividing collections
Worksheet 5.1
Temporarily stacking collections when there is not enough time to interfile

INSTRUCTIONS
Enter the requested data in columns B and C

	Shelves	Strings
Measured length of main run	1,216	250
Measured length of second run	820	160
Total capacity of destination shelves in number of shelves	2,200	
Number of shelves in each single-faced section in destination shelves	6	

You have barely enough growth, consider another method.   Growth   15.8%

Use the bottom 4 shelves for the main run.

Figure 5.6 Example worksheet tab 5.1, temporary stacking.

5. Make a collection map for the second run, using the same method and the same set of floor plans for the collection map. Do not count any of the sections you marked off for the main run. When you put the number of shelves per section into the spreadsheet, use the number of empty shelves you did not allocate to the main run (E – F). This number is always half or less of the total shelves in the section.

6. Now make another map for the interfiled collection on a new set of floor plans. Use this map when you interfile. Follow the instructions in chapter 4 without any exceptions. Count all of the shelves, even the ones you marked off. Use the spreadsheet to determine growth just as if you were working with a single collection. You can use different growth rates for different parts of the collection. Use the same waypoints you established when you set up the main run.

When you move, you put the main run on the bottom F shelves, observing the waypoints and leaving every seventh section open. If you had 30 percent growth or more, you will leave a bit of space on each shelf. Otherwise the shelves will be fairly tight. Then you load the second run on the top shelves. It won't be perfect, but if you have two copies of the same book, one in each run, they should end up on the same section of stack or very close. Then, when you interfile, all of the books that belong together should be right in front of you, and you should not have to move them more than one or two sections onto the shelves you left open, or the ones you opened when you interfiled the books in front of them. The more growth space you have, the easier the interfiling will be.

7. Flag both runs and put the waypoint markers on the new shelves. Make some signs reminding movers which shelves to use for each run. Mark off with a note or caution tape the first and every seventh section to indicate that those shelves are to be left open.

8. Move one run at a time. It doesn't matter which is first. If you try to move both runs at the same time, you just cause a traffic jam. Starting at a waypoint, pack the shelves tight until you come to a collection flag. If you had enough overall growth—(D – C) / C—that you were able to put a growth factor into cell C23, you will not have to pack tight. The spreadsheet calculates how much room you can leave on each shelf. Give each reshelving crew a ruler or other gauge to measure this distance.

9. Move the other run in the same way. Note that if you did use a growth factor, it may not be the same for both runs. You may be leaving more or less space on this run. No matter. It would be a rare occurrence if both runs happened to be exactly proportional in size to the share of shelving allocated to them.

10. After everything is moved, you can begin to interfile. This can be done while the library is open if necessary. Each interfiler is working in a very small space and not moving books any great distance. Use the set of floor plans on which you built the second collection map. Go through the shelves and place the waypoint markers for the combined collection. These should be close to, but not necessarily identical with, the waypoint locations you marked for the main and second runs. If the library is open to the public, you may want to mark only a few waypoints at a time in case the markers get moved.

11. You can assign an interfiler to start at any shelf after an open section. Interfile the books from each run and put the interfiled books into the first shelf of the open section, leaving the appropriate amount of growth space per shelf as calculated by the spreadsheet. If everything was laid out perfectly, each time you interfile and shift a few books you open up a space for the books that follow them. You start with a full section of shelves open, and the amount of space slowly dwindles as you spread the growth over each shelf until, by the time you get to the next open section or next waypoint, you have only a shelf or two open in front of you.

In the real world, it isn't this easy. The books are not perfectly distributed, and there are times when you are working over three or four sections, not just one. It works best if each interfiler has one or two book carts to use as mobile sorting tables.

An advantage of this method is that you can assign many interfilers to work simultaneously; in fact, you could assign one to each group of seven sections. The individual assignments are short, which lets you fit them in around other jobs and helps alleviate mental fatigue.

INTERFILING ONE OR MANY SMALL COLLECTIONS

"Small" here is a relative term. In a tight collection of 10,000 items, a few hundred interfilees will have some impact. A loose collection of a million items may be able to absorb ten thousand items without undue crowding. The essence of this scenario is that the collection to be interfiled is so small that it will fit comfortably into the growth space left in the main collection.

Wait until the main collection is moved and reshelved. Then assign one crew to move the small collection and interfile it directly into the main run. As simple as that.

If you don't have time to complete the interfiling, you can move the books into a back room or storage area until you can get to them. When we move with the big move carts, we often save any small interfiling collections until the end and then just leave them on the carts until we can get to them.

CONSOLIDATING COLLECTIONS

I have encountered this situation a few times. In one instance, a university nursing school's library was to be consolidated into a new library building that would house all library materials for the campus in one collection. The nursing library had a few nonmedical reference books that were to be integrated into the general reference collection, and the main library had a few medical books. The bulk of the nursing collection fit intact into the general collection.

Shortly before the move, we took the reference books to the main collection, interfiled them, and eliminated the duplicates. At the same time, we took the few medical books to the nursing library, deduped, and interfiled them.

When we built the collection map, we made the start of the nursing collection a waypoint and also set a waypoint where the regular collection resumed. The spreadsheet combined the two collections and calculated the waypoints. We flagged each collection. When we moved, the only noticeable difference was that we had two origin buildings. The reshelvers just loaded the books according to the waypoints, without even needing to know where the books originated.

Another version of this scenario occurs when a library has pulled out a small subset of the collection, often because of space limitations in the origin building. I moved an extremely cramped branch that had coped with years of space problems by filling every possible nook with shelves. Collective biographies (929.2XX) were in a former broom closet. Cartoon collections (741.5) were in shelves running up a stairway.

We measured this collection as if it were one continuous entity. When we came to a spot where one of the disconnected collections should have been filed, we went to that collection location, measured it in place, and returned to the main run. We used the spreadsheet to calculate a single set of waypoints, some of which fell in the middle of one of the disconnected sections.

Just before we moved, we made up special flags for each of the disconnects. The flag was nothing more than a sheet of colored paper that said something like "Go to 929.2 in the broom closet." We inserted the flag right after 929.1XX in the regular collection. When the unshelvers came to one of these flags, they moved their cart to wherever the disconnected collection happened to be located and put it on the cart in order. At the end of the subset, they returned to the main run and continued. In effect, they were interfiling as they unshelved. The reshelvers never saw any interfiling.

MATERIALS RETURNED WHILE YOU WERE CLOSED

Do what you can to encourage your patrons to return books before your move or to hold them until after. Still, some patrons return materials while you are closed, and these must be interfiled. A high percentage of these materials will be current, popular, high-circulation items.

The best way to deal with them is to wait until nearly the end of the move, then box or cart the books to the new building and interfile them. In many cases and particularly in a high-circulation library, the returns fill most of the space you left for future growth. Not to worry. These are, after all, the current, popular, high-circulation items. As soon as you reopen, they will go right back out again, freeing up the growth space. In most cases circulation increases in a new library, so there will be even more growth space after a few days. I have been involved in many moves where the shelves we so carefully filled seemed to be half empty after a week or so.

If you cannot fit all of the returns onto the shelves at first, just wait a few days. There will be room.

DIVIDING COLLECTIONS

You may encounter a situation where there are more books on the shelves in the origin building than you have room for in the destination. In this case, you have to divide the collection and put some portion of it into storage or another location.

If you reduce the collection by taking some contiguous portion of it to another location (say you put the collective biographies in a broom closet), you can treat that as a separate collection and use the standard process for measuring, laying out, and moving each collection separately.

More likely, you will find that you have to put duplicate or less used titles into storage and move the rest to the open shelves. This work needs to be done well in advance of the move. Here's what you do:

1a. Determine how many books you have to remove: Measure your existing collection using the shelves-and-strings method. Total the number of shelves. Divide the strings by three and subtract that number from the total shelves. This gives you the size of your collection in shelves, packed tight.

1b. Count the number of shelves in the new shelving arrangement. Detailed instructions are included in chapter 4. Double-check. Don't make any mistakes.

1c. Decide how much growth space you want to have in the new shelves as a percentage of the capacity of the shelf. Multiply the number of shelves in the destination by the percentage of growth you want. Subtract that number from the number of shelves in the destination. The result is the number of shelves of books you can house in the new building.

2. Subtract the number of shelves you can house in the new building from the size of your collection. That is the number of shelves of books you have to remove.

3. Calculate the proportion of books you will have to remove. You can do this manually by dividing the number of origin shelves by the number of shelves you have to remove. Call this number X. You need to remove one out of every X books (see the box for an example). Alternatively, go to www.ala.org/editions/extras/fortriede 09942 for a spreadsheet that does this calculation for you; use the 5.2 tab (figure 5.7). **WEB** Enter the length of the collection and the number of shelves in the destination. Also enter the percentage you want to leave open for growth. The spreadsheet tells you to remove one book in every X. If you have nearly but not quite enough shelves, the spreadsheet suggests that you try a lower growth percentage and allows you to enter trial percentages and shows you the results.

> **CALCULATING HOW MANY BOOKS TO REMOVE: AN EXAMPLE**
>
> - The origin collection measures at 12,280 shelves and 1,428 strings.
> - The destination building counts out to 11,000 shelves.
> - You want room for 15 percent growth in the new building.
>
> Calculate thus:
>
> 1,428 feet of strings / 3 = 476 shelves equivalent, empty in origin
>
> 12,280 − 476 = 11,804 shelves of books in origin, packed tight
>
> 11,000 × 0.15 = 1,650 shelves of growth required
>
> 11,000 − 1,650 = 9,350 holding capacity of shelves in destination
>
> 11,804 − 9,350 = 2,454 shelves of books to remove
>
> 11,804 / 2,454 = 4.81: You need to remove a little less than one book in every five.

4a. Determine which books you are going to remove. Assign this task to librarians who are familiar with the collection. Go through the collection and tip one book out of every X spine down in place on the shelf. In our example, it would have been one out of every five. You do not have to tip literally one in every X, but you do have to average this percentage of books tipped. If you tip the books in place, you can review your work, reconsider any title, or tip more if necessary to get to the total necessary.

4b. When all the books are tipped, a move crew pulls the tipped books and moves them on carts or in boxes to their new location. This can be done well in advance of the major move. It must be done before you can do the final shelves-and-strings measurement and establish the waypoints for the move.

As you plan the timetable for the move, pay particular attention to this segment of the work. You need to move the tipped books as soon as possible after the staff has finished tipping them so the patrons don't straighten them up for you. You may want to pack and move the tipped

> **Interfiling and dividing collections**
> **Worksheet 5.2**
> Dividing collections
>
> **INSTRUCTIONS**
> Enter the requested data in columns B and C
>
> | | Shelves | Strings |
> |---|---|---|
> | Measured length of origin collection | 1,216 | 250 |
> | Total capacity of destination shelves in number of shelves | 1,400 | |
> | Percent of growth desired in destination shelves | 20.0% | |
>
> **You have nearly enough shelves. Try a lower % of growth and your books may fit.**

Figure 5.7 Example worksheet tab 5.2, dividing collections.

books when the library is closed to keep patrons away from the movers for their own safety. You need to remove the tipped books early enough that you can measure the remaining books, set the waypoints, and build the collection map before you have to start the main move.

Chapter 6
Recruiting and Training Move Workers

A library move is a labor-intensive task. There is no good way to automate it. We can make it as efficient as possible with good planning and the proper tools and techniques, but it comes down to people doing the work. Professional move consultants usually bring two or three of their own people as supervisors and then hire unskilled labor locally. If you are reading this book, we assume you have decided to organize your move yourself. Your decision is whether to use your own staff or hire laborers for the job. Consider these points:

- In most cases it is least expensive overall to use your own staff for much, if not most, of the work. They tend to be more motivated than other workers because they have to live with the results.

- Your own staff *will be* involved at some level, in the planning phase if nothing else. No one knows your collection as well as your staff. No one does a better job measuring the collection; identifying all of the separate parts of the collection; or planning growth, displays, and all of the decisions that go into setting up the new shelving arrangement.

- Is your staff physically able to handle books, push carts, or lift boxes and do the hard work of the move? Don't underestimate the physical labor involved, but don't underestimate your staff. Also note that there are many less physical tasks that can be done by those unable to move books.

- How much are you willing to trust strangers with your move? Will you use your staff as supervisors and, if so, will they be working leaders or just supervise the job? One advantage of the waypoints system is that persons unfamiliar with the classification scheme can work accurately with moderate training and supervision.

- Does your staff *want* to help? My experience is that most librarians welcome the chance to get a little dirty and physical with the books. Many librarians have told me that they learned something new about their collection in the move. Many more have vowed to weed after seeing their collection up close and personal.

- Do you have enough staff available to do the move in a reasonable time?

- If your staff does not move books, what will they do during the time the library is disrupted? I strongly suggest they not be allowed in the destination building unless they have specific move-related tasks. First, there is a safety issue: the more people, the greater the chance someone will get hurt. Second, the temptation to direct or advise the movers may prove irresistible; the more "supervisors" you have, the greater the chance that someone will make a major mistake.

Some staff simply may not be up to the task. Provide a process so people can opt out, and find work for those who want to help but can't.

If you have enough staff willing and able to do the move, you can skip the next section. If not, where will you get extra help?

NONSTAFF MOVERS

Volunteers

I love volunteers. Volunteers are the backbone of many a library. My own library has 1,200 active volunteers right now. We couldn't operate without them. But, except on a small, one-day, move, I would rather not use volunteers. I have used volunteers for moves, many times, but I would rather not. The reason is workflow. We need the whole crew to work together, start together, stop together, and go to lunch together. If I am paying the crew, I can set their work hours. With volunteers, I would want to have a commitment to work all day and preferably every day of the move, to save retraining. This is a lot to ask of volunteers.

Make sure any volunteers know what is expected of them, especially with regard to lifting, pushing, pulling, and grasping. Also, talk with them about the pace of work required. Some people who would happily volunteer may not be able to keep up with the workload.

Try to recruit volunteers from organized groups—a church, PTA, service club, or similar. Look for groups where the members are committed to the group as well as to your project. The extra commitment may help attendance and give you a head start building morale.

Check with your insurance company before you commit to using volunteers. Make sure you and your volunteers are covered and find out what special requirements may be imposed on you. You may be expected to log their exact hours or to provide documentation that you have passed each of them through a safety class.

Paid Workers

Even if you are paying workers, you may want to consider recruiting from organized groups. Some of the smoothest moves I have worked on were done for universities using students over a class break. They tend to be young, strong, intelligent, and easily captivated by the adventure of it all. It is also easy to recruit them. A few flyers, an ad in the student newspaper, a call to the campus employment office, and word of mouth usually do the job.

A twist on that one: Two fraternities. One sorority. Instant motivation.

I did another move where most of the work was done by a high school baseball team trying to earn money for a new batting cage. Think about your own community and what groups you might approach to help with your move. If you get lucky, you may be able to assemble your entire crew with one phone call.

You can instead contract with a temporary services company for the workers you need. You pay a premium for their service, but they do all of the interviewing and administrative work. Beyond that, they carry the insurance and workers' comp responsibility, and it is relatively easy to replace someone who cannot handle the work. Even if we are using students or other organized groups as workers, we often contract with a temp agency to do the personnel administration. It is usually cheaper to pay the agency than to hire the workers yourself, set up personnel accounts, and deal with FICA, taxes, and other red tape.

Alternately, you can take on the hiring yourself. Advertise that you are hiring workers for the duration of your move. Interview and hire the best of the applicants.

JOB DESCRIPTIONS

Here is a list of the various jobs you may need to fill. Depending on the size of your move, you may not need all of them.

The basic work unit is a crew that consists of one or two unshelvers at the origin; one or more pushers in each building; and one or two reshelvers in the destination. Usually a crew rotates between loading and pushing for variety and to rest muscles.

Unshelvers

Unshelvers usually work in pairs to load the books. It works best if one person takes the books off the shelves and hands them to the other person to put on the cart or in the box. A single person soon gets out of sync, with books from the top shelf going on the bottom of the cart or vice versa. With two people, both save a lot of bending and stretching. This is an unskilled position with little or no decision making. Unshelvers need to

- make sure to start each cart or box from the proper (BLACK) end
- follow the flow of the collection at the ends of each range
- number the carts or boxes sequentially
- include all waypoint markers with the books

Pushers

Pushers move loaded carts or stacks of boxes between the shelves and the loading dock or elevator and return with empties. This is an unskilled position with no decision making. Strength and size are not particularly important. Pushers need to

- keep carts or boxes in order
- bring back empties
- be very aware of safety issues pushing heavy loads

Reshelvers

Reshelvers work in pairs to reshelve the books. They work in pairs for the same reasons as the unshelvers. This is an unskilled position but with slightly more decision making than the unshelvers. Reshelvers must

- make certain to start each cart or box from the proper (BLACK) end
- make absolutely certain to unload carts or boxes in numerical order
- follow the flow of the collection at the ends of ranges
- watch the waypoints carefully and call for a supervisor if they miss one
- leave the required amount of space on each shelf

Reshelvers assigned to periodicals need substantially more ability to make judgments about how and when to break runs and leave growth. I usually try to assign a skilled periodicals librarian to work with this crew.

Supervisor

If you have four or more crews working simultaneously, it is useful to have a supervisor for each building. On a big move to or from a multistory building, I prefer to have a supervisor on each floor. In a small move with fewer crews, the move coordinator can do this job.

The supervisor should be familiar with the shelving plan and the overall plan of the work. If possible, I try to assign a librarian to this role. This is a skilled position and requires considerable on-the-spot judgment. The supervisor is responsible for

- monitoring the working crews
- shifting or adding staff as necessary if a crew is slow or if extra people are needed to form a human chain in a narrow aisle
- monitoring workflow in the area and making adjustments as needed
- making sure crews are hitting waypoints and answering questions if they miss
- filling in where and as needed

Interfilers

If you have collections to be interfiled, you might use conscientious volunteers or outside hires, but most libraries assign this work to regular employees who are familiar with the classification system. Staff who have to work with or retrieve books from the finished collection have an extra motivation to get it right.

Interfilers sort the books from two or more collections into one order. They usually work with one or two helpers who bring books from the shelves and load the sorting trays. Another removes the carts of interfiled materials and takes them to the reshelvers. The work requires long periods of intense concentration, all the while working as quickly as possible. You may need to recruit many people for this job and assign them to work in shifts. Interfilers are responsible for

- sorting books from two collections into a single order strictly according to the classification system
- removing sorted books to a box or cart or onto another sorting tray in the case of multiple sorts
- monitoring their own performance and calling for relief when they begin to lose efficiency

The job requires an aptitude for the work and the ability to concentrate mentally while performing a physical task. This is a skilled and somewhat difficult position. The interfiler must be thoroughly familiar with the classification system, including any local anomalies; pay meticulous attention to detail; and understand the absolute necessity of placing books exactly into order.

Dockmaster, Origin Building

This person loads books onto the truck for shipment and unloads empties. The dockmaster also shrinkwraps carts or straps on the cardboard side panels if you are using my version of move carts. The most important task is to make sure there is an even flow of all materials. That means the lowest-numbered cart of each color needs to go on the truck first, and there needs to be a mix of collections (colored sequence cards) on each truck. At times the supervisor in the destination building may ask to have a specific collection held or rushed. The dockmaster needs to keep all of these elements in mind.

This is a skilled position. The person needs to master the intricacies of the shipping issues and needs to be strong enough to move carts, dollies, or pallets of boxes around on the dock. Pushing carts is relatively easy, once you get them moving. Jockeying carts around on the dock involves much starting and stopping and does require considerable strength. This job becomes more critical, and much harder, as the number of crews working simultaneously increases.

If others are using your dock during your move, your dockmaster should be granted absolute power to determine who gets to use the dock, in what order, and for how long. The dockmaster should have the authority to order someone to vacate the dock to allow a truck to slip in, unload, reload, and pull away. It may be difficult to get this authority, but you should insist on it early in the planning process and negotiate for as much authority as you can get. Many delivery persons are accustomed to leaving their truck in the dock while they deliver within the building. Also, some contractors use their truck to store tools and supplies and prefer to have it close at hand, at the dock. Either can tie up the dock for hours and cause a significant interruption in your workflow. Having one person in charge, with responsibility to see that all users have a fair chance at this limited resource, benefits everyone. The origin dockmaster is responsible for

- keeping track of all collections being moved at any time by tracking the color-coded sequence cards
- developing a sorting plan and sorting carts or boxes into an observable order so that the dock crew can load a truck without skipping any books
- strapping cardboard sides to carts or shrinkwrapping carts as needed
- unloading empties and placing them for the pushers to return to the unshelving areas
- loading books into the truck via dock plate, ramp, or forklift
- maintaining safety among the dock crew and bystanders
- keeping material flowing through the dock, including the work of non-move-related persons
- responding to the changing flow of work at the destination building by holding or advancing transport of specific materials as requested
- making certain that the lowest-numbered carts and boxes of each color are transported before higher-numbered ones of that color. Books do not have to be loaded in strict order, but we do not want, for instance, carts 7 and 8 on the truck while number 6 is still on the dock. The reshelvers cannot finish 7 and 8 until they get 6.

This position requires more judgment, decision making, understanding, and strength than any other except the move coordinator. In bad weather, the dockmaster may be exposed to the elements. The longer the move and the more crews working simultaneously, the bigger and more critical is this position.

Dockmaster, Destination Building

This position is responsible for unloading full carts, boxes, dollies, or pallets by dock plate, ramp, or forklift; unwrapping or unstrapping them and getting them started on their way to the shelves; and returning empties to the origin building.

This is a skilled position, but it requires much less judgment and decision making than the dockmaster at the origin building. This position requires less strength since there is less pushing and sorting. In bad weather, the dockmaster may be exposed to the elements. This dockmaster needs the same authority to manage access to the dock and for the same reasons. The destination dockmaster is responsible for

- unloading full carts, stacks, dollies, or pallets and reloading the truck with empties, including straps and sides
- removing sides and straps or shrinkwrap from incoming carts
- maintaining safety among the dock crew and bystanders
- keeping material flowing through the dock, including the work of non-move-related persons and including a steady flow of empties back to the origin building

Dock Assistants

Depending on the size of your move, you need one or more dock assistants at each building. These positions assist the dockmaster. They carry out the same tasks but do not have the authority and decision-making responsibility.

My general guideline is that, at the origin building, a dockmaster and two assistants can handle up to three simultaneous crews. For every two additional crews, you need one additional assistant, up to a maximum of four assistants. At the destination building, you usually need one assistant less than at the origin. The extra work of shrinkwrapping or strapping and sorting requires a little more help on the origin side. If you use an elevator located some distance from the loading dock, you need additional assistants to act as pushers. These numbers are adequate for planning purposes. As you get into your move, you may find that you need more or less help on the dock.

Elevator Operator

If you have an elevator that serves three or more floors, or if your elevator is not close to the loading dock, it is helpful to assign one person to load and unload the elevator and ride it up and down. If the elevator is controlled by whoever pushes the call button first, its use becomes inefficient and the upper floors often don't get sufficient service. Also, the pushers spend too much time waiting for the arrival of the elevator. With a dedicated elevator operator, pushers can just drop their loads and return for more.

With only two floors, an elevator operator is useful but not necessary. The pushers and dock crew can be instructed to load the elevator and then send it to the other floor. As soon as you load, *always* send the cab to the other floor. The elevator operator is responsible for

- loading and unloading the elevator
- maintaining an even flow of full carts or boxes and empties, making sure that all floors are serviced evenly
- installing and removing the walk-off mat or other floor covering used to protect the threshold of the elevator car
- making sure the elevator is not overloaded

This is a position with a short learning curve. The elevator operator should be large and strong enough to jockey carts and pallets on and off the elevator.

Forklift Operator

The forklift operator loads or unloads the truck if a dock plate or shallow ramp cannot be used. OSHA requires that forklift operators be trained and certified. The training is not difficult and almost anyone could be certified. The most important traits for a forklift driver are maturity, an emphasis on safety, and patience. The forklift operates with loads of up to 1,500 lbs, 5 feet in the air. Slow, smooth, steady movements are much more important than demonstrations of skill. The operator should be chosen with this in mind. The forklift operator is responsible for

- loading or unloading full and empty carts, dollies, or pallets between the truck and the dock area
- maintaining safety within the area of operation
- ceasing operation immediately if anyone, crew or bystander, moves into the operating area of the forklift
- assisting the dock crew as needed

Driver

The driver helps load books onto the truck and drives between buildings. The driver must have a valid driving license. Be sure that a regular, personal license covers this type of activity in your state and that the driver does not need some sort of commercial license. As with the forklift, smooth, steady, and careful are the important traits. We can block or strap the carts in place, but violent movements cause them to shift. I once had a substitute driver get careless while turning a corner. A cart broke loose and put an 8-inch bulge in the side of the rental truck.

During the loading operation, the driver works in the truck, removing loads from the forklift or the dock plate and placing them in the truck. It is not necessary to keep the loads in order in the truck. During unloading, the driver pulls the loads onto the forklift or to the ramp or dock plate. The driver is responsible for

- driving the truck between buildings
- assisting in loading and unloading the truck
- strapping, blocking, or otherwise restraining the movement of loads within the truck during transport
- carrying information, supplies, and other items between the buildings as needed
- monitoring the condition of the truck, reporting problems, and keeping the truck gassed and running
- notifying the move coordinator of any potential problems that might cause the truck to be out of service for any time, including the need to go for gas
- keeping a count of carts or boxes moved each day

Dispatcher

If you have more than three or four crews working, it is helpful to place a dispatcher at a central desk in each building. This person keeps track of what crews are working, what parts of the collection they are working on, and what colors are assigned to each collection. The dispatchers communicate back and forth about backlogs, shortages, or supplies needed to keep up a smooth workflow. As crews finish their assigned work, they report to the dispatch desk for a new assignment.

At the origin building, the dispatcher keeps a chart showing what crews are working on what collections and the colors assigned. The desk should also have a list of collections still to be moved. When a crew has finished an assignment, they report to the dispatcher, who assigns them a new collection and a color. The move coordinator is responsible for setting the overall assignments and order of the move, but the dispatcher is usually the one to hand out actual assignments. Whenever the dispatcher assigns a new crew and color, he or she should call the dispatcher at the origin building and alert that person that a new stream of material is arriving soon.

At the destination building, the dispatcher works primarily from one of the collection layout drawings with the waypoints marked. When the first load of a collection arrives, the dispatcher assigns a reshelving crew and shows them where to start. The dispatcher also interacts with the pushers to make sure they know where to take materials, based on the color of the sequence cards. The dispatchers and move coordinator need to work together to make certain that the appropriate crews are available and that there are adequate elevators, aisles, and access for them.

The dispatch desks are good places to keep coffee, snacks, supplies, assignment lists, and other necessities.

Move Coordinator

Someone has to be in charge. Ideally the move coordinator is involved in the planning from the beginning. The move coordinator must have a clear and detailed concept of the move and absolutely must have the confidence to carry out the plan, including the confidence to activate backup plans or make adjustments on the fly. The coordinator must spend time in both buildings, concentrating on the places where the workflow is less efficient. During the actual move, the coordinator is responsible for

- determining which collections move in what order
- assigning the work crews to specific collections
- monitoring the progress of the crews, adding, subtracting, or changing personnel as necessary
- preparing crew assignments in advance so that, when a crew finishes one collection, they can be reassigned quickly to another assignment
- providing a running list of assignments to the origin dispatch desk
- training personnel
- monitoring the flow of work for maximum efficiency and shifting workers as needed. This is an ongoing activity. There is always one point in the workflow that is less efficient than any other. It is

up to the move coordinator to do whatever is necessary to improve efficiency at that spot, in which case some other point becomes the bottleneck.
- working with the supervisor in the destination building to arrange a skipahead if a crew gets backlogged
- being ready to revise the move plan if necessary in case of a major disaster
- being everywhere, all of the time

Personnel and Morale Officer

This is the person in charge of staff. Workers should report to this person first thing each day. The personnel officer keeps a list of all staff, and their hours worked if necessary. If you are using workers from a temporary service agency, the personnel officer is the point of contact for that relationship. This person is also in charge of snacks, lunches, contests, drawings, and other amenities. This is an excellent job for someone who wants to participate in the move but is not up to the physical demands of the work. It is important to identify this person early in the planning, for the work requires considerable preplanning and preparation. This person also coordinates efforts to secure donations of food and prizes. If you are kind, you will assign this person one or more assistants.

Night Crew

On a large move it is useful to have a small crew that can work after normal hours to clean up loose ends and prepare for the next day. One crew member should be capable of supervising the others, while working from a specific task list.

HOW MANY STAFF DO YOU NEED?

This is a time versus people equation. It is like a story problem. If twenty people can move a library in six days, how long will it take forty people?

Start with a count of how many books you have. Count books, not shelves. This can be a fairly rough count. If you come within 10 percent, that is close enough. If you are going to be wrong, guess high.

With move carts and moving between buildings, we figure a single crew—two unshelvers, two or more pushers, two reshelvers—can move fifty-five carts per day, or 12,000–14,000 books. With book carts, I reduce that estimate to 10,000 per crew per day; with the smaller carts, you spend more time moving carts around and less time loading. Usually one pusher per crew in each building is sufficient. If a crew is working a long way from the dock, you may need to add an additional pusher. Figure seven to eight minutes on average for a crew to load a move cart. If the pusher can walk to the dock and back in that time, you need only one pusher for that crew.

An experienced, highly motivated team working with adult fiction can work much faster. The "fly" team at Allen County Public Library loaded forty-eight carts in a four-hour period. This is unusual, but if your collection is heavily weighted toward adult light-reading materials, you might use a slightly higher average loading rate.

Most crews seem to load children's books at about the same rate as they load adult materials. The books are thinner and you can get more books per cart, but they are often awkward, slippery, odd-size, and harder to load quickly. In a given time period a crew loads fewer carts but more books than one loading adult materials.

Periodical collections take a bit longer than average to load. You load long runs of same-size books, which is easy, but they are usually heavy and often oversize for the cart or box, which cuts productivity. The slowest move I ever participated in was a large collection of city directories—huge, heavy, oversize books that filled a cart quickly. We had to handle the books one at a time, and we spent a lot of time just jockeying carts in and out of place.

There is no magic formula to calculate how many workers you need for your move and where to deploy them. So much depends on the exact layout of your building, how many books you are moving, and how long you have for the move. Here, I describe two staff schedules, one for a move between buildings and one for a move within a single building. These are only rough outlines. As you plan, you make changes; once the move starts, you make constant adjustments to fine-tune the operation.

TIP

If you need to save on staff, cut back on the number of pushers and assign them to rotate among the crews. Make certain they service all the crews evenly.

As a general rule, take the total number of books, divide by the number of days you have for the move, and divide that by 1,300 (books / days / 1,300 = crew). This should give you a safe figure for the total number of workers needed for a move between buildings. Figure at least 25 percent fewer staff for a move within a building. If you have a very small move, you may need one or two more than this formula; for a very large move, or one with a lot of children's books, you may be able to get by with slightly fewer.

It is possible to have too many people, but it is far better to have too many than too few.

Staff Schedule for a Move between Two Buildings

Figure how many crews you will have working simultaneously. There are six people per crew. In addition, you need

- one dockmaster at each location and one or more assistants at each
- one driver per truck
- one forklift operator per forklift
- one elevator operator per elevator, if your elevator serves three or more floors
- two dispatchers, if you have three or more crews working
- two supervisors, if you have three or more crews working
- one move coordinator

Staff Schedule for a Move within a Building

Moves within a building are much more efficient because you eliminate much of the overhead and most of the people are directly moving books. They are also much easier to supervise. Calculate how many crews you will have working simultaneously. In this case a crew consists of five people—two unshelvers, one pusher, and two reshelvers. In addition, you need

- one elevator operator per elevator, if your elevator serves three or more floors
- one dispatcher
- one move coordinator
- one supervisor to assist the coordinator, if you have more than five crews working

Chapter 7

Assembling Tools and Supplies

This chapter contains a list of tools and supplies you need during your move. You should assemble these items well in advance of the move.

CARTS

If you are going to move on book carts, you need enough of them to keep your work crews busy. If you are borrowing carts from neighboring libraries, make arrangements well in advance. You may have to pick up the carts at the last minute, but the total number of carts you have affects your moving schedule.

Plan some time before the move to prepare the carts. Check the wheels to make sure they turn and run freely. Oil the wheels if necessary. Tighten screws and bolts. Identify the "starting" end of each cart. The templates and other materials included in this book assume that you put black tape on the top edge of one end (figure 7.1). If you use some other method, be sure to rewrite the various signs and instructions to match. Put two book card pockets on the "starting" end of each book cart. You use only one at a time, but they do get ripped, and the extra pocket keeps the workflow intact.

If you are using move carts (figure 7.2), which I recommend for most moves, make arrangements well ahead of the move date. You have three choices: rent, borrow, or build. You should investigate each method and determine which best fits your need and budget. As you check sources, consider the length of the carts in relation to the width of your aisles. It is *by far* more efficient to load and unload carts if you can wheel them right up to the shelves you are unloading. This means that the carts need to be shorter than the width of your aisles. If you have short ranges—six sections long or less—cart length won't matter. With longer ranges, if you can't wheel the cart to the shelf, you have to leave it at the end of the aisle and hand the books along a human chain. The cost of the extra crew to handle the books rapidly exceeds the cost of renting or building more, but smaller, carts. Also, check to see what provisions are made to retain the books on the cart shelves as the carts are being moved. Some have angled shelves. Some have a lip on the front of the shelf. Some require the whole cart to be shrinkwrapped. Some have nothing. If a vendor tries to tell you books will not rattle off their flat shelves, I'd suggest you look for your carts from another source.

Figure 7.1 Black tape indicates starting end for all carts.

Assembling Tools and Supplies

Figure 7.2 Cart designed specifically for library moves.

Rent

Several national companies rent carts. Rental rates vary, and in some cases the cost of transporting the carts to your location may exceed the rental cost, for the carts are quite bulky. If you have a contract with a moving company to move your furniture, equipment, and staff effects, ask how much it would cost to have them pick up and deliver carts.

Most of the rental companies and general moving companies have what are called "machine carts." These look like move carts but have only one or two very wide shelves. They are not suitable for moving books.

I do not know of any rental companies that supply carts with both pockets for the numbering system and side panels. I have seen rental carts that have a flag system to carry a number. If you rent carts, you may want to plan time to tape one end and to add card pockets.

Make sure the length of the carts is suitable for your aisles in both your old and new buildings.

Borrow

You may be able to find a library that has purchased or built carts and will loan them to you. Also, it may be worth asking local moving companies to loan you carts before you offer to rent them. Your move is likely to be a visible event in your community, and companies may be willing to help you in return for the publicity value.

Build

It may be to your benefit to build some or all of the carts you need. Compare the cost of construction to the rental rate, including delivery costs, and consider any extra time you may have the books on the carts after the move. Appendix B includes plans and specifications for the carts I use. The construction is simple; a skilled handyman can do it in a home garage workshop. The only special tool needed is a large table saw.

If you have carts left over after the move, there are uses for them. Cataloging departments love them, especially for special projects. They are handy for temporary shelving, shifting, or subsequent moves. They are a great way to store books for book sales. Arrange books on the carts as you weed or accept gifts. On sale day, just roll the carts into the book sale space. No reshelving, no books on untidy tables. You may be able to sell unwanted carts to local office moving companies or to other libraries to recoup a portion of the costs.

If you have the carts built, be sure that the builder uses the heavy-duty casters specified in appendix B. I know of two instances where the builder tried to save money using cheap wheels; in both cases the light-duty casters would not bear the weight of the books.

Quantity

You need eight to fifteen book carts or six to twelve move carts for each crew, the higher numbers if you are moving between buildings and have carts tied up on the dock or in transport. It is much better to have too many carts than too few. The cost of having crew members standing around waiting for carts rapidly exceeds the cost of a few more carts.

A 32-inch move cart, the size suitable for ADA-minimum 36-inch aisles, holds 240–250 adult books. A 36-inch cart holds about 300, a 48-inch cart about 400. A good move crew can load fifty-five 32- or 36-inch carts in an eight-hour day. One highly motivated crew from the reshelving department at my library pride themselves on loading a minimum of eighty trucks a day. I personally have never used 48-inch trucks, but I would expect the loading rates to be more like forty to forty-five per day, assuming you can get them all the way to the shelf where you are loading and unloading.

The capacity and loading rates of book carts vary. You can calculate capacity based on the carts you have available. Measure the total length of the shelves on the cart in inches. We figure about one book per inch, then round up a bit. Children's books can be figured at about three per inch, two for fiction. The loading rate is related to capacity, but it is not a direct ratio. Crews move relatively fewer books with the smaller carts over the same period.

SIDES AND STRAPS, SHRINKWRAP

You need some way to keep books from rattling off the carts as you move them. The problem is that the books slide around as the carts are moved, forklifted, or being transported between buildings.

Shrinkwrap works. Get rolls about 12–14 inches wide and applicators to hold the rolls. You can wrap about twenty-two 36-inch carts with one standard roll.

If you rented move carts with slanted or lipped shelves, the books should stay on those shelves through normal moving operations.

The move carts I prefer have a unique retaining system (figure 7.3). Sides of cross-linked cardboard are strapped around the cart. The sides are made of two sheets of cardboard glued together with the grain running at right angles. This makes for a light but strong panel without the potential for splinters. The shelves are inset slightly, and there is a lip at the bottom to retain the side panel. A ratcheting tie-down strap holds the panel near the top. The whole construction is easy to put together and remove and holds books in place even if the cart is tipped on its side.

Full specifications for the sides are included with the cart specifications in appendix B. The sides can be made by a corrugated paper manufacturer. The straps are available at many hardware and home improvement stores.

PALLETS

If you move or store books in boxes on pallets, you need a supply of pallets. New ones are fairly expensive. Often you can buy reconditioned ones at a fraction of the cost.

Figure 7.3 Side panels and a restraining strap hold books in place on a move cart.

Standard pallets are 48 by 40 inches. Make sure you get all the same size. Unless you are storing books for a long time, you may be able to borrow enough pallets for a shelf-to-shelf move from a local manufacturing or shipping company.

Not all pallets are created equal. Some have slats that are only about ¼ inch thick, or are spaced 3 inches or so apart, or both. These are light-duty and not suited to moving a heavy load of books. Get pallets with solid ¾-inch board slats. If you are using the pallets for long-term storage, the width of the gaps becomes more critical. Jim Kelly, of Kelly Box and Packaging, recommends filling in all gaps larger than ¾ inch. You may be able to buy used pallets and even sell them back to the vendor when you are done.

DOLLIES, PALLET JACKS, AND HAND TRUCKS

If you are moving with boxes, you need a way to move them. Pick a method of transportation and start locating the tools you need. The likely choices—hand trucks, dollies, or pallet jacks—are discussed in chapter 12.

If you use hand trucks, you need one for every pusher and three or four for each dock. It is unlikely you will find enough hand trucks from one source to meet all of your needs. Many businesses and other organization have hand trucks, and you may be able to borrow them—but you will have to make a lot of contacts to get the number you need. If you rent, you may have to work with several different rental agencies.

If you use dollies, the number you need depends on their size. Figure that a good crew can load one hundred boxes an hour and it takes at least an hour to cycle a load between buildings. For each crew, you need enough dollies to carry one hundred boxes. One dolly holds three stacks of four boxes, so you need nine dollies for that crew ($100 / [3 \times 4] \approx 9$). If at all possible, try to give each crew only one size of dolly so they can always load in the same pattern. This helps the unshelvers and reshelvers keep the boxes in order.

You may have to contact many sources to find enough dollies. Think about a manufacturing or warehousing operation in your area that might use a lot of dollies and might be willing to loan or rent you a supply. If at all possible, get dollies with four swivel wheels. They are much easier to maneuver in a tight spot than those with two fixed and two swivel casters. If you are using pallets, you need pallet jacks. This is the most expensive method of transport you can rent, but many different types of businesses have pallet jacks, and you may be able to borrow enough to do your move.

You need one jack for each crew in each building, at least one for each dock crew, and one in each truck unless your truck matches the dock height at both buildings. If you have a short route between the shelves and the dock, you may be able to use one jack to service two crews. A pallet holds thirty-two boxes stacked four high. It takes longer to drag and maneuver that load to or from the dock, but it takes a lot longer for each crew to load that many boxes, and you may be able to make the jacks do double duty.

TRUCK

If you are moving between buildings, one truck is sufficient if you have up to five or six crews working simultaneously. If you have a larger move, you may need a second truck and driver, or even a third. I have done moves with fifteen crews that required three trucks to keep up with the flow. Rental trucks work well. You should shop around to find the best truck for your needs.

Height

Height of the floor of the truck is critical. If you have a loading dock, try to find a truck that is the same height as your dock so you can roll loads on and off without using a forklift or ramp. A simple plywood plate can be used to bridge between the dock and the truck, making loading and unloading much faster. Some docks have load levelers, a small platform that can be raised or lowered to match a truck bed. These do not help much and certainly are not a substitute for a truck that matches the dock. You have to operate the leveler like an elevator, taking one pallet and three or four carts at a load. You still need a plate between the truck and leveler, and you may need another to bridge a gap between the leveler and the dock. Spend the extra time to find the right truck.

If the two loading docks are not the same height, evaluate the area around the docks and determine whether one of them is better suited to use a forklift truck. A level paved surface and plenty of turning radius are most important. A covered working area could be important if it rains. When you determine which dock area is best for a forklift, look for a truck that matches the height of the *other* dock. "Matches" in this case means no more than an inch of difference and too high rather than too low. The weight of the carts brings the truck down to the dock height.

Length

The length of the truck affects its capacity. My biggest moves were done with a 14-foot U-Haul. Smaller trucks make more trips but keep a smoother workflow. Longer trucks cause a start-and-stop flow at both docks. Unless you are moving several miles per trip, the added capacity of a longer truck does not seem to matter. With 32- or

TIP

Go look at the truck and measure it yourself. The ideal situation is when you have two loading docks of the same height.

> **TIP**
>
> A diesel truck can be a problem if you have a small, enclosed dock. Diesel fumes can make some people ill. Even if your dock has good ventilation, make certain the truck will not be parked near an air intake for the building. Gas engines are usually turned off when the truck is parked; diesel engines are usually left running.

36-inch move carts, you can load about one cart per linear foot of truck bed length. Some trucks have flat floors. Others have internal wheel wells that cut capacity by one or two carts. If you have a choice, opt for the flat floor.

Angle

Ideally you want the front of the truck to be slightly lower than the back, so the carts can nestle against the front of the truck box. However, many loading dock ramps slope down toward the dock. This creates a difficult situation for the loaders, because the carts may roll back out of the truck. If this is the case, you must block the wheels of each cart as it is loaded. Cut some pieces of 1-by-4-inch board about 8 inches long and keep them handy in the truck. Sometimes a longer truck evens out this angle and eliminates the need for wheel chocks.

Dock height is the most important factor. Length of the truck is the least.

Liftgate

You may be tempted to rent a truck with a liftgate (figure 7.4) to avoid all the extra work with docks, forklifts, and so forth. *I have never seen a liftgate that was safe for any wheeled conveyance.* The carts roll easily. If the truck is parked at an angle, or if the liftgate is not perfectly level throughout its entire range of motion, the cart may roll off. I stress safety as the most important part of every move, but after 100 carts, or 10,000 carts, if only one person gets careless, then we have a cart weighing half a ton or more, 4 feet in the air and moving, with half a dozen people standing around. I have seen two jobs where people tried to use liftgates to load move carts. In each case they eventually gave up and used a different method for the sake of safety.

Figure 7.4 Don't do this! A liftgate is dangerous if you are loading carts or dollies.

Maybe, if a liftgate could be modified with a railing at least 4 inches high all the way around, it could be made safe. Part of the railing would have to be removable to allow the cart to move on and off the gate. I have never tried this method.

You can use a liftgate to load individual stacks of boxes or a pallet of boxes if the stacks are tied together and the liftgate can handle the weight.

DOCK PLATE

If you can find a truck that matches your dock, you need a dock plate. When you back the truck against the dock, there is still a small gap. The dock plate covers this gap. Most commercial dock plates are made of heavy metal. If you have one, fine. For moving books, we can use a plate made from plywood (figure 7.5). Get a 4-by-8-foot sheet of ½-inch BC (sheathing) plywood. Cut it in half, making two plates. To make it even easier to load carts, sand down the edges of the sheet. The plywood is much lighter and easier to move than a metal plate.

Figure 7.5 A 4-by-4-foot piece of plywood makes a light, strong dock plate.

RESTRAINING STRAPS OR BARS

You need a set of heavy-duty straps or a cargo bar to keep the carts from moving around inside the trucks. Both should be available from the rental truck supplier. I prefer the bars. A cargo bar is an extendable bar that is either spring-loaded or locked into position with a cam lever. It is braced against the sides of the truck to restrain the cargo. If the truck supplier does not have a cargo bar, you can usually find them at a good truck stop store. They are not expensive.

RAMP

Unless you are able to match the truck to the dock height at both buildings, you need some method to get carts on and off the trucks. Most rental trucks come with a loading ramp. You can use the ramp to load and unload empty carts and most book carts. I do not recommend pushing loaded move carts up a truck ramp. The carts are heavy, and it may require several people to push one up a ramp into a truck. In addition, every truck ramp I have seen has a short, steep section right at the bottom end. This creates a sudden jolt to the loaded cart that can buckle the wheels or throw the cart off to one side of the ramp, spilling it.

Caution: If you do a test, loading up a cart and pushing it around your route, be careful not to assume that all carts are as easy as the first one with a fresh crew. For some reason as yet unknown to modern physicists, but common knowledge among the pyramid builders, each load in a move gets heavier than the previous one. By the time you have pushed fifty, or five hundred, carts up a ramp, you feel the full effect of the weight. At that point people get tired and careless and mistakes can happen.

If you have elevation changes within your building, you may be able to use either existing ramps or a temporary ramp you build. You can move loaded move carts and dollies up and down a 1-in-12 ramp, *but*

- You will not be able to make any turns on the ramp, and you will need room at the bottom so that a runaway cart does not hit something it can damage, including a wall. A scrap piece of heavy shag rug nailed to the ramp helps slow the truck on the slope.
- The ramp must have an edge or rail to prevent a load from falling off the side.
- You need two people to control the cart on the slope. One person can walk behind the cart on the ramp. There must be room for another person to walk beside—never in front of—the cart to help slow it down.

FORKLIFT

If you cannot get a substantially level path for loaded book carts, the best alternative I have found is a forklift. It is safer than ramps because the crew can stand away when the cart is being lifted and because a hydraulic lifter does not get tired. A forklift is also surprisingly quick. We can load empties into a truck about as fast with a forklift as we can by pushing them up a ramp, and we can do it with fewer people.

Forklifts come in two main types, propane and electric. Electric forklifts are battery-powered. They are easy to use but need to be recharged every day. Before you settle on an electric, make sure you have enough of the right kind of power to plug in the battery charger. Most do *not* just plug into a handy wall outlet. Propane trucks are only slightly more complex—you have to remember to turn the gas on and off. They do not have to be recharged, but you do have to change fuel tanks from time to time.

You can rent forklifts from many local sources, and you may be able to borrow one free of charge for your project. If your building is new construction, the contractor may have a truck on site that you can use for free or a fee. In any case you need a trained operator. The training is simple and oriented to safety, but OSHA requires it.

You do not need the biggest forklift. One rated for 2,500 lbs is just fine. This may be either the ride-on or walk-behind type. The forklift should have adjustable forks, meaning that the two tines that go under the load can be moved together or apart to fit between the wheels and provide a stable base.

The operator may not be able to see exactly how high the load has been raised in relation to the truck bed or loading dock. If the operator has the cart too low and runs the wheels into the truck bed or the dock, the impact *will* rip the wheels off the cart. Here's one way to deal with this:

The lift mechanism has one upright that stays constant and one or more that travel up and down. Put a load on the fork, then raise it an inch or two above the surface (truck bed or dock) where it is to be deposited. Then put a piece of painter's tape on the fixed upright and another on the moving upright so that both pieces of tape are level when the load clears the surface of the dock or truck. The lift operator can then just match up the two pieces of tape instead of trying to judge when the load clears the surface.

Forklifts are agile. Many can turn in their own length or spin in place. You don't really need this capability. The most efficient way to use one for unloading carts is just as an elevator. The operator raises the fork to the mark and moves forward to hang the tines over the back deck of the truck. One of the crew moves a loaded cart onto the tines. Always put the cart on the tines. Don't move the tines under the cart; if you do, sooner or later you snag a wheel and damage it. The operator lifts the load slightly, backs straight back about 6 feet, and lowers it to the ground. Another crew member on the ground pulls the cart off the tines and starts it on the way to the shelves. The operator raises the tines again and moves forward about 6 feet to put the tines inside the truck. Do this over and over. No fancy turns. No demonstrations of skill. Just patience.

Loading the truck is the same process. The forklift just moves up and in, back and down. The topography of your loading/unloading area may force the forklift driver to turn, back, pivot, or otherwise maneuver. If so, that's what you do, but it will be slower than the back-and-forth routine.

On one library's move out, using a forklift to load from ground level, we found we could cycle a truck quickly with four or five people—driver, forklift operator, and two or three dock crew. This was our procedure:

1. Back up the truck.
2. Pull out the ramp and set in place.
3. Open the door.
4. Unload down the ramp thirteen empty carts, a stack of cardboard sides, and a box of straps.
5. Unhook the ramp and push it back in place.
6. Load thirteen full carts via forklift.
7. Strap them in.
8. Close and lock the door.
9. Drive away.

Elapsed time, 4 minutes, 20 seconds. Over and over.

On the move back, we had a loading dock matched to the truck. The sequence went:

1. Back up the truck.
2. Open the door.
3. Set the plywood dock plate across the gap.
4. Unload thirteen empties across the dock plate, with sides and straps.
5. Load thirteen full carts across the dock plate.
6. Strap them in.
7. Kick the dock plate out of the way and pull down the door.
8. Drive away.

Elapsed time, about 3 minutes, 10 seconds.

You may not need to cycle your trucks this quickly, but you can see that the loading dock is much faster than the forklift option. In safety as well I would judge the dock plate to be the safest method, followed by the forklift, with the ramp last.

BOXES

Move Boxes

Move boxes may be reused many times. Boxes for moving books should be strong, easy to build and tear down, with handholds at each end. Integral tops are a distinct advantage. You need some sort of top so the boxes stack solidly. Separate tops work well, but then you have two pieces to keep track of. A box about 16–20 inches long is easiest to handle. One dimension of the box should be at least 12 inches to allow 8½-by-11-inch books to fit. All boxes must be the same size so they stack solidly. Copier paper boxes are the right size but are not strong enough to handle the weight of books. Appendix A includes specifications for a move box I have used.

It is difficult to predict how many boxes you need for a move. One box holds only about half a shelf of books, so the loading goes fast. A good crew can load 800–900 boxes in a day, and a fast crew loading fiction can load 1,000 or more, the equivalent of sixty-two move carts. The unpredictability lies in how quickly you can expect to recycle boxes, that is, move them, unload them, and return the empties. Every place the box stops moving—both loading docks, the transport vehicle, and whatever backlog develops at the reshelving area—increases the number of boxes you need to keep the crews working.

For an average move, I would obtain not less than 150 boxes for each unshelving crew working simultaneously. For a more complex move, I would up that number to 200–250. The problem is the delivery time. If you get into the move and find that you have crews standing around waiting for boxes, you may not be able to get additional boxes immediately.

If you are moving within one building, you need fewer boxes. Even so, it is better to have too many than too few.

Storage Boxes

You can store books for up to a year in regular move boxes, but boxes for long-term storage have different requirements. They are likely to be used only once, but they may have to hold the books for several years. The most important feature of these boxes is an extremely high crush weight so that they can carry the weight without sagging.

Appendix A includes specifications for an engineered cardboard box storage system we used at Allen County Public Library. We stored over a million books and government documents in boxes for a period of four years. This system worked well. It gave us maximum density of storage, and not one stack of books collapsed. The system used extra-heavy boxes, without tops, stacked in layers of eight boxes, with a single sheet of cardboard between the layers and a formed top to help hold the stack together. We built stacks of boxes seven layers high, on pallets, fifty-six boxes to a 40-by-48-inch pallet, about 1,100 books per stack. These boxes have a capacity of about 20–25 books each (for more details on this storage project, see "Long-Term Storage," chapter 12).

Microfilm/fiche Trays

Most microfilm cabinet manufacturers void their warranty if you move the cabinets when they are full. The cabinets are engineered to hold a tremendous weight straight up and down, but they warp or twist the drawer slides when they are tipped.

We use a cardboard tray (figure 7.6) to move either film or fiche. The tray is the same length as a standard film cabinet drawer and is wide enough to hold two rows of film or one of fiche. We number each cabinet and write that number on the tray. Then we load the trays onto a move cart for transport. Appendix A includes specifications for the microfilm trays, and chapter 14 contains detailed instructions for moving microforms.

You need one tray for every two rows of microfilm or one row of microfiche in your collection. You can recycle them. To estimate how many trays you need, count the number of rows of film in the collection—rows, not drawers—and divide by two. Add to this the number of rows of fiche. Then estimate how many times you can recycle them during the move. Consider how many people you can devote to this part of the move, the transport time, and other factors that affect the movement of the material. Divide the total number of rows by the times you can recycle. That's how many trays you need.

If you are moving only one or two cabinets of film, forget about the trays and move them on carts as if the

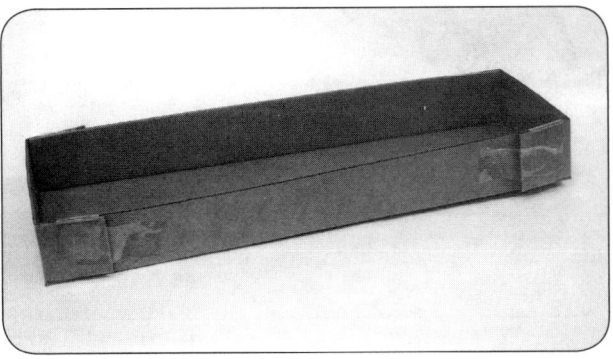

Figure 7.6 Microfilm tray.

film boxes were just like books. Fiche must be moved in some kind of container.

FLOOR AND WALL PROTECTION

You may need to protect walls, floors, and other surfaces in your buildings. Accumulate the necessary supplies and plan time to install them before the move.

The best floor covering is 3/8- or 1/2-inch plywood or chipboard. Masonite only works over a hard floor, not over carpet. For smaller areas, pieces of walk-off mat work well. See the discussion in chapter 8 to determine how much material you need.

The most likely places for wall damage to occur are doorways, elevators, and other choke points. The basic wall protection is cardboard in flat sheets. You can buy it from a box manufacturer, but if you are buying new furniture, check with the furniture or shelving installer. Typically they have a *lot* of cardboard to dispose of.

The technique for corners, doorways, and the like uses cardboard bent and taped around the area you are trying to protect. Smaller sheets and especially the boxes your shelving came in work well for this. You can also purchase edge protectors made of heavy paperboard (figure 7.7). These are designed to be used with metal strapping systems to protect palletized materials. They are useful to protect corners and doorways. You can buy them from strapping suppliers.

Stockpile a lot of rubber wastebaskets, from the small desk kind to large trash cans. These make excellent bumpers wherever there is a danger of carts running into a wall. They work like the stacks of cans used to protect highway overpasses, absorbing the energy and deflecting the cart.

Elevator walls are a special case. If yours have pads or if the contractors have protections in place, leave them there. If not, the best protection I have found is 2-inch-thick foam insulation, which you can buy in 4-by-8-foot sheets at any building supply store. I like the blue better than the pink; it doesn't crumble as much.

SIGNS AND PAPERWORK

You can prepare the signage and other paperwork in advance. Appendix D shows examples of many of those needed. Electronic versions are available at www.ala.org/editions/extras/fortriede09942. WEB Included are

Collection flags and waypoint markers. See chapters 11 and 12 for details.

"TOP, BLACK, LEFT." The cart system relies on a piece of black tape on one end of the cart to provide a quick visual reference for the starting point for each cart. If someone inadvertently loads or unloads the cart from the other side, a couple of hundred books end up out of order. I include two templates for signs reminding the crew to load and unload carts from the black end. I make many copies and post them all over both buildings as a constant reminder.

Elevator weight limits. You may need to post a sign in your elevators to remind crew not to load too many books at one time. The template has a blank where you fill in the safe number. Figure loaded trucks at 1,200–1,500 lbs each; most weigh a little less. Check the weight limits on your elevators and set the number of carts, pallets, or dollies accordingly.

Sequence cards. These are 3-by-5-inch cards numbered 1 through 100. You need at least one set of numbers for each collection you are going to move. In practice you need about double that. Each set should be on different-colored paper to identify the separate collections. If you have large collections, you can run several sets of the same color. You need seventeen pages for each set of one hundred numbers. The templates are arranged so that, if you run them in sets of seventeen, then cut them apart on a paper cutter, they will all be in order—that is, numbers 1–17 in one stack, 18–34 in another, and so on. Stack up the stacks, rubber-band them, and you have a stack in order, 1 to 100, with two

Figure 7.7 Edge protector.

extras. If you have many collections, you may run out of colors. Here are a couple of things you can do:

- You can reuse some colors, but only after the first collection you assigned to that color has been moved and reshelved.
- You can run extra copies of the template on plain paper. Then take a wide-tip marker and mark a stripe across the top of each card in one set. Mark a diagonal line on each card of another. Any marks must be on the top of the card above the number. The bottom of the card is hidden by the pocket. Now copy each marked-up template onto each of your available colors of paper. You can assign "plain pink" to one collection, "pink line" to another, and "pink slash" to a third.
- You can modify copies of the template to add some easily recognized symbol to the number.

COMMUNICATION TOOLS

You need a good communications system between your two buildings. At a minimum, you need phones at both loading docks, at both dispatch desks, and with the move coordinator and any supervisors. Cell phones work well, but make sure everyone has enough minutes and check for areas where there is no signal.

If you have working telephones in both buildings, you have a good start. If you do not have phones in the dock area, you may be able to buy a long cord and use a nearby extension.

Radios work well, even in some places where cell phones cannot get a signal, but make sure all of the users know how to work them.

In any case make up a contact list with the number (or radio contact) for each position and post it at each location. Give copies to each roving supervisor.

DISPATCH DESK SETUPS

Set up a central communications and control location in each building. This is where crews receive their assignments, report progress, come for help and questions, and generally hang out. You need a telephone, cell phone, or radio at each location, along with a table and a few chairs.

The color-coded sequence cards are assigned at the origin building desk. The destination desk should have one or more copies of the Layout spreadsheet printout for each collection. Both desks should have a copy of the destination floor plan, marked with all the waypoints. If you have a floor plan of the origin building, you can cross off blocks of shelving as they are emptied, providing a visual reference. If possible, hang the floor plans on easels or tape them to the walls so they can be consulted easily (figure 7.8).

A large whiteboard or dry-erase board is useful at the origin building to keep a running log of which crews are currently working, which collections they are working on, and which color numbers are assigned to each crew.

Telephone lists should be available at both desks.

FOOD

Okay, I generally have to do some convincing here, but there are good reasons. There is a dynamic to every move, a sense of camaraderie and teamwork that is essential to success. I like to build on this whenever possible.

Then there is a practical reason: Think of a well-organized move as a production line. A book starts on the shelf and moves through the various steps until it eventually rests on its new shelf. Empty carts and supplies flow back to start the process all over. So long as the work keeps flowing smoothly, the move continues rapidly and efficiently. Smooth is fast. If one workstation gets backed up, the entire system gets out of sync. One of my crew describes this situation as "the pig in the python of progress." The flow works best if we all start

Figure 7.8 Dispatch desk—the nerve center of every move.

and stop at the same time. If one crew loads "just one more cart" before lunch, they cause a backlog at the next station. Then, if they come back from lunch late, they cause another glitch.

If people go to lunch on their own, they straggle back at different times, some early and some late. For this reason, I strongly recommend my clients consider providing lunch, at least part of the time. This also brings the entire crew together in one (or two) places. It is a chance to talk about problems and progress, hand out prizes, build teamwork, and celebrate successes.

The menu can be simple. Pizza is always good, as are sub sandwiches. Often you can get a local restaurant to donate or sponsor a lunch, especially if your move is well known in the community. I have done university moves where we arranged meals in the cafeteria. One popular meal is a "chili cook-off." Often there are staff members who want to help with the move but are physically unable to load or push carts. We have enlisted them to make their signature chili, and the crew votes for their favorite. Be creative.

Whenever possible I prefer to provide snacks and drinks for the crew. They are usually appreciated, and it keeps people from wandering off looking for a vending machine. It's amazing how a plate of warm cookies improves productivity in the middle of the afternoon when everyone is getting really tired. Again, it is often possible to get donations. Coffee? I don't touch the stuff myself, but lots of people do. If you provide it, they won't go off looking for it on their own.

PRIZES

Okay, more explaining. Moving a library can be fun, or it can be incredible drudgery. What makes it fun is the morale of the people doing the move. The most important morale booster is a smooth, well-planned move in which the crew can see the books just melting away. Next after that are little amenities that break up the day and show appreciation for their work. Lunch or snacks are one such. In addition, we often organize contests, prize drawings, and the like.

I usually set up a pool and let the crew guess how many book carts we will load each day. We have also had cart-loading races. Which team can load one cart fastest? We usually do this over the lunch break with two or three crews racing head-to-head.

If we can get a lot of small prizes donated, we do a straight drawing in which everybody who works on a particular day has a chance to win a prize. Prizes are easy to come by. You make a lot of phone calls and ask people. Many businesses are willing to give coupons or "buy one, get one free" offers. Restaurant coupons, theater tickets, and passes to local attractions are usually easy to get. Your library may have T-shirts, ball caps, mouse pads, or other logo items. I worked for one university that donated tickets to see its undefeated, nationally ranked football team. Massage gift certificates are especially welcome—particularly about the third day of the move—and surprisingly easy to get. Many massage therapists give away a free session, expecting the recipient to return on a regular basis.

The trick is to start early, work your way through the yellow pages, and don't get discouraged if you get rejected now and then. Many people will want to be associated with your move, and the opportunity to build goodwill works in both directions. Check with contractors and suppliers. They made a lot of money from your project, and they may even expect you to ask for a few favors.

The amenities become more important on larger, longer moves. On a one-day move, I'd do lunch and let it go at that. On a two-day move, I'd do lunch the first day and a snack the second; no prizes. If the move is to last three days or longer, I'd start contests and drawings from day one and do lunches and snacks as frequently as possible. On an eight- or ten-day megamove, I'd pour on all the goodies I could get. This is hard, dirty work; a show of appreciation is welcome.

OTHER SUPPLIES

Duct tape. Fixes anything, buy it anywhere. The black kind makes good tape for marking the start end of carts.

Painter's tape. Paper tape, usually blue, sticks like masking tape but leaves little or no residue on your new walls and furnishings. Get the 2-inch-wide roll. Buy it at any paint, hardware, or home improvement store.

Card pockets. Attach to carts and boxes to hold the numbered, color-coded cards. Get the self-stick kind. Paper lasts longer than plastic. Buy from Demco or Highsmith if you no longer have them in stock.

Step stools. Not everyone is tall enough to reach the top shelf.

Measuring blocks. Use these to help shelvers leave the right amount of space per shelf. It doesn't matter how much work you put into calculating growth space if the shelvers leave 8 inches where they are supposed to leave 6 inches. I cut 1-by-3-inch lumber to the lengths called for by the Layout spreadsheet and give each reshelving crew a block to match the space they are supposed to leave. Wood is easy to use and lasts forever, but you can do the same with paper, cardboard, or many other materials. Write the length of each block on the block (figure 7.9).

Figure 7.9 Measuring blocks help reshelvers leave the proper space for growth on each shelf.

Caution tape. What the police use at the crime scene. Use it to block off shelves you want left open or to mark unsafe or unused pathways. Buy it at home improvement and hardware stores.

Toolbox. Sooner or later you will damage a cart or you have to take apart, fix, remove, or unstick something. Collect a set of basic tools—hammer, screwdrivers, pliers, wrenches, box cutter, power drill—along with some spare screws and bolts. Set up a "hospital" in a convenient location where you can make repairs to damaged equipment.

Floor plans. Have at least two sets, fully marked with all collections and waypoints.

Chapter 8

Preparing the Workspaces

As move day approaches, you are likely to become inundated with last minute details. Many of these have to do with the building and its furnishings. Shelving, wall and floor finishes, and elevators are among the last items completed in many building projects. Unfortunately, these are all critical to your move and must be completed and functional before you start.

This is a time when you need to maintain close, even daily, contact with the contractor's representative, the shelving installers, and other trades still working in the building. You need to assure yourself that, not only will their work be completed on time, but so are the paperwork and inspections required before you can move into the space.

THE BASICS

As the contractors are winding down their work, you are ramping up yours. Listed here are several activities in which you will be involved during this time. Some require no more than a phone call; others take a full crew and should be incorporated into the overall plan.

1. Confirm the rental truck. Make sure the rental company has a truck to match your dock on the day you need it. Impress upon the company that a different truck is not acceptable unless it is the same height as your dock. I have had rental companies offer me a longer, but higher, truck at the same price, calling it a good deal. It is not.

2. Negotiate with your elevator repair company to have a technician on site, or at least on call, during your move. This is especially critical during the first day of the move. *This is important.* On most of the jobs I have done in the past five years, we have needed elevator repair on the first day. The problem seems to be that elevators are set for normal pedestrian traffic. When we use them constantly to move heavy carts, even when we stay well within the load limits of the elevator, they get out of adjustment. Usually it is a quick fix, but you need someone available to do the fix. While you are waiting, you are very nearly out of business.

3. Get an elevator lockout key. Unless your elevator is very old, it has a little control panel behind a locked door. One of the switches on the panel can be set to hold the door open until the switch is reset or the floor button is pushed and held. There may also be a switch that prevents someone on another floor from calling the elevator. The door hold-open feature is critical. If the door starts to shut while you are loading a 1,500-lb cart, you may nudge the door out of alignment. Correction: you *will* knock the door off the track. Then you will need a repair person to fix it and the elevator will

be out of service until that is done. The call lockout is especially useful if you have assigned an elevator operator. It allows the operator to control where and when the elevator goes.

Insist on having a key to the control panel and get someone to show you how the controls work.

While you're thinking about elevators, arrange to have a vacuum cleaner available. During the move, dirt, little pieces of paper, pieces broken off the wall or floor protection, and other crumbs collect in the door track. They can cause the electric eye to assume the doorway is blocked and prevent the door from closing. Every now and then you may have to vacuum out the track.

4. Negotiate with other users of the loading dock—mail and delivery services, trash haulers, furniture movers, and contractors. Make sure all users know they are subject to the instructions of your dockmaster. Try to get them to make their deliveries or pickups before or after your moving day hours.

5. Prep the shelves.

5a. If you are moving into a new building or have had a lot of construction, you probably need to clean the shelves. This can be a major project in itself. You want to do it fairly late, so the shelves don't get dirty again, but you have to allow time to get the job done. Drywall dust is about the worst cleaning problem you will face. Drywall dust from sanding is extremely fine and clings to anything. Dust from cutting drywall is coarse, fibrous, and highly abrasive. If it gets wet, drywall dust forms a cementlike film that cannot be brushed or vacuumed away. Brushes, dust rags, feather dusters, and most vacuums are an excellent way to redistribute dust—redistribute as in "spread around," not "remove." Even a water- or HEPA-filtered vacuum does not get all of the dust. The only really effective way to remove drywall dust is by washing it off with a damp rag. Issue masks and plastic gloves to the cleaners. Provide ladders or step stools. Wash the shelves with a damp rag and change rags frequently. At that, you will probably have to wash each shelf twice to get it really clean. With dark shelves, you can see if there is a film of drywall smudge left after the first washing. With gray or tan shelves, the film is not visible. Wash them once, allow time to dry, and rub your hand over the shelf. If the shelves are still dirty, there will be a line of dust on your hand.

5b. Check the stability of the stacks to make sure they don't tip when you begin to load books. Stability problems occur most often when you remove very heavy books from one side of an old range or when there has been a faulty installation. Check the new shelves for stability and be wary of the old ones. Look especially for ranges where a considerable number of large books overhang the base shelf. You may have to stabilize such stacks, or you can remove books from both sides simultaneously to prevent tipping. In my experience, problems have been rare.

5c. Make certain the shelves are set at the proper vertical distance apart. Vertical shelf spacing should have been specified at the design phase, but mistakes can happen. Except possibly for fiction, you need at least 11 inches between shelves, and 12 inches is much better. When the shelves are empty, it is easy to sight through the rows to spot an occasional shelf that has been misadjusted. The bigger problem is when all shelves at one level are set at the wrong height. Installers often set up one range and key everything else from that. If the first one is wrong, they may all be wrong. If someone set the gap between the bottom two shelves at only 10 inches and all of the others at 11 inches, you have to raise every shelf in the room by 1 inch to get enough room to raise the bottom shelf. The preferred solution is to make friends with the shelving installers and check their work as they go, before a massive shelf-changing project becomes necessary.

5d. Make sure the bookends are in place. Installing the bookends is usually an item in the contract for purchase and installation of shelves. Unless the contract specifies that the installer put the bookends on the shelf, you should expect to do it yourself. This is another big job, and you need to assign people to the task. It is much easier to install bookends before you get the books on the shelves.

5e. Flag the collection. Install the flags in the collection in the origin building (details in chapter 4). Do this

TIP

You can stabilize a range of shelving temporarily using a board and clamps at the top of the shelves. Get a 1-by-3-inch board long enough to lie across the tops of three ranges. If your aisles are 3 feet wide, this will be a 10-foot board. Clamp the board to the top bar or an upright of each of three adjacent ranges. This stabilizes the stack enough to allow you to remove or load the books.

in the last week or so prior to the move. The longer you wait, the less chance a flag will get lost or moved.

5f. Mark the waypoints on the shelves in the destination building. Do this after the final cleaning of the shelves. Make sure you tape down the waypoint markers so they don't get moved accidentally (see chapter 4).

5g. Block off shelves that you are not going to fill. This lets the reshelvers work quickly without having to watch the drawings. Yellow caution tape works well for this.

5h. Place step stools where they are easily accessible when needed.

6. Interfile everything possible—newly returned books, office collections, displays, and so on. Lay them on top of the books on the shelves if necessary.

7. Set up a holding area for returned materials. If any materials are returned from circulation during your move, you need a place to store and organize them. In a large public library, you need to allocate an area of shelving. Pick some shelving that is convenient for returns and arrange your plan so you move those materials first. Try to keep the returns interfiled in good order. When the move is over, you can put them on carts and move them.

8. Make sure the communications system is working. Make up the telephone list. Make sure the phones in the loading dock areas ring loud enough to be heard. If you are using radios, check their operation, make sure you can get reception in all areas, and train the users.

9. Install signs, route markers, and the like. Use painter's tape to avoid leaving residue.

PREPARING FOR A MOVE WITH BOXES

Boxes take up a lot of space, even empty. Plan accordingly.

If you are borrowing or buying ready-made boxes, try to take delivery a day or two prior to the move and detail a crew to pre-position the boxes as close as possible to where they are needed. Because the unshelving location moves as books are removed from the shelves, you can save time for the unshelvers by spotting boxes along the route. Because one person can't move many boxes at one time, even empty, you may need to assign several people to this work, and it can become a project in itself.

Also, put card pockets on the boxes prior to the move.

If your boxes came unassembled, you need one or more "box factories" and people assigned to build boxes. Establish factories near the place where books are being unshelved so you do not have to transport boxes over a distance. It is easiest to build boxes on a table or other standing-height work surface. We usually give the box makers a folding table so they can change locations easily to stay near the unshelvers. In a multifloor building, set up at least one factory on each floor. You would need more people to transport empty boxes between floors than you do to staff a factory on each floor.

Unassembled boxes usually arrive on pallets with four to five hundred boxes per pallet. If your doors are wide enough, take the pallets right to the factory. If you have standard doors, not wide enough to pass a pallet, you have to break down the bundles and hand-carry the cardboard sheets to the factory. Issue leather gloves to the people carrying the cardboard. Fresh-cut cardboard is sharp. Staff the box factory according to the number of unshelving crews it is to supply. Generally one box maker can just about keep up with one unshelving crew. Add one additional person per factory to manage supplies, take away waste, put on card pockets, and stack empty boxes. If your boxes require taping, you may need additional workers to keep up with the unshelvers. I can load and number a box faster than I can form and tape one. If you are making lids, you must double the factory workforce; a lid is just a shallow box, and it takes as long to make one as it does to make the box.

Stock the factory with plenty of tape, tape guns, staples, card pockets, and other supplies. Make sure you have leather gloves for the box makers. Cheap jersey gloves last only a few minutes and provide almost no protection.

Unless you are boxing for storage, the box factory operates only at the start of the move. Once the boxes have been built, loaded, transported, and unloaded, the process becomes one of recycling and the factory goes

TIP

Lids are usually cut with flaps on each end. The flaps are bent and taped to the sides to form the lid. Always tape the short flap to the *outside* of the lid. This does not look as finished as putting it inside, but the inside of the lid is smooth and won't catch on the box. Whoever is putting lids on the boxes will be grateful for your kindness.

TIP

Start the move with a supply of boxes and lids on hand. If possible, make up a starting supply of boxes prior to move day, or at least start the box makers working while you are training and orienting the rest of the crew. You do not want an entire crew standing around while the factory gets organized and tools up for production.

out of business, freeing the workers for other move tasks. On a large, multiday move, this is a convenient way to ramp up to full speed. You start with fewer move crews the first day or two while the dock crews, drivers, and pushers learn efficiencies, then reassign the box makers when the process can handle an increased load.

PROTECTING YOUR BUILDINGS

Early in the planning process, and then again when the new building is close to completion, you should evaluate the routes you will use to move books in and out. Identify every turn, choke point, and elevation change and any point where a cart could damage a wall.

Selecting Routes

Move carts, book carts, and dollies roll easily but are hard to control in tight areas and around corners. The wheels rotate freely, and if they are not aligned in the direction of travel, the cart moves slightly sideways each time you start or change direction. The problem arises if you get a cart partway through a doorway or into an elevator and have to pull it back for another try. It will likely rub the door frame, perhaps enough to damage it. If that doorway has a threshold, the cart is more likely to get caught. In an elevator, the gap between the car and the floor outside is a particular problem. When you pull back for another try, the wheels can fall into that gap. It is hard to lift a loaded cart out of that gap. Pallets are especially likely to rub doorways and tight spaces. Pallet jacks don't roll so easily, and they are even more difficult to control. In general:

- A longer flat route is faster and takes fewer people than a shorter route with ramps, stairs, tight turns, or other impediments.
- A longer route over a hard floor is faster, and requires less effort from the pushers, than a route on carpet.
- A route with a side slope—as with a sidewalk that is not level from side to side—causes carts and dollies to run askew and may require two pushers per cart.
- A longer route with aisles at least 6 feet wide is preferable to a slightly shorter route with 3- to 4-foot aisles. Pallets require an aisle at least 9 feet wide to pass two abreast.
- Narrow aisles leave no room for carts to pass, and there is a greater chance that carts will damage walls or other surfaces. If you have to use narrow aisles, try to set up a pair of one-way routes.

Floors

Once you have selected the best routes, you may need to protect walls, floors, and other surfaces from damage. We'll start with the floors:

Protect new carpet from wear and dirt, especially in those areas that are heavily traveled by loaded carts. In addition to wear, there may be another problem if you have carpet squares. The weight of the carts and the pressure of the pushers' feet can shift carpet squares. Once they have shifted, it is difficult to get them to lie smoothly again.

The basic floor protection is 3/8- or 1/2-inch plywood or chipboard. Masonite does not work over carpet. Cart wheels cut right through Masonite if it is used over carpet. Masonite is just fine to use over a hard floor.

You may not have to purchase all of the floor protections. In a new building, the contractors may have protections in place. Also, shelving or furniture installers may install protections for their own purpose. It is worth your time to organize a cooperative venture with them.

Carpet protection is not absolutely necessary. The larger the move, the greater the likelihood of wear or damage. The floor protection does not have to go all the way to the end of each aisle; just worry about the main path for full carts. Empty carts don't wear the carpet nearly as much as loaded ones. Put the floor protections over the main walkways and the places where carts or dollies will be turning.

Plan extra width at corners. Carts and dollies roll easily once they are moving, but they are hard to stop and start. Pallets are hard to turn in a tight space. A route that involves a lot of right-angle turns is slow and physically difficult for the pushers. Provide enough width so that pushers can make wide, sweeping turns.

Plywood or chipboard creeps on carpet and slides on a hard floor. It may help to use duct tape to fasten adjacent panels together. Use lots of tape and press it down tightly. You might also use the nonskid mats sold to put under throw rugs, especially on corners.

Elevation Changes

As you walk the routes, notice *every* elevation change. Even a 1/2-inch threshold in a tight doorway can be a problem. The reason is that the cart is moving slowly through the doorway. If it hangs up on the threshold and the pusher pulls it back for another try, the wheels swing sideways and the cart hits the doorway.

Whenever you encounter an elevation change greater than about 1/2 inch, you must ease the transition. Most small changes (like thresholds or carpet-to-tile transitions) are easy to fix. A piece of walk-off mat can be thrown over the transition. The plastic mats used under office chairs also work well. Cut them to fit as necessary.

A slightly taller transition—an inch or two of elevation—needs a bit more work. You can use a walk-off or chair mat, but you must build up the low side. Use strips of 1/2-inch plywood to build steps about 6–8 inches wide (figure 8.1), then put the walk-off mat over that.

For an elevation change greater than 2 inches, you need a more substantial ramp. At most, you can ramp down one or two steps; for greater elevations, use a lift, forklift, or human chain. The ramp must be heavy enough to carry the weight of the loads, and it should have sides at least 4 inches high to prevent the carts and dollies from slipping off the side. The ramp should match as closely as possible the height of the floor at the top of the ramp. The slope of the ramp should be no greater than 1 in 12—that is, a 2-inch-high ramp should be at least 24 inches long, a foot-high ramp 12 feet long.

Walls

The basic wall protection materials are cardboard, rigid foam insulation, and rubber wastebaskets. Cardboard is easy to get. You can purchase it from a box manufacturer, but your shelving and much of your furniture will come in cardboard boxes. Talk to your suppliers; perhaps you can save them the trouble of disposing of their packaging material.

Doorways are the most obvious problem spots. The best way to protect a door is to remove it entirely. You might leave double doors in place and just prop them wide open. This provides a safely wide space if there is no center mullion. If you leave the doors propped open, set a rubber wastebasket in front of each door (figure 8.2). These act as bumpers to deflect an errant cart. What you are trying to accomplish with the wastebaskets is the same thing the highway department does to protect bridge supports on an interstate. The wastebaskets absorb impacts and deflect the carts.

Figure 8.1 Plywood strips ease carts over a low bump. Cover with a piece of walk-off mat.

Figure 8.2 Rubber or vinyl wastebaskets protect doors and corners.

You can purchase paperboard edge protectors from vendors that sell industrial pallet supplies. Furniture items, shelving end panels, and some other items may come palleted with heavy edge protectors. These are excellent protection for doorways and corners. Collect every one you can find. Tape the corner protector tightly to the corner with painter's tape. Wrap another piece of sheet cardboard loosely over the corner guard and tape it securely (figure 8.3). This double wrap provides very good abrasion resistance and surprisingly good impact protection.

Usually you do not have to protect regular flat walls along hallways, unless the hallway is very narrow or carts will be stored along the walls. If you must protect walls, use flat sheets of cardboard taped to the walls with painter's tape (figure 8.4). Don't use duct tape or you'll be cleaning the residue off the walls for weeks.

Look for protrusions into a hallway, no matter how wide it is. Drinking fountains are vulnerable, and it can be messy if you hit one with a cart. Set a rubber trash can or large wastebasket on either side of it. If the protrusion is part of a solid wall or column, you can use

Figure 8.4 Floor and wall protections in place.

an office-size wastebasket. Fire extinguishers are another common protrusion. Remove them or set a trash can to protect them.

Another danger point is a crossing wall at the end of a hallway if the carts have to make a tight turn. The danger is that a pusher can be going too fast and miss the turn, damaging the wall. A row of rubber trash cans protects the wall.

While you are watching for danger points in hallways, consider the dangers to people not associated with the move. Someone opens an office door and steps into the hallway in front of a cart or walks down a connecting hallway and into the middle of your cart route. Pushers get a safety lecture on these dangers, but you might consider blocking off some hallways, creating "safe-travel" lanes for pedestrians, or at least posting obvious warning signs. A couple of days before the move, send a "be careful" memo to everybody you can think of.

Elevators

Elevators pose at least three problems:

Narrow entrances. Protect them with a double wrap of cardboard and, if they are really decorative or if they protrude, set wastebaskets as well.

The gap between the car and the floor. Treat this as an elevation change. The track acts as a threshold and may stop a cart that is pushed slowly. The gap itself is wide enough to trap a wheel if you try to pull the cart back for another try. Cut a piece of walk-off mat or the plastic mat

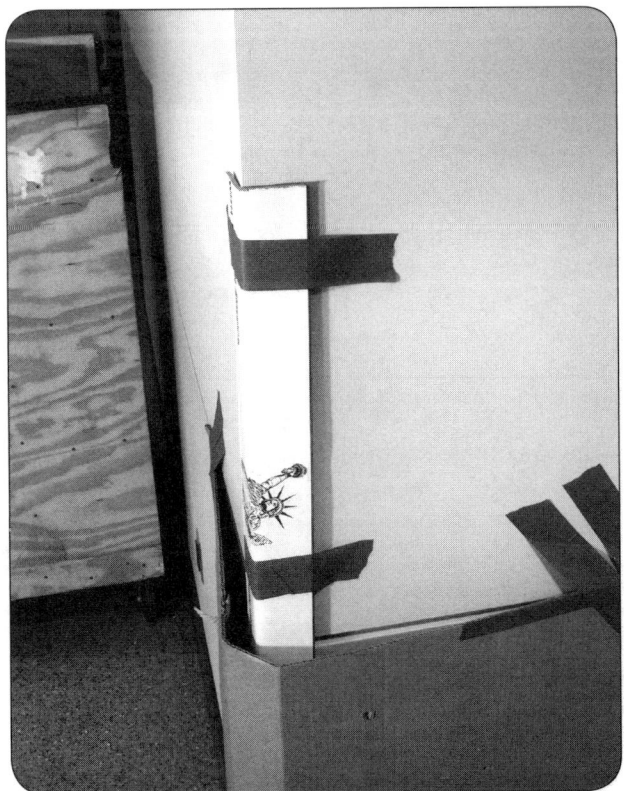

Figure 8.3 Edge protector prevents damage to corners.

that is used as a carpet protector under an office chair to throw across the entire opening. Make one for each floor and a couple of spares.

The elevator car walls may get bumped by the carts. If your elevator has protective pads, leave them up throughout the move. If not, use 2-inch rigid foam insulation. It comes in 4-by-8-foot sheets and is light and resilient. Cut it to fit and tape it inside the elevator with lots of duct tape. Cut out gaps for the controls if necessary. You don't have to protect the walls any higher than about 4 feet. If there is a railing in the car, the insulation should stick out far enough to protect the railing.

The Other Move

Chapter 9

So far, we have discussed moving books. But someone also has to move the FFE—furniture, fixtures, equipment, supplies, files, and personal and professional effects of your staff.

You should hire a professional office mover to move your furniture and staff effects for the same reason you *don't* hire an office mover to move your books. You move the books yourself because the library staff has the experience to handle them correctly and to keep them in order. When it comes to FFE, the movers are the experts. They have the experience, the expertise, the equipment, the trucks, the trained manpower, and the insurance to do the work efficiently. Let the furniture experts do what they do best.

In a small library, you may have no option but to move the FFE with whatever equipment and whatever help you can muster. Even then, there are companies that specialize in small moves at a reasonable price. Some universities may have a department that specializes in moving offices.

It is not necessary to hire a company that specializes in moving libraries. Look for a mover with experience moving offices and one that has done projects approximately as large as your move. There is a high degree of similarity between a move of library FFE and the move of any similar size office in a public- or private-sector setting. A desk in a library is very much like a desk anywhere. A table is a table; a chair, a chair. Even quintessential library furniture has its counterparts in an office environment. Microfilm readers appear in many offices. Everyone uses file cabinets. The tools and techniques needed to disassemble and move a reference desk are much like those needed to move any reception desk.

FINDING A MOVER

So where do you find such a mover? Yellow pages. Call around, describe your move in general terms, make sure they understand you are not asking them to move the books, and compile a list of companies that think they can handle the job. Usually it is less expensive to hire a local mover. The cost of getting workers, trucks, and equipment to a distant job site is considerable. A local firm has a financial advantage in this matter.

The information in this chapter comes primarily from several recent moves for which I was actively involved in planning the furniture and equipment move as well as the move of the books. Many of the specifics here were drawn from conversations with and materials supplied by Susan Stoneburner of Colen Moving and Storage in Fort Wayne, Indiana. Susan and her crews moved the staff and furniture of the Allen County Public Library into a temporary building in 2003 and back into the new building in 2007.

Yours is likely to be a high-profile move. The community will be interested, with considerable notice taken in the media and around the various office watercoolers. It would be valuable advertising for a mover to have its trucks sitting in front of your building, and movers are happy to have a library on their list of references. All of this can translate to intense competition for your business and potentially into a lower price.

How you go about hiring the mover depends on several considerations, some of which may be beyond your control. The degree of formality of the process you can use is often determined by the anticipated cost of the project. A large move may require a formal bidding process; a small one may escape formality altogether.

The formal process is structured for you by local or state law. Your attorney can provide the format and help you to prepare the bid documents, most of which are in standardized language. You, however, have to provide a full and descriptive inventory of everything to be moved.

> **LIBRARY MOVERS AND FFE**
>
> Many library moving specialists are happy to prepare a detailed inventory for you and to write extensive bid specifications, evaluate bidders, recommend the most suitable mover, and even manage the contract for you. If you absolutely cannot do this work yourself, hiring a professional may be an option. Be aware that you will still have a significant role and time commitment in the process. At the very least, you still have to make the go/no-go decisions.
>
> The reason library movers are so eager to help with this part of the project is that it is profitable, with little downside risk. They can charge an hourly rate for as long as it takes to complete the inventory. Bid specifications are impressive documents, but most of the content is boilerplate that changes little or not at all from one bid to another. There is not much cost to customize bid documents for a specific library.
>
> Another reason library movers offer to help with an FFE move is to establish a relationship that may lead to a contract to move your books as well.
>
> A better alternative may be to require the FFE mover to do the inventory and design the move for you. This is the way they have to price most of their jobs. They do only the work they need to provide you with an accurate price at a cost much lower than paying someone to produce a full inventory.

FURNITURE INVENTORY

Preparing the inventory is time-consuming. In chapter 2, I recommend that one member of the move team be given responsibility to coordinate this portion of the move. If you can afford only two people on the move team, one of them should have the FFE responsibility.

Movers are used to a situation in which they are taking everything in sight. If you are not taking all of your furniture and equipment, it helps them visualize the move if you can clearly and obviously mark the go and no-go pieces. Visibly marking every item to be moved helps the movers to see at a glance the scope of the work. Consider it this way: You're a branch manager. You walk in on Monday morning, glance at the drop box, and know right away how long it will take to check in all those books. You don't count them, measure them, or weigh them. One glance tells you what it will take. That's the way movers look at a room. Do what you can to make sure they see what you want them to see.

The inventory must be complete and accurate on both quantities and descriptions. The need to have an accurate count of items should be obvious, but the descriptions may be just as important. There may seem to be little difference between moving "Table, library, 35 by 44 inches" and "Table, library, 38 by 48 inches." But the difference becomes a real problem if the doorway is 36 inches wide or your elevator cab is 47 inches deep and the larger table has to be carried down the stairs. For some items you may need to indicate the weight as well, particularly if the item is unique or may be outside the experience of the movers. Microfilm cabinets, for instance, don't *look* that heavy. Don't worry too much about measuring every item. Concentrate on the unusual pieces and on anything that may present a problem getting it out the door.

You can find many suggestions for ways to build a thorough FFE inventory. If you talk to professional movers, however, you find that they measure a move in terms of how many workers and how many trips it will take to clear a room. A floor lamp and a file cabinet are the same size to a mover—one worker, one trip. A 3-by-5-foot desk takes one worker and a dolly. A 3-by-5-foot table takes two workers, one to carry each end.

Here are some tips to help you prepare your inventory:

- Make up some stickers: "Go" and "No-go"; "Move" and "Stay"; or just use stickers with different colors or shapes.

- Put a sticker on every piece of furniture and equipment, in some visible location. Then wait a few days for staff comment. This is an interactive process. Often a library purchases some or all new furniture for a new building but finds there is considerable staff pressure to move favored or iconic items that really have no place in the new building. The rationale "But it's in perfectly good condition" or "It's a shame to throw it away" does not apply. If the item is not needed, there is no reason to move it. On the other hand, premarking items does give staff a chance to see what is going and to urge reconsideration where a truly critical item has been missed. It also makes the inventory process much easier.

- Make up an inventory sheet with columns for the name of the item, the size, and for each room or area where the items are located. A sample page of an inventory is shown in appendix E. Work in a team of two. One person counts, measures, and marks the items. The other records the counts on the inventory. Note that, although it is not hard to measure furniture, weighing it is another matter. Don't lift it up and put it on a scale; the easiest way to get the weight is to look up the item in a catalog. A few pounds one way or the other won't matter. If an item is unusually heavy and you can't find the weight, note that the item is "Heavy" and make sure you point it out during the walk-through.

- As you count each item, make some sort of mark on the "Go/No-go" label. After you think you're finished, have someone go through the building with a fresh set of eyes to make sure you didn't miss anything. It is surprising how easy it is to overlook everyday items like clocks or wastebaskets. Make sure to include things like janitor's equipment and lawn care supplies. Include pictures of items that may not be familiar to the prospective movers. Pictures are also useful to distinguish among items of similar descriptions, such as chairs.

- If you plan to empty a file or other container and move the contents separately, make that notation.

- Describe artworks thoroughly. Include not only size and weight but a description of the composition (wood, metal, plaster) and any handling or crating requirements.

OFFICE CONTENTS AND STAFF EFFECTS

Staff effects may be but are not necessarily the personal property of staff. We extend the term to include all of the nonfurniture items usually found in an office and that are associated more with an individual than with the library. Some libraries require that staff members move their own personally owned property. Staff effects may include personal file contents; reference books, catalogs, or other book materials kept in an office; decorations and memorabilia; personal assistive devices; building- and move-related items such as floor plans and spec books; and desk accessories.

Office contents are particularly time-consuming to inventory. Each is different, and you end up measuring file drawer contents and trying to visualize how a wide variety of items can be packaged so you can get an accurate box count, office by office.

In a small library, or if you are committed to a formal bid process, you may just have to take the time and do the work. Be aware that many, but not all, movers want to verify your work or even do their own inventory before they commit to a price. You may need to allow time for this process. You may also need to assign each of them a staff person as a guide, just to help them locate everything in your building.

If you have a larger library staff and are not required by your process to prepare a comprehensive inventory, you can use a shortcut method to describe the office effects. It works like this:

Every librarian has an office, cubicle, or other "personal" space. Some have more or fewer files, mementos, and so forth, but the variation is not great and you can identify one or two staff who have the most, one or two who have the least, and one or two who are about average.

A department manager probably has a larger space with more files and perhaps a small table and some extra chairs. The director and some senior administrators have even more. Part-timers, shelvers, and housekeepers may have only a locker. Within each group there should not be much variation in the overall number of boxes and amount of furniture to be moved.

Your first step is to divide your staff into categories, roughly based on the amount of "personal" space they have. Your particulars may vary, but a list of categories might look like this:

Senior administrators: individual office, executive desk, table and six chairs, 40–60 boxes

Department managers: private office, desk, 25–40 boxes

Librarian: private cubicle, no desk, 15–25 boxes

Clerk: shared cubicle, no desk, 5–10 boxes

Other: locker only, 1–2 boxes

Now count the number of persons in each group. If an individual within a category has substantially more than the average, make a note to that effect or count them in a higher category. Don't overlook yourself. As the move coordinator, you will accumulate an amazing amount of paper.

Prepare a list that shows the definition of each category and how many staff are at each level. Include the list with the physical inventory and ask for bids or quotes. Invite all bidders to walk through your buildings with a library representative—they should insist on this anyway. Make a point of showing them one or two "average" workspaces at each level so they can judge for themselves that you have described it accurately.

This method saves much time and expense and is surprisingly accurate. I first used it on a move that involved 225 staff but little furniture, because that library had bought all new. At the end of the job, the head of the moving company told me her actual costs were within 1 percent of her estimate. Even the losing bidders were happy with the method, because it cost less to prepare their bids. Each bidder wants to verify the amount of material to be moved so they can price it accurately. Normally this means they have to visit every office and measure or estimate the contents. They need to see if file drawers are full or nearly empty, judge how many personal mementos there are, and determine how many other things not on the inventory are actually moving. With the shortcut method, they can carefully evaluate your "average" spaces, check a few others to make sure those were indeed average, and prepare their bids. There is a significant expense of staff time to calculate a price for a large move. If the company is not the successful bidder, they lose that investment. With the streamlined process, we had a larger number of bidders and the prices were lower because the bidders did not have to cover so many prebid expenses.

CONDITIONS OF THE MOVE

No matter how formal your pricing process, you have to prepare some statement describing the conditions of the move. This statement becomes part of the contract. The move company is bound to its quoted price if the conditions are met; you'll probably be charged more if conditions change. Appendix E includes a sample request for quotes. Yours should reflect your own situation. Some things that should go into a statement of conditions are

location or address of both buildings

description of loading docks or other exits in both buildings

description of elevators including size, door opening, and weight capacity

what other work will be done simultaneously, especially describing how the other work may interfere with the office furniture movers. Movers usually base their pricing on unlimited access to the entire area and increase the price to account for lost time if they have to share resources.

timetable for the move, including earliest and latest dates and any dates when the mover may not work

times when mover is allowed to work: nights, weekends, holidays, or other times when the library is closed? This may be your only option if you have limited loading space.

specification of who is responsible for boxing, crating, or otherwise preparing items for shipment

insurance the mover is required to carry, on workers, on the material being moved, and on the building

description of protections the mover must provide

description of what the mover is expected to clean and remove

other requirements, anomalies, and potential problems that may be unique to your situation. Watch particularly for situations that require additional workers or more time. The biggest expense for most movers is the time they spend walking back and forth carrying one load or going back for another. They base their cost estimates on the number of people and the number of trips. If you have offices on a mezzanine with no elevator, it costs more to move those offices than the "average." Mention them specifically. Note anything that requires disassembly. It is not unheard of that some part of the building may have to be modified—a door taken off its hinges or a railing removed, for instance. On one move, we had to get an 8-foot globe through a 7½-foot doorway—the ultimate round peg in a square hole. It was the featured story on the evening news.

OTHER CONSIDERATIONS

Copiers and leased equipment. Check your lease agreement. The owner may require that you use a particular mover or the vendor's service department to transport and set up the equipment.

Vending machines. Vending machines are usually moved by the owners.

Computers. In my experience libraries are about evenly divided. About half of the time the IT department staff prefer to move computers themselves; the rest prefer that the mover does the work. Get this issue settled internally before you ask anyone to give you a price for the move. Computers are such a big piece of a library move that their presence or absence can change the scale of the move and affect the overall markup. When the movers have a lot of high-volume, easy-to-move items, they can schedule staff more efficiently and use the computers to fill in when they do not need the full crew for other moves. If you do have the movers transport your computers, be sure to specify in the contract who packs them and who reassembles them.

INSURANCE

There are several insurance issues related to a move. These should be spelled out in your request for pricing:

- The mover should be required to provide insurance for its own staff and equipment, including workers' compensation insurance.

- The mover should be required to provide a reasonable amount of general liability and property damage insurance to cover the building and contents and any other damage.
- In most states, licensed movers must provide moving valuation insurance. There may be several levels of coverage, the minimum of which is included in the base price of the move.

The following summary of Indiana requirements is a useful example; all states have some version of these requirements. Costs are as of date of publication.

Released Valuation. All licensed movers provide a basic amount of carrier liability, even if you are insured through your own insurance carrier. In Indiana, our maximum liability is sixty (60) cents per pound per piece of parcel. Settlement Example: If a table weighs 100 pounds and was damaged or destroyed, the settlement would be $60. This coverage is provided at no cost to you.

Replacement Valuation. You may elect to purchase this coverage by declaring a full replacement value for your shipment. The value must equal no less than $5.00 per pound times the weight of the shipment. This coverage is provided at a cost of $0.75 per $100 of value declared (i.e., $5,000 coverage—cost $42.50).

Check with your own insurance agent to determine if your current policy provides any protection during a move.

WALK-THROUGH

Schedule at least one opportunity for potential movers to tour your building with the FFE move coordinator.

TIP

If your insurance agent recommends additional insurance for your collection while you are moving, make sure the quoted priced is based only on the risk to that portion you are moving at any one time, not on the whole collection. Remind your agent that nearly all of your collection will be safely on the shelves at one building or the other. The only extra liability is for that small portion that is in transit at any one time.

Movers need to see the buildings to judge for themselves how best to design their move. They will have many questions, and you may need to identify for them equipment with which they are not familiar. The walk-through must include both origin and destination buildings. I prefer to start with the new structure and finish at the occupied building.

There are two schools of thought on the walk-through. One holds that each potential bidder should get a private tour. This gives the bidder a chance to ask questions, or propose solutions, without fear that a rival will learn a trade secret or otherwise benefit. The opposite school holds that it is more important, and fairer, to ensure that all bidders hear the same information in the same way; otherwise proposals made and agreed to in a private tour could constitute an illegal modification of the conditions of the move for the benefit of one bidder.

Both views have their adherents. I prefer to err on the side of fairness and do group walk-throughs. I also require that any questions posed after the walk-through be presented in writing, and I either e-mail the question and its answer to all potential bidders or post the questions and answer on a website accessible to all.

Many movers request a second walk-through or some time to explore the library on their own. A large library is a lot to absorb on one tour. The mover may need to clarify notes made on the tour, measure a route, verify a first impression, or any of a dozen other things. If you are doing a formal bid, each bidder may want to verify your inventory item by item, a task that can take many days.

Because much of the mover's work on a repeat visit is in nonpublic areas, I assign each one a guide. I emphasize to everyone that the guides have no part in the decision process; they are authorized only to answer specific, factual questions about the items to be moved and have no authority to make any agreements or to modify any conditions of the request for quotes.

In a large library, it would not be unreasonable to plan a second group walk-through a few days before the bids are due. Poll the potential bidders to determine if they feel a second tour is necessary. If you simply schedule a second visit on your own, some bidders feel obligated to spend time and money to attend even though they have no further questions.

CONTRACT PRICE

At the end of the process, you come to an agreement with one mover. You have a list of everything that is to be moved, a timetable, a list of who is responsible for what, and a price. Typically the inventory is incorporated into the agreement by reference. All of these, taken together, become a contract between you and the mover.

The contract price covers the listed items and responsibilities. Almost certainly there will be modifications during the move. You will find something that was not listed on the inventory; you may decide not to take some substantial item; or the timetable may change. As part of the negotiation process, you should ask the mover to state the costs for any work beyond that included in the contract. This is usually provided as a rate sheet listing the hourly charge for workers and supervisors and a list of hourly rental rates for trucks and other equipment. Get this negotiated before you sign the contract. Once the contract is signed, you lose most of your negotiating leverage.

LABELING AND PACKING

Your mover should supply you with boxes and with labels for your furniture, equipment, and the boxes. Typically the labels have spaces to enter the floor and room number and perhaps the name of the owner or a cubicle number. Often they are color-coded as well. The mover should specify where the label should be placed on the various types of furniture and boxes. It is important, for instance, not to put a label on the top of a box, because another box may be stacked on top of it. If the furniture is labeled consistently, the movers won't have to hunt all over a chair to figure out where it goes.

Movers must be able to read the labels from a short distance. Write the floor and room number of the destination on the labels with a dark marker. If there are multiple destinations within a room, you may add the cubicle number, the name of the staff member, or some other designator to the label.

Your mover may conduct a packing seminar for your staff to explain the labeling system, to show how to pack boxes or to pack and label computers and accessories, and to discuss which file cabinets can be moved with the contents intact. They also tell you how high to stack boxes. Their quoted price is based on the assumption that your staff stack the boxes to a standard height so the workers can just take the stack away. If the movers have to restack boxes, the price goes up.

One of the jobs of the move team is to make certain that all staff have their own spaces packed and labeled before the movers come for them. The move team should also assign staff to label all items that are to be moved from common spaces and public areas. The move team should prepare a schedule showing when each office and each public area is to be moved. Typically we require that an area be packed and labeled the day before it is to be moved. We schedule an inspection midafternoon of the day prior to the move. This allows time to finish up anything that might have been missed, or to schedule another area if necessary.

DURING THE MOVE

The move team is responsible for preparing the buildings for the move:

- Check that all rooms are numbered. If not, post temporary signs.
- Post floor plans of each room in the room or at the doorway.
- Post general floor plans at central locations within the building.
- If necessary, post directional signs at the entrance or at points where movers may have a choice of routes. Anything you can do to eliminate confusion helps to keep the price low. Remember, the movers do not know their way around your buildings.

Designate one or more of your staff to be the guide and single point of contact with the movers. These persons are responsible for ensuring that all of the furniture and equipment gets placed properly according to the floor plans and that all staff personal effects get to the correct location.

Assign at least one guide for each floor, two or more if the space is large. Carefully delineate their areas of responsibility so there is no overlap. The idea is that there is one and only one source of information for any given space.

Find some way to identify the guides. I like to equip each of them with a reflective vest such as those worn by police officers or crossing guards (figure 9.1). They are cheap, easily seen from a distance, and convey an immediate sense of authority. Movers should be told that they are to take direction only from the staff vested (sorry) with that authority and to ignore instruction from any other person. Staff should be told to direct all communication with the movers to the designated guide for their area. The middle of a move is no time to redesign a space.

I prefer that staff be required to stay away from their home department and workspace until their part of the move has been completed and also that higher administrators stay away from the space. The time for staff input and administrative decision making was long ago, in the design phase.

Still, sometimes it is necessary to make a change from the accepted plan. The guide should contact the coordinator of the office move if a change seems required. Some changes can be approved on the spot by the appropriate person. Others may require discussion among the decision makers or even a redesign of the space.

Many staff will be eager to get into their new space, set up their desk and work area, and begin to feel some control of their new situation. Ask for their patience, emphasize the safety issue, and reinforce the authority of the designated guides. Better yet, find something for them to do elsewhere. If possible, schedule a specific time when each staff person can be away from assigned duties to unpack and set up their spaces. This may help them find patience.

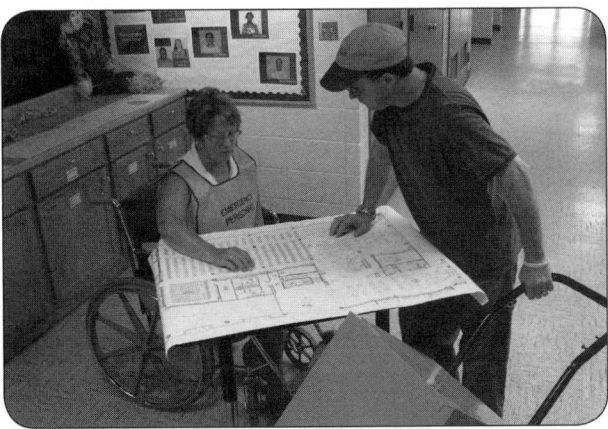

Figure 9.1 Staff who do not move books may help in other ways, such as directing the movers.

SUMMARY ADVICE

It is to your benefit financially and otherwise to make an FFE move as easy as possible for the hired movers. Here are some ways to make the move work as smoothly as possible, from the movers' perspective:

- Supply a good, complete inventory, organized room by room. It is easiest for movers to clear one room at a time; it takes more time and gets more expensive if they have to keep going back to the same space.
- Supply a clear timetable or an order in which the spaces should be moved if timing or sequencing is critical. The mover has a plan of work, developed in consultation with you. If you keep changing the plan at the last minute, the mover may not have the right equipment and crew available.
- Block off safe travel lanes away from staff and patrons. Assign elevators, stairs, doors, and other passages for exclusive use of the movers.
- Have everything packed and labeled in advance of the move.
- Provide one person to answer questions and give directions; movers cannot work effectively if they get conflicting instructions from different staff.

Part 2
MOVING

> *They see the size of the elephant and they forget how fast they can chew.*
>
> Curt Witcher, dockmaster

Preparing to Move

Chapter 10

In the last few days before move day, you are likely to be very busy with final preparations. Here is a short checklist of some tasks you need to include:

1. Set up the dispatch desk at the origin building.
   - Set up a whiteboard, blackboard, or just a large sheet of paper ruled into three columns: "Collection," "Color," "Done to." This is used to make and track assignments.
   - Keep the supply of sequence cards here.
   - Post drawings of the origin building shelving plan if you have them.
   - Make sure the phones and radios are working.
   - Post the telephone list.
2. Set up the dispatch desk at the destination building.
   - Post drawings of the shelving layout, with waypoints marked.
   - Make sure the phones and radios are working.
   - Post the telephone list.
3. Spot the carts, boxes, pallets, dollies, and other equipment near where you plan to start each crew. Stock sides, straps, or shrinkwrap in the origin loading dock. Set up the box factory(ies) and stock with tape, staples, gloves, tape guns, card pockets, and anything else needed to build boxes. Make up a starting supply of boxes and distribute them where the first unshelving crews will begin work.

The first three are big jobs. Make sure you allocate enough staff to get them done.

4. Post signs and instructions. Templates or samples for many of the signs you may need are available in appendix D at www.ala.org/editions/extras/fortriede09942. **WEB** Put signs in the elevators to advise the maximum safe loads. Post routes, doors, elevators, and exits reserved for the movers and safe-passage lanes for the civilians. If you are using carts, post TOP, BLACK, LEFT reminders in conspicuous places. Post a work schedule with break and lunch times.
5. Make sure the forklift is charged to capacity if it is electric.
6. Send a notice to all of the crew telling them where and when to report. Make sure to remind them not to wear open-toed shoes.
7. Make sure you have the elevator lockout key.
8. Decide how to start the move (see below).

9. Make the starting assignments (see below).
10. Prepare the introduction for move day (see below).

DECIDING HOW TO START A MOVE

One of the secrets to efficiency is to achieve and maintain a smooth workflow. One of the reasons we want everyone to start and stop together is so the workflow does not get backlogged. This is particularly important at the start of the first day. If you do not plan otherwise, everyone else will be standing around waiting while a crew loads the first books. Then each of the positions will come online one at a time as that first load makes its way along the route. It could be an hour before the reshelvers get access to any books. The last thing you want is to get people all fired up and then give them nothing to do. There are two ways to get most everyone involved right away. Either one works. Pick the option that works for you.

Option One: The Shotgun Start

Pick several collections to start, one for each crew. Make up a list of assignments so you know who is doing what jobs, at least at the start. A day before the move, have one small team load six carts or about thirty to forty boxes of material from each of the collections you picked to start. Spot two loaded carts or eight to ten boxes from each collection at each loading dock and take the same number all the way to where they will be reshelved. Every time we do this one, someone always wants to go ahead and reshelve those books. That doesn't help.

The idea is that, when the crew starts on move day, there is work waiting at each major station. You assign people to each position and they can go to work immediately. They may not be at full speed, but there is something on which they can practice before the rush starts.

This option presumes that (1) you have access to a small crew, transport equipment, truck, and the new building a day before the move; and (2) you are able to pretrain at least the leaders at each of the stations. If you can do these premoves, you can get a smooth start where you call everyone together, do the safety lecture and general instructions, hand out the assignments, and dismiss everyone at the same time. This one works especially well if you have good supervisors. It is the method you will use on the second and succeeding days as everyone just picks up where they left off the previous day.

Option Two: Everybody Loads

Pick several collections to start, one for each crew. Then pick an equal number of small collections. Small collections such as ready reference, displays, current copies of magazines, course reserves, or whatever fits on one to five carts, or twenty-five to seventy boxes, are perfect for this purpose. Make up a list of starting assignments as in the first option. Assign the reshelving half of each crew to one of the small collections. Instead of going immediately to the destination building, the reshelvers start the first day by unshelving small collections in the origin.

The idea behind this option is that you get everyone, including the reshelvers, started loading something right away and that you move the reshelving part of each crew to the new building about the time their work catches up with them.

At the start of the first day, do the safety lecture and general instructions (see below) and show everyone how to load. Then call out the crews one at a time and assign them their work. Start with the reshelvers and the small collections. Instruct those crews to load all of their assigned collection, then take it to the loading dock and get all of their books on one truck, go with the collection to the new building, and reshelve the books. When they finish they report to the dispatch desk for a new assignment. By that time, a good working supply of the regular collection materials has arrived.

 TIP

There is a third way to start. Just have the crew at the destination report a couple of hours after the crew at the origin. Get the unshelvers started, then move over to the destination, do another introductory meeting, and get that crew started about the time the first books show up. I have tried this a couple of times with poor results. Just about the time the origin crews start to identify problems or misunderstandings and really need assistance, the move coordinator is over at the other building doing the opening day meeting and not available. I would use this method only if I had good, experienced supervisors and the two buildings were some distance apart.

TIP

If you have a really big move, say more than eight crews working simultaneously, it is a good idea to phase them in rather than trying to start them all together. This gives the elevator and dock crews time to get up to speed and gives you time to get the move under control while it is still a manageable size. On a big move, I might start five crews, then add two more every two hours.

Next assign the origin building part of each crew (the unshelvers) to a collection and send the dock crews to organize their dock spaces.

This option works well if you have to make up crews on the fly from the available workforce and if you can't get a head start in the new building. If you have tasks well defined and sequence card colors assigned ahead of time, the start-up process goes quickly. (I timed Option Two start a couple of weeks before I wrote this. With forty-four crew members, it took eleven minutes to get everyone working productively.)

This approach is the one I use most on contract jobs where I am often the only person familiar with the process. The move coordinator can get everyone started to work quickly, then follow the first loads and spend a few minutes instructing the crew at each position as the books work their way through the process.

MAKING STARTING ASSIGNMENTS

Decide which collections to move first. Generally I prefer to start with the larger collections. I can start a crew working and not have to worry about reassigning them for a long time.

Some move carts are designed with only three shelves to accommodate taller books. If you are moving with boxes, you may have purchased a few larger boxes for the oversize books. You should start a crew working on oversize or periodicals (which have a lot of tall books) right away. The idea is to get as few as possible of the oversize carts or boxes, but to keep them steadily busy throughout the move.

You also need to think about staff with specialized knowledge. If you have only one person who can oversee periodicals and reference, you should avoid scheduling those two collections at the same time. You don't want to save all of the small collections to the end, but you don't have to do them all first, the exception being whatever quick-shelve collections you assigned if you picked Option Two.

Also, think about collections that are hard to move or do not fit neatly into the regular process. An example might be materials stored in an area not accessible by elevator. If you have to human-chain materials up or down steps, you may want to do a little at a time over several sessions to provide variety and give people the opportunity to use different muscles.

Microfilm is sufficiently different from the regular process that I treat it separately (see chapter 14). In any case it seems to be easier to start everyone on a common process and then introduce the variations once the flow is established.

If you have to start with an odd collection, go ahead. You might have to do a bit more training at the outset, but that's okay. I did a library where 80 percent of the books were on floors that had no elevator. We based the move plan on a human chain up and down the stairs and treated all the ground-floor materials as the oddities.

If you know all of the people who are working, you can make up exact crews, by name, in advance. Try to match people with their abilities and attitudes. Two slow people working together may get as much done as one fast and one slow. The team can't work any faster than the slowest member. It generally works better to pair fast with fast and slow with slow.

In a cart move, don't assume that the physically largest or strongest workers should be the pushers. Book carts don't hold much weight, and move carts roll easily so that a 100-lb seventh grader can push a 1,200-lb cart quite easily (and see figure 10.1). (Strength does count on the origin loading dock, where carts are being started and stopped and jockeyed about.)

If you are moving with boxes, the physical abilities of individual staff will affect your assignment decisions to a greater extent. Assign as pushers people who are large enough and strong enough to handle whatever equipment you are using to move the boxes. Height is an advantage when you are using hand trucks. Strength is necessary to maneuver a pallet with a pallet jack. If the pushers will be stacking and restacking boxes, assign people who can handle the weight. Great strength is not required for stacking, but stamina is, and this is not a job for someone with a weak back.

Figure 10.1 The cart weighs 932 lbs; the pusher weighs 28 lbs. He pushed it about 40 feet before losing interest.

As you make up the crews, consider how many pushers to assign to each crew. If someone can push a cart from the assigned shelves to the loading dock (or elevator) and back in seven minutes or less, you need only one pusher. If you have a crew working close to the dock or elevator, one of the unshelvers can push a loaded cart to the dock while the other sets up the next cart to be loaded, and you do not need a third person assigned as pusher. In a cart move, I prefer to start everyone with a pusher and make adjustments later, once I see how the crew is working.

With a box move, there are more variables to consider. The number of pushers depends on the method you are using to transport boxes. Hand trucks can take only one stack at a time, but they go quickly and are easy to maneuver. They require more pushers than other methods. Pallets take eight stacks at a time but may require two pushers each. They take longer than other methods to travel the same distance. Dollies fall in between.

Consider how far the pushers have to go to and from the loading dock or elevator. Also consider the floor covering. A longer route or one over carpet takes more time than a short route or one over a hard surface. This requires more pushers. The impact is greatest for pallet jacks, which have smaller wheels and are not easy to maneuver around corners.

Each situation is different. I prefer to assign more pushers than I really think it will take and make adjustments later. You can always reassign pushers to make up a new unshelving crew if you don't have enough work to keep them busy as pushers.

If you have ranges more than seven sections long and you cannot wheel the pallets or carts down the aisles, assign extra crew to help human-chain the books out to the end of the aisle. You won't need these people all of the time. When the unshelvers are working near the end of the aisle, they can load without help. As they move down the aisle, you need to add one more person for every two sections after the fourth to maintain the chain. You need to plan only enough help to reach halfway down the aisle. After that, move the supplies to the other end of the range and start reducing the length of the chain.

Sometimes you do not know all of the crew. Perhaps you hired through a temporary service, or you are using volunteers, or you hired additional staff just for the move. In that case your assignment list may take this form: "Crew of 3 to start at 326.8 (waypoint) using pink slash cards."

With luck, you will have staff or other familiar people as crew leaders. Then the list might read: "Jane and 2 strong crew to Art Books with oversize carts (boxes) and blue cards."

The noted "strong" reflects the extra weight of large art books and the "oversize" notes that this crew is to use the three-shelf carts or oversize boxes.

List enough assignments for every crew and a few extra to be assigned to whichever crew finishes first. This way the dispatch desk can make the assignments and you won't have to make them up on the fly. On a one-day move, you would probably list all of the collections more or less in the order they are to be moved. On a multiday move, you make a new list at the end of each day, updated to reflect progress made the preceding day. In this case a second-day entry might read: "Crew of 3 to continue at 392.4 using pink cards starting with #56."

INTRODUCTION FOR MOVE DAY

Before you start your move, get everyone together for a welcome and general instructions. A prepared agenda keeps this meeting informative, productive, and short. Figure 10.2 is my agenda for a recent move.

AGENDA

Welcome everybody—Thank you for helping

Safety I (Safety Director or EMT)

Proper lifting   Push vs. pull
Forklift safety   Fire alarms

Safety II (Move Coordinator)

Cart/dolly/pallet safety   Hands and feet
Safe routes for movers and other staff   Moldy books

Housekeeping details (Personnel Officer)

Communication tree   Saturday work
Work times and break times   Keep out of the construction areas
Amenities   Pop and snacks
Bathrooms   Don't write notes on the carts!

Rule Number One!! Everything is in order; everything stays in order. There is no Rule Number Two!!

How to load a cart or box

Assignments

1. Sara—take two dockmasters and go get the destination dock set up

    Mike K
    Jason T

2. Jane take 5 people from LP team and start bringing up microform trays using public passenger elevators. Store them in 317 and around the microfilm area. Check other floors for them. When done, go to LP and report to the desk for reassignment.

    Tabatha W
    Ashly D
    Charles J
    Courtney H
    Elizabeth K

3. 5 people from destination team. Load 13 carts of 940s onto the first truck. Take them to destination and start shelving them. Stay there. We'll send you more.

    Steve M, Leader
    Tim D
    Blaise O
    Damon H
    Natalie R

4. 3 people from RENCEN team. 2 loaders, 1 pusher. Load 940s on new white trucks, using purple cards.

    John B
    Vicki T
    Estanislao Q

    .
    .
    .

12. 5 people from RENCEN team. 2 loaders, 3 pushers. Start loading city directories, new yellow carts, using lime green cards.

    Robert R, Leader
    Elaine K
    . . .

Drivers: Ian McK
          Andrew R

Forklift: Mike C

Figure 10.2 Sample agenda for first move day briefing.

TIP

Print a list of the duties for each position and give a position description to each person (see chapter 6). You can also include the most critical safety reminders. This option is most appropriate on big moves.

Safety

The safety lecture is the most important part of this meeting. A library move is not particularly dangerous, but negligence and recklessness can cause trouble at any time. Because your crew members are inexperienced, they may be unaware of potential dangers. Whenever possible, I like to bring in an "authority" for this portion. The contractor's safety officer is a great choice. An EMT or nurse is also good. Here are some things you should cover:

Basic lifting. Lift with the legs, not the back. Squat down, don't bend over. Lift with the weight close to your body, not out away from you. Get help if you can't lift something comfortably by yourself. If you are moving with boxes, this part is even more critical.

Transport safety. Move carts and dollies weigh 500–1,500 lbs, loaded; pallets are even heavier. If you hit a door at a walking pace, you can tear it off its hinges. If you hit a person, that person will get hurt. Pushers must watch for people, especially people who might step into their path from a hallway or office. Even book carts, which are much lighter, can do a lot of damage.

Push, don't pull. Pulling puts a strain on shoulder and elbow joints, and you can accidentally pull a cart over your foot. Pushing, you can lean your body against the load to get it moving; then it pushes easily. The handles on a pallet jack are designed to be pulled, but turn it around and follow it down a slight slope. *Never* get in front of a load going down even a slight slope.

Shoes. No open-toed shoes at all. Tennis shoes or sneakers are the minimum acceptable. Work shoes are preferable. Steel toes are nice but not necessary. If you are working in a construction site, OSHA requires hard-soled shoes. I do not allow open-toed shoes on my work sites, even for visitors.

Hands. The most common danger is hands getting caught between a load of books and something else. Grip a cart by the middle of the end panel, not by the outer edges (figure 10.3). Grip a dolly in the middle. This prevents pinches and scrapes from narrow aisles or walls. Dock crews and the people loading trucks must be careful not to get their hands caught when two loads are packed against one another.

Hands, again. If you shelve or unshelve books all day, your hands and wrists can get sore. The tendency is to grab two or a few books at a time and squeeze them to keep them from sliding. Most people's muscles are not used to that action, and repeating it over and over can cause strains. The solution is to vary the number of books you take each time. We illustrate three methods in figure 10.4. Believe it or not, taking a larger number of books, even a whole armload, is less tiring at the end of the day than handling them one or two at a time.

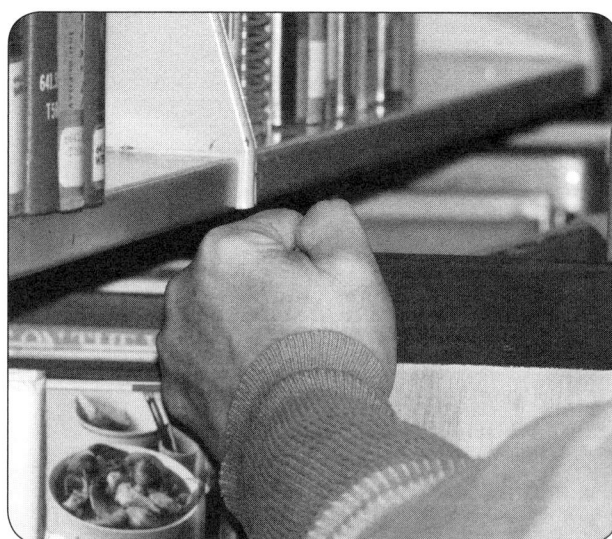

Figure 10.3 Right (left) and wrong (right) hand placement for pushing a cart.

Figure 10.4 Wendy, Jane, and Keri, the "fly" team at Allen County Public Library. By varying the number of books in a handful, they reduce muscle fatigue.

Another solution is to rotate jobs between shelvers/unshelvers and pushers.

Moldy books. Unshelvers and reshelvers should watch for moldy or mildewed books. Such books should be cleaned and not packed with the rest of the collection. Do not touch moldy books with bare hands, and, if you do, wash your hands before you put them near your mouth or eyes. Call a supervisor to take care of these books.

Loading dock. Stand clear of the forklift. Stand away when the forklift is working. Do not walk behind the forklift any time the operator is in the driver's seat. Do not use the loading dock as an entrance to the building. If a load starts to fall or tip when it is on the forklift, get away fast; *do not ever* try to stop it from falling.

How to Load

While you have the entire crew present in one place, demonstrate to everyone the proper way to load a cart or box. It is important that everyone know how to load and how to keep the loads in order, even those who will be doing other jobs. One well-meaning person trying to find a "better way" can cause untold time and labor if that person does not understand how the process is supposed to work. (For this discussion, I assume you followed my advice and marked each cart or box, using black tape for carts and card pockets for boxes. If you did something else, change the instructions accordingly.)

When I do the loading demo, I stress the importance of keeping the books in order at all times. I have found that a significant number of hired laborers do not realize that the books are in order and that it is important to keep them that way. I go through the entire process for them:

- The books are in order on the shelves.
- We take them off the shelves, in order.
- We put them on the carts (boxes), in order.
- We number the carts (boxes), in order.
- We put the carts (boxes) on the truck, in order.
- We take the carts (boxes) off the truck, in order.
- We take the carts (boxes) to the shelves, in order.
- We take the books off the carts (boxes), in order.
- We put the books back on the shelves, in order.

I stress Rule Number One: "Everything stays in order."

If we are moving with carts, show them a cart and point out that one end is always marked BLACK. I stress that we always start loading from the TOP shelf with the BLACK end to the LEFT. That way, everyone who handles the cart throughout its journey knows immediately which is the first book on the cart.

If we are using move carts, I demonstrate how to fill one side, then spin the cart and fill the other.

If we are using book carts, I demonstrate the agreed-on loading process, whether it is to fill one side, spin, and do the other, or to fill two rows on each shelf from the same side.

For a box move I show a box and point out the pocket end. I stress that we always load left to right with the pocket to the right so we always know which book comes out of the box first. I show how to put the books in the box, upright on their bottom edge.

I stress the importance of building a stack to the agreed height and make sure everyone understands never to take a box from one stack to another.

Finally, I show the sequence cards and stress the importance of numbering every cart without skipping any or missing any numbers.

Moving with Carts

After all of the planning, the preparation, and the paperwork, we come now to the fun part. In fact, this is the only part of the move most of your staff, patrons, and the press will ever see, and it is the part they will talk about for years. As the move coordinator, your job now is to see that all of the steps stay in order, that no one invents a "better way" all on their own, and that the stages of the move follow through a smooth, balanced process. You must constantly adjust people, processes, routes, and resources to ensure that the move is under control as much as possible.

MOVING BOOKS, STEP BY STEP

You are ready to move some books. Here is how the flow should work:

1. Assign each crew a starting point and a pack of colored sequence cards. The starting point does not have to be the beginning of a collection, but it must be a waypoint. In a large move, it is not uncommon to have several crews working in one collection. Try to spread the assignments so the crews are not all using the same aisles, elevators, and other facilities.

2. In each crew, one person takes books from the shelf and hands them to the other unshelver, who puts them on the cart, starting on the TOP shelf with the BLACK end to the LEFT. Two people working together are more efficient when the books are coming off the top shelves and going onto the bottom shelves of the cart, or vice versa. When the books and the cart shelves are at the same level, crews often find it is easier for one person to grab an armload of books and put them directly onto the carts. Don't be too rigid about the roles. The main idea is to provide the opportunity for a variety of lifting and turning motions. Typically a two-person crew moves more books over the course of a day than two individuals working separately. Rarely you may find a person who prefers to work alone and who can work as fast, and for as long, as a two-person crew.

3. Fill one cart from TOP, BLACK, LEFT to the bottom right. Spin that cart and load the other side from TOP, LEFT to bottom, right. As the crew works along, they come to the waypoint flags inserted in the collection. They take the flag along with the surrounding books and put it on the cart exactly where it falls in the collection, leaving some portion of the flag sticking out so it is readily visible. Pack the books tight on the carts. Loosely packed books slide off the shelves when the carts are moved.

4. Once the cart is filled, the unshelving crew removes card number 1 from the pack and inserts it in a card pocket on the cart. Pull the last two cards, marked "XXX," from the pack, write the name of the collection and the call number of the starting

waypoint on each card, and put these cards in the pocket as well with the XXX card showing.

5. The pusher takes the cart to the elevator or loading dock. If there are any empty carts there, the pusher takes one back to the unshelvers.

6. The elevator operator loads carts onto the elevator and takes them to the loading dock level, then offloads them. If there are any empties, the elevator operator loads them and takes them to the floor(s) where they are needed. The elevator operator must be careful to get the lowest-numbered carts of each color sequence onto the elevator first and to service all of the floors evenly.

7. The dock crew takes over next. They take the carts from the elevator or place where the pushers drop them onto the dock. They remove one of the XXX cards from the first cart of each color and post it in a convenient spot. This provides a visible reference for what collections are in process at any time.

8. The carts first go to the packaging area. If you are shrinkwrapping, it is best to work in pairs; one person holds the cart while another applies the shrinkwrap. It is easiest to wrap horizontally around the cart, but you should take at least one wrap vertically under and over the cart to strengthen the wrap.

If you are using move carts that accept cardboard side panels, one person can do the packaging alone, although it is much faster with two (figure 11.1). With two, each person takes one panel and sets it in place inside the retainer at the bottom shelf. Holding the panel in place, they pass the strap around the cart and ratchet it down tight.

If you rented carts with slanted or lipped shelves, you may be able to skip the packaging step.

9. The dockmaster should establish some way of sorting carts on the dock so that it is easy to determine which carts are next to go on the truck. This may be as simple as a designated area for each color sequence card (each collection). The actual system develops through trial and error and is determined more than anything by the size and shape of your loading dock area.

One method is to designate an area for each color series using tape on the floor, caution tape on stanchions, or some other indicator.

Another way is to establish one line for each color. The pushers drop the carts at the tail of each line, and the shrinkwrap or strapping crews work back and forth from line to line. In this method, the pushers need to be careful to drop the carts in the proper lines. This method is easy and works well if you have several routes to your dock or if you have a small dock area, because the lines of carts can extend out into a hallway or approach.

A third method, also useful when the dock is small, is to establish a single line for all carts. The line can run out of the dock and down an approach hallway. This reserves the dock space for offloading empties and supplies. With this method, it may be difficult to find a particular cart or pull it out of line if it is needed at the destination building.

Pushers should be trained to leave the carts end to end in one row (figure 11.2, left). When the strapping or shrinkwrap crew finishes their task, they can turn the carts side by side with the numbered card end facing out (figure 11.2, right). In most cases the dock crew takes the carts in order, right down the line. However, if they need to hold a color, or advance the transport of another, the dock crew can walk along the row and pull out the carts they need.

10a. Load the truck, with dock plate. If you have a loading dock and a truck that nearly matches it in height, you can use a dock plate to roll the carts into the truck. This is, by far, the fastest and safest way to load a truck. See "Dock Plate," chapter 7.

Roll any empty carts off the truck and get them out of the way. Any available pushers can start taking carts back to the unshelvers, but the first priority is to get the truck reloaded and on its way. Wise use of the truck is

Figure 11.1 Two people working together can strap a cart quickly.

Figure 11.2 (left) Pushers leave carts parked end to end. (right) Carts set side by side allow easy access to every cart.

one of the keys to a smooth, fast move. Use the truck to help balance the workflow. Sometimes this means sending the truck off half full if the origin is slow and the reshelvers are calling for work. You might unload a truck and send it back immediately and empty if empty carts are starting to pile up at the destination. Keep your trucks moving and you will have an efficient move. This is why we want a lot of communication between the dockmasters. Each dockmaster should know almost as much about conditions at the other dock as about those at his or her own.

Roll loaded carts onto the truck. They do not have to go in order, but it is vitally important that the lowest numbers of each color sequence go on before the higher numbers. If the crew skips a cart, the shelvers have to wait for it. Worse, if the shelvers lose track of the numbers, they may just skip the forgotten cart. If that happens, you will have to shift anything they shelved until the mistake was caught or the next waypoint was reached.

10b. Load the truck, with forklift. If your truck does not match the dock height, you need to load the carts with a forklift. You may be able to unload empties using a ramp supplied with the truck. If the ramp is not too steep, it is fastest to unload empties down the ramp. *I do not recommend loading full carts of any kind up a truck ramp.* You will not be able to load full move carts up a truck ramp.

If you can, deploy the ramp and unload the empties. Then stow the ramp and load full carts using the forklift.

The loading dock is defined as that area where you are loading and unloading. It may not be a space designed as an actual loading dock. It could be the sidewalk outside your door, a narrow aisle leading to your service door, or almost anywhere else. Often you have three heights to deal with: the truck bed, the street, and the curb or loading dock.

The most efficient way to load and unload is to put the forklift on the dock surface itself and use the forklift as a simple elevator. Back the truck up until it overhangs the dock level. Back the forklift away from the truck far enough that one of the dock crew can swing a loaded cart around to and onto the forks. Always put the cart on the tines; do not drive the tines under the cart. Otherwise sooner or later you will snag a wheel and damage it. The dock crew member signals when the cart is set. The forklift operator just raises the forks enough to clear the truck bed and moves straight forward against the truck, then lowers the tines so the wheels of the cart rest freely on the truck bed. The truck driver or one of the dock crew pulls the cart off the tines and guides it into place in the truck. The forklift operator backs up enough to clear the truck and lowers the lift to allow the dock crew to swing another cart onto the tines. If you can use the forklift this way—up and in, back and down—you will find loading to be fast and safe.

You may not be able to put the forklift on the dock level. In that case the driver has to turn and maneuver the forklift. Proceed in this manner: Raise the tines until they just clear the dock surface, and move the forklift against the dock. One of the dock crew places a cart on

TIP

If you work outside, you may have to deal with wet weather. A creative dockmaster laid one of the cardboard side panels on top of the cart for the short run between the dock and the truck. The cardboard absorbed the light rain and kept the books dry. Three or four panels lasted an entire afternoon.

the tines. Lift the forks just enough to get the cart wheels off the dock and maneuver so that the forklift lines up with the truck. Raise the cart until the wheels just clear the truck bed and move forward against the truck. The truck driver or one of the dock crew pulls the cart off the tines and guides it into place in the truck. The operator backs up and maneuvers to accept another cart at the dock.

At all times the forks should be kept as low as possible while they are carrying a loaded cart. If it is necessary to keep the cart high to clear obstructions, all crew must stand out of the area during the movement.

11. Block or strap the carts. You need to restrain them so they do not roll around during transport. You can use a heavy strap hooked to the sides of the truck and ratcheted tight. Make sure whatever you are using as an attachment point is strong enough to take the strain. Some trucks are made with a reinforced track for a tie-down strap. The light straps we use for the move carts are not strong enough to restrain carts. I recommend a strap at least 2 inches wide.

You can also use a cargo bar, sometimes known as a "load lock." See "Restraining Straps or Bars," chapter 7.

12. Transport the carts. The driver takes the loaded carts to the destination building, driving slowly and being careful on hills and corners so the carts do not roll. If you are running a prize pool or just want to measure progress, the driver is responsible for keeping a count of the carts or boxes moved each day. Keep a clipboard in the truck and write down the number for each trip. The driver is not eligible to participate in any pool based on the number of items moved.

13a. Unload the truck, with dock plate. If you have a loading dock and a truck that nearly matches it in height, you can use a dock plate to roll the carts out of the truck. As when you loaded, this is by far the fastest and safest way to unload a truck. Roll empty carts onto the truck. Make sure to include any straps, side panels, wheel chocks, or other reusable supplies. It is just as important to return empties and supplies as it is to move full carts.

Strap or block the empty carts so they do not shift in the truck.

13b. Unload the truck, with forklift. If your truck does not match the height of the loading dock, you need to unload the truck with a forklift. The most efficient way is to put the forklift on the dock surface itself and use it just as an elevator.

Always put the cart on the tines; don't ram the forks under the cart. When the cart is unloaded, the dock crew pulls the cart off the tines and sets it aside for the pushers.

If you cannot put the forklift on the dock surface, the operator has to turn and maneuver the forklift. Lower the cart as soon as possible and before you turn the forklift. If some obstruction requires the maneuvering to be done with the cart high in the air, everyone in the area must stand back well out of the way.

Use the forklift to load empty carts onto the truck. Be sure to load any straps, side panels, wheel chocks, or other supplies.

13c. Unload the truck, with ramp. You may be able to use the ramp supplied with the truck to unload book carts. *It is not safe to unload move carts down a ramp.* The

LOADING ON A HILL

The ideal situation for loading is with the front of the truck level or just slightly lower than the back. Carts roll easily and hold against the front of the truck.

If the truck angles down sharply, you may need to use two or more crew members to hold the cart back to keep it from slamming into the front of the truck. Control the cart from the sides. *Do not get in front of the cart.*

If the truck angles up sharply, you may need two or more crew members to push the carts up the slope. Also, you have to block the wheels of each cart to keep it from rolling back out of the truck. I use pieces of 1-by-3-inch board cut 8 inches long. Keep a supply in the truck and block at least one wheel of every cart.

You may have a situation where the truck sits level or nose down at the origin building but angles up at the destination. If so, you still need to block the wheels of every cart you load. Otherwise the carts roll out of the truck as soon as you remove the restraining strap or load lock.

only exception is if there is only a slight slope between the truck bed and the loading dock, in which case the ramp serves as a kind of dock plate.

Be careful to line up the cart with the ramp. Most truck ramps are only slightly wider than the wheels on a cart. If you miss the ramp with a wheel, the cart falls.

With book carts, roll the carts carefully down the ramp. You may need two people for each cart to ensure that a cart does not get away from you. Be extra careful at the bottom of the ramp. Most truck ramps have a steep section right at the end. If the cart is going too fast at the end of the ramp, the wheels may be damaged. Handle the carts from the sides. Do not get in front of a loaded cart.

If you are using move carts, you need two people per cart to prevent a runaway even on a slight slope. If two people are not enough to hold the cart, don't use the ramp. It is too dangerous. Be extra careful not to damage the wheels on the steep section at the bottom of the ramp. *Do not get in front of a loaded move cart.*

14. Unwrap the carts and start them on their way. The dock crew and driver remove the restraining straps or cargo bars and move the carts off the truck onto the dock. On the dock, other crews remove and dispose of the shrinkwrap or unstrap and remove the sides. There is no need to keep the carts in order. The pushers can sort out the carts for their particular crew by color and number. Pushers should take the lowest-numbered carts first, but even this is not absolutely vital. Often the higher-numbered cart of a color comes off the truck first, and the pushers can get it started on its way while the dock crew is unloading the rest of the truck. Pushers can take the carts all the way to the reshelvers or to the elevator if you are using a dedicated elevator operator. Whoever pushes the first cart of any new collection must remove the second XXX card from the pocket and take it to the dispatch desk in the destination building; this serves as a notice that a new collection stream has arrived and the dispatch desk staff can direct the pusher to the correct location for the new material.

15. If you are using a dedicated elevator operator, that person takes the carts to the appropriate floor and brings back any empties. The elevator operator must make an effort to keep an even flow of work to all floors and to return all empties promptly.

16. Push the carts to the reshelving area. If there is an elevator, the dock crew is responsible for taking carts as far as the elevator. Otherwise the pushers pick up carts at the dock and take them all the way to the reshelvers.

As soon as the truck arrives, all available pushers should congregate at the dock area or at the elevator on their floor. Pushers retrieve carts and take them to where their reshelvers are working. If pushers are assigned to a particular reshelving crew, they should move carts only for that crew. The colored sequence cards indicate which carts belong to which crew. Pushers do not necessarily need to take carts in strict order; often the low-numbered carts are last off the truck. However, at the reshelving location pushers do need to sort the carts into order.

Pushers should leave carts in an area close to where the reshelvers are working. This location moves as the shelvers progress, and the pushers need to plan ahead to place the carts where they are most convenient for the reshelvers. If the carts are in strict order, they can be placed in a line, end to end, with the sequence cards facing forward. Another option is to place the carts side by side with the sequence cards visible.

Pushers return any empty carts to the dock area—or elevator—as soon as possible. Train the pushers that it is just as important to return all empties as it is to bring full carts to the shelves.

17. Reshelve the books. The reshelving crew must watch carefully the numbers of the sequence cards to make certain they unload the carts in strict order. In addition, they must make certain to unload each cart from the TOP with the BLACK end to the LEFT. This

TIP

Sooner or later you have to get a loaded cart up onto the plywood you laid down as floor protection. Even the ½-inch elevation change can be difficult to surmount if the cart is heavy. Here's the trick: Set the cart alongside the floor protection with the wheels parallel to and touching the plywood. Stand at one end of the cart; grab the cart at the top of the end panel with the hand that is away from the plywood and under the second shelf with the hand on the floor protection side. Slightly lift and twist one wheel up onto the plywood. It is the combination of the lower hand lifting and the top hand tipping the cart back just the slightest bit that shifts the weight off that first wheel. Once you have the first wheel up, the rest twists up effortlessly.

should be ingrained in them through repetition and training.

The reshelving half of each crew finds the starting collection flag on their first cart. They match the flag with a waypoint marker taped to the shelf where the first book is to go. The waypoint marker also indicates how much space the crew must leave empty on each shelf up to the next waypoint.

One person takes the books from the cart starting with the first book on the TOP shelf with the BLACK end to the LEFT, then hands them to the other reshelver, who puts them on the shelf, leaving the amount of space indicated on the previous waypoint marker. It is necessary to provide each crew with a ruler or other way to gauge this distance. A consistent error of 1 inch per shelf will cumulate to two or three shelves by the next waypoint.

Efficiency in reshelving parallels that for unshelving. Two people working together and trading off jobs are more efficient and get more work done with less effort than two individuals working separately.

Empty the cart from TOP, BLACK, LEFT to the bottom right, then spin the cart and empty the other side from top left to bottom right.

When the crew empties a cart, they should remove the sequence card and keep it, in order, in a convenient place. The cards may be useful to diagnose a shelving error. A missing number might indicate a forgotten cart. Also, you may be able to recycle the deck of sequence cards to use on another collection if you have a large move.

18. Measure accuracy at each waypoint. As the crew works along, they come to the waypoint flags left between the books by the unshelvers. If you measured the collection and calculated waypoints accurately, the reshelving crew should reach the next waypoint on their shelves just as they reach the flag left in the books by the unshelvers when they loaded the cart. In practice, because we calculated growth conservatively, they may reach the flag on the cart one or two shelves before they get to the waypoint on the shelf.

If the crew does get to the flag before they reach the waypoint marker, they should skip to the shelf with the marker, match the flag to the marker, and continue reshelving from that point. If they reach the waypoint marker on the shelves while they still have books left on the cart ahead of the flag, there is a problem and they must call for the move coordinator or their supervisor. Likewise, if they get to the flag four or more shelves before they get to the waypoint, they need to call for help. See chapter 13 for the corrective steps.

Chapter 12

Moving with Boxes

If you are moving with boxes, you have some additional considerations not required with the cart move and a few more general lessons to be learned. From there we can move on to the step-by-step instructions and, finally, a review of topics related to storing books in boxes.

BOX BASICS

Methods of Moving Boxes

Before you can plan your move, you must decide how you are going to move the boxes. Here are the methods I have used:

- hand-carry or drag them
- hand truck
- dolly or cart
- pallets and pallet jack

Hand-Carry

This is the low-tech, minimum-preparation way. It works for a very small move, within a single building. It is best to have plenty of young, strong help; that five hundredth box gets very heavy.

Just pick up the boxes, more or less in order, and carry them to the new location. This is actually easier if you grip the box by the bottom rather than using handles.

The drag variation of this method actually works well in limited circumstances. The move must be in one building. The boxes must be sturdy and have strong handholds. You need a hook with a handle. I make them out of an old broom handle that has a hole in the end where you can hang it. Wedge a piece of dowel rod into the hole so it sticks out about an inch and you have a hook (figure 12.1).

Catch the hook in the handgrip hole of a box and you can drag the box easily. In fact, you can drag a stack of four or five loaded boxes over vinyl or carpet with surprisingly little effort. The handle lifts the leading edge of the bottom box just enough that it glides over thresholds, bumps, and other irregularities in the floor.

You do need to brace the stack near the top with one hand. With a bit of practice, you can even take a stack of loaded boxes down three or four steps without spilling them. Just pull straight out and let the whole stack bounce down one step at a time. No, we never figured out how to get them up the stairs or even up or down a ramp.

Figure 12.1 A homemade handle moves boxes efficiently.

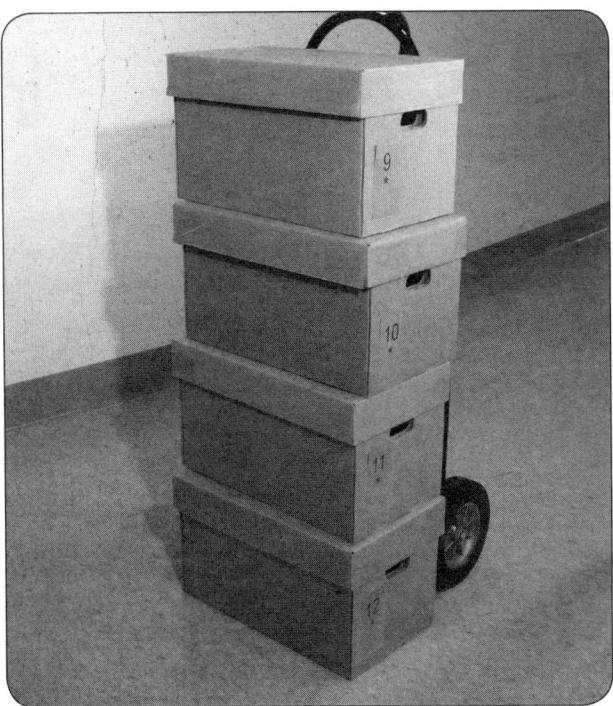

Figure 12.2 Hand truck moves one stack at a time.

This is my preferred way to move empties. I think the record is a stack of twelve beer cases.

It is also a good idea to have hooks available for the reshelvers to place stacks of boxes exactly where they need them.

Hand Truck

A hand truck (figure 12.2) can take one stack of boxes from the unshelving area all the way to the move truck and from there to the destination shelves. Elevators, ramps, dock plates, and rough surfaces are not impediments. A strong mover can negotiate a hand truck down three or four steps and up one or two, although I would look for a flat route if possible. They can be loaded and unloaded from a truck by ramp if necessary.

The big advantage of the hand truck is that you stack the boxes only once and the hand truck does not have to be present when the boxes are stacked. The books arrive at the destination shelves with the boxes in the same order in which they were packed. You need to plan ahead so the unshelvers stack the boxes to a height that fits the hand truck, but that is a simple calculation and an easy instruction. Hand trucks are common. It should be easy to find enough to do the job.

The disadvantage is the limited capacity of a hand truck, about one-eighth that of a move cart, so you need more pushers to move the same number of books in the same time. Because each stack is moved separately, the dock crews spend more time and care to make sure they are dispatching and receiving the stacks in order. It is more difficult at every stage to make certain that an individual stack was not overlooked.

Dolly or Cart

There are many types of four-wheeled carts that can be used to move books (figure 12.3). If possible, get carts on which all four wheels swivel; they are easier to maneuver in tight places.

Dollies are easy to move and maneuver. They usually pass through a doorway or down an aisle. With large wheels they can handle irregularities in floor surfaces. They may be able to move up or down on a slight slope. They usually fit into an elevator.

Dollies are too heavy to load up a ramp and have less capacity than a pallet. You may find it difficult to assemble enough dollies to do the job, and it may be

Figure 12.3 Dollies come in many versions.

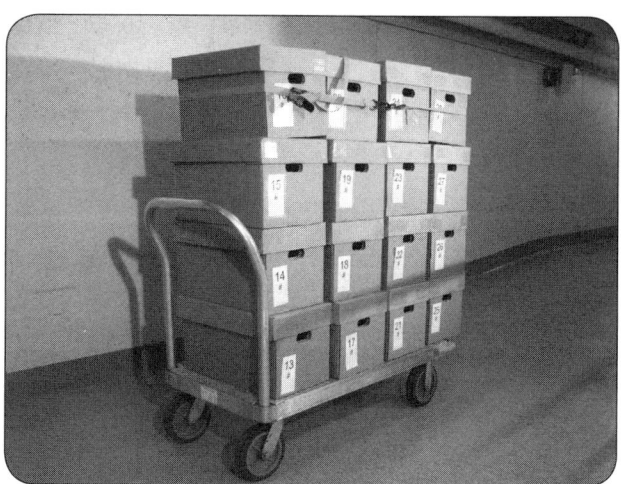

Figure 12.4 Strap stacks together to keep them from toppling.

impossible to find dollies all the same size, in which case you have to train crews how to load and unload each size. If the dolly cannot pass an obstruction, or if you do not have enough of them that you can afford to leave the books on them all the way from the unshelving to the reshelving locations, you may have to do a lot of restacking.

Dollies are not safe to load with a liftgate, nor can they be used on a ramp without danger of toppling the stacks. One solution is to strap the stacks together near the top using the same type of ratchet tie-down straps we use for move carts (figure 12.4). A 15-foot strap can contain up to six stacks.

Depending on size, a dolly can move three to six stacks of boxes. Be careful not to overload a dolly with boxes hanging out over the sides. Unless stacks are fully supported, they may topple when the dolly is moved or bumped, and you may find they won't pass through a doorway.

If you have enough of them, you can assign several dollies to each move crew and they can stack boxes directly onto the dolly as they fill them. In this case the boxes can stay on the dolly all the way to the destination shelves.

On most moves there are not enough dollies to assign a set to each crew. In this case the unshelvers have to stack boxes in the aisle as they fill them, and a crew of pushers has to restack them onto the dolly when they come to move the boxes.

Depending on the exact circumstances of your move, you may stack and restack the boxes several times. It would not be uncommon to have the following sequence befall a four-high stack of boxes:

1. Unshelvers fill boxes and stack them, #1 on the bottom, #4 on top.
2. Pushers restack boxes on dolly, #4 on the bottom, #1 on top.
3. Dock crew stacks boxes in truck, #1 on the bottom, #4 on top.
4. Destination dock crew restacks them on another dolly, #4 on the bottom, #1 on top.
5. Pushers remove boxes from the dolly and stack them at the reshelving location, #1 on the bottom, #4 on top.
6. The stack is now upside down, so someone has to restack it to get the #1 box on top.

This sequence points up an important lesson: dollies require fewer pushers and fewer trips than hand trucks, but they may require much more lifting and stacking. You really need to plan out the move in detail to save steps. In the example above, the unshelvers could have been told to fill all four boxes first and then to build their stack with the #4 box on the bottom. At the end of step 5, the stack would have had box #1 on top, saving the final restacking.

Pallet

You can stack boxes on pallets and then move the whole pallet with a pallet jack. Essentially the pallet is a dolly without wheels. You should be able to get enough pallets that you can stack the boxes once and leave them on the pallet until the books are reshelved. This, by itself, can save much labor.

Pallets are cheap and easy to obtain. They have high capacity and, if you have a clear path, the boxes never have to be restacked. They are relatively easy for the dock crew to keep in order, if only because there are so few of them for the number of books they move. Pallet jacks, however, are expensive and relatively hard to find. They are heavy and hard to move, even empty. Because of their small wheels, they do not easily handle rough surfaces, carpet, or other obstacles. They do not fit down most aisles or through most doorways. You may have to carry boxes down the aisle to stack them on the pallet. You may have to restack the pallet at every choke point. Because they are hard to maneuver, pallets require the heaviest floor, wall, and doorway protections.

A standard pallet is 40 by 48 inches and holds eight stacks of boxes, or the equivalent of two move carts. With the largest footprint of all the moving options, pallets are difficult, or impossible, to move in tight spaces. A standard door, for instance is 32–36 inches wide. A 40-inch pallet won't go through that door. You can't take a loaded pallet down a ramp safely. I can't imagine how many people you'd need to get one up a ramp.

Because pallets rock and tip as you move them, especially on rough surfaces, you must strap the stacks together at the top to prevent them from toppling. Use ratchet-type tie-down straps around the whole load; you need a strap at least 16 feet long (the standard 15-footer just is not long enough).

Hybrid Systems

You may well use more than one method to move your books over the whole route. You might use hand trucks to move single stacks through the narrow aisles and around the tight corners in your origin building, then restack them on dollies or even pallets at the destination where you have wide aisles and a big freight elevator. Just from a practical standpoint, you may not be able to assemble enough pallet jacks or dollies or hand trucks to handle the workload at both locations, and you may be forced to use some of each.

I do not describe in detail every combination of circumstances you may encounter. You may have to combine elements to design a move that works best for your buildings. These are the important points to consider:

- Minimize the number of restackings. It is hard work and there is always the potential for error.
- Hand trucks are the most versatile method, but they require more crew as pushers and more time and care at the loading docks.
- Pallets utilize the fewest pushers but require 50-inch doorways and aisles and lots of pallet jacks.
- Dollies are a compromise. They have less capacity but are easier to maneuver than pallets.
- Make sure you can get enough equipment to complete the move efficiently.
- Plan thoroughly and walk through the plan well in advance. Think about the five hundredth or five thousandth box, not the first. It is difficult to change the system in the middle of the move if you find your plan is inefficient or unworkable.
- Before it is too late, you might reconsider the whole box idea and decide to use carts.

It is also possible that you may conduct part of the move with carts and another part with boxes. This is particularly likely if you have to store a portion of your books for some time and move the rest to open shelves. Try to separate the moves in time, or at least in space. A simultaneous box and cart move in the same space would be confusing for all concerned. If you absolutely have to do both moves at the same time, try to set up two loading docks with separate crews.

Plans for Packing and Stacking

Whatever conveyance you use, you must decide how many boxes go to a stack and train the unshelvers accordingly. The decision is based primarily on the weight the pushers can handle. Four boxes is usually a reasonable number in all methods. Five gets to be heavy on a pallet and may be difficult for some pushers using a hand truck. Make certain the pushers, dock crew, and everyone else knows that there are *no* circumstances under which it is appropriate to add a box to or take one from a stack to adjust a load. That guarantees a box out of order.

Determine how many times each stack will be removed and restacked. We want the books to arrive at the destination shelves with the lowest-numbered box on top of each stack. As we saw above, some types of conveyance may require that the boxes be stacked and restacked several times. We need to know the exact number, which may be different for different parts of the collection in different locations.

Walk through your entire route with your chosen conveyance. Count every time you cannot pass a choke point without handling the boxes. Is a doorway too narrow to pass a pallet? Is there a ramp? How wide is the elevator door? For that matter, is the elevator deep enough to take a dolly and, if not, is it wide enough to turn the dolly to fit? Don't just measure, try it. Many elevator cabs are 48 inches deep. A 48-inch dolly may not fit inside one and still allow the door to close. How wide are your aisles? Can you get a pallet or dolly anywhere near the spot where the unshelvers will be working, or will you have to build a human chain just to get to a place where you can stack boxes? Most pallets are accessed from the 48-inch side; you need a 48-inch opening to pass through, and 50 inches is the practical minimum.

Count all of the restackings, but not the building of the original stack by the unshelvers. If the total is an odd number, the unshelvers should build the stack with the low number on the bottom. If the total is an even number, they should build the stack with the low number on top.

Now consider the total number of restackings. If it is anything greater than zero, you might remember that I prefer moving on carts. This would be the reason. Boxes are cheaper and probably easier to obtain, but the extra crew needed to move boxes and the cost and effort to acquire the necessary trucks, dollies, or pallet equipment may well offset the cost and effort required to beg, borrow, buy, or build carts.

How to Pack

When we pack boxes, we put only one row of books in each box. Yes, we could pack more books into a box, filling it completely, but the extra time and expertise required at the reshelving step to get the books back into order more than makes up for the savings in transport costs. With a single row of books per box, replicating the arrangement of the shelf, we can use even minimally trained unshelvers and reshelvers with every expectation that the books will be reshelved in the proper order.

Start at the beginning of a collection or at any waypoint. Load the boxes, left to right, with the front of the box to your right. The front is the end with the card pocket. The first thing that goes into the box is the flag for the waypoint at the start of the collection. Then fill the box, not tight, but snug. Put as many books as possible into the box without jamming them in so tightly that the reshelvers damage them getting them out again.

Whenever possible, set the books into boxes on their bottom edge, upright, as if they were on the shelf. This position affords maximum support and protection to the books. Sometimes you use boxes that are wider than they are tall. In that case you may have to put the books into the boxes spine up. Over time this can damage the spine, but it is safe for the short duration of a shelf-to-shelf move.

You may come across books that are too tall to fit in the box. *Do not allow them to stick up above the top of the box,* which makes a stack unstable. If you have an occasional tall book, you can put it into the same box, but slip it in front of the row of books, spine down, or lay it flat on top of the other books (figure 12.5). Yes, I said not to pack books into the empty spaces, out of order like this. But for the occasional large book it does little harm. If the reshelvers are familiar with the classification scheme, they can file it in the proper order. If not, instruct them to lay it on top of the books on the shelf and assign someone to tour the collection occasionally to shelve these odd items.

You may find books that are too large to fit in the box in any direction. Set these aside for now. We deal with them in chapter 15.

When the box is full, fold in the top flaps or put on the lid. Remove the first card from a deck of numbered sequence cards and put it in the card pocket. Then pull the last two cards, marked "XXX," from the pack. Write the name of the collection and the call number of the

Figure 12.5 Infrequent tall books can be moved in the box with their shelf mates.

starting waypoint on each card. Put these cards in the pocket as well with the XXX card showing.

It is convenient to know which boxes contain collection flags in case you need to check the accuracy of the reshelving or to set up a skipahead. An easy way to pinpoint the flags is to mark the sequence card with a marker. A simple check mark or slash alerts reshelvers to the flag.

Now load the second box and number it. If you are stacking boxes with number 1 on the bottom, you can build the stack as you go, putting each box on top of the preceding one, up to the agreed-upon height. If you are stacking with number 1 on top, you should fill four or five boxes, then stack them in reverse order.

Each time you come to a flag, mark the sequence card.

Because the boxes are small, you use up a lot of sequence cards, one deck for every twenty to twenty-five stacks. It is entirely possible that you will run through a full deck of one hundred cards and start another before the first number 1 card has cleared the loading dock. You would not want to change colors in the middle of a run, and you don't want to use a duplicate card number if there is any chance that someone will misunderstand the proper order. The book's website (www.ala.org/editions/extras/fortriede09942) has templates for card sets numbered up to two hundred. **WEB** By the time you get through two hundred cards, you should be able to start over with another deck at the number 1 card again.

How to Stack

If you are stacking boxes to be moved by hand cart, or if the pushers will restack them onto a cart or dolly, just leave the boxes stacked in the aisle behind you as you move along the shelves. Stack boxes against the shelves you just emptied with the card pocket end out into the aisle. This lets you see at a glance that the numbers are in order and lets the pushers approach the stacks from the side with a hand truck or from in front for restacking by hand.

The aisle fills quickly. A fairly full, seven-high section of shelving requires fourteen boxes. This is three or four stacks and takes up more floor space than the width of the shelf. Make sure you assign enough pushers to keep up with the unshelvers. If you have room, start stacking a few feet out into the cross aisle at the start of the range.

If you are stacking directly onto a dolly or pallet, you must complete each stack to the agreed height before you start another. You should not load in horizontal layers, nor should you build up the stacks by interlocking them like bricks to increase stability (figure 12.6). Either of these procedures gets the boxes out of order. See figure 12.4 for the correct method.

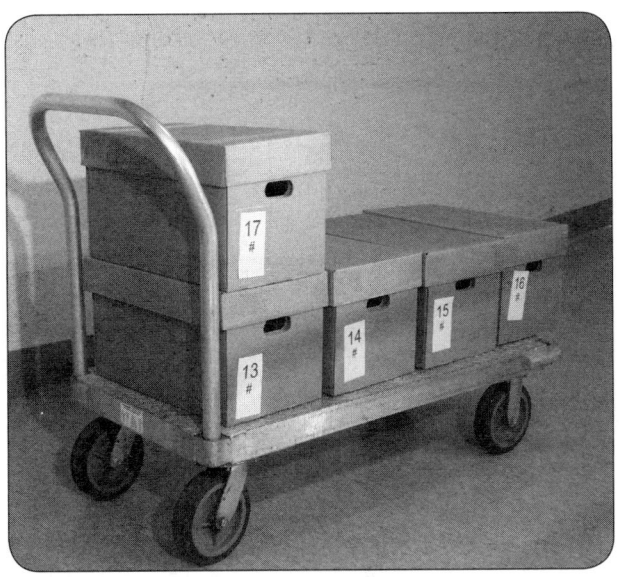

Figure 12.6 There is a right sequence for stacking boxes on a cart. These two are both wrong.

If you have a dolly that holds only one row of boxes, load the stacks in this pattern, as viewed from above:

1	2	3	4

Front

If your dolly holds two rows, the loading pattern is

6	5	4
1	2	3

Front (left side)

This is not the most satisfactory pattern, for the sequence cards face only the "front" so the cards for stacks 2, 3, 4, and 5 are hidden. However, the 1 and 6 stacks are usually enough to identify the contents of the dolly. If we turn the boxes so that all the fronts face outward, they overhang any dolly I have ever used. We once tried to reverse the boxes 3 and 4 but found that this caused trouble for the reshelvers. Reshelvers get into a rhythm of removing the boxes, and having them all oriented the same way facilitates the workflow.

With pallets, the loading pattern is

Front

8	7	6	5
1	2	3	4

Front

All of the card numbers are visible. This pattern works only if the outside dimension of your box is less than 20 inches; otherwise the box overhangs the pallet. Make certain you arrange the pallet so the pushers can approach it with a pallet jack. Most pallets are accessed from the long side; some can be approached from the side or end.

Yes, you can create your own pattern to fit whatever you are using to move the boxes. The critical point is that you establish only one pattern and that everyone uses exactly the same sequence loading and unloading. If you are using dollies of different sizes, you are using different loading patterns, so you must be extra careful as you train the crews. We usually make up large posters showing the loading sequence and hang them all around the unshelving and reshelving areas to reinforce the training.

MOVING BOOKS, STEP BY STEP

There are three situations where you might move using boxes: a shelf-to-shelf move; a move to short-term storage, followed by a move into a new or renovated space; and a move to long-term storage. I consider the shelf-to-shelf move in detail, then discuss special considerations that apply to the two storage scenarios.

Use the methods and processes in chapter 4 to build the reshelving plan. It does not matter whether you move in boxes or on carts; these steps remain the same. If you have to divide or combine collections, you can follow the instructions in chapter 5. Chapters 6 and 7 describe how to assemble crew and supplies; follow those instructions that pertain to a box move or to moves in general.

A move with boxes follows the same steps as the cart move (chapter 11), but it is somewhat more complex because of the potential stacking and restacking of boxes and the various means used to transport the boxes. At nearly all positions, the actual work done depends on whether you are transporting boxes on hand carts, dollies, or on pallets with pallet jacks. At some points it is necessary for me to describe each one separately.

We must take even more care to make sure boxes do not get out of order at any point in their journey. Here is how the flow should work:

1. Assign each crew a starting point and a pack of colored sequence cards. This does not have to be the start of a collection, but it must be a waypoint. In a large move, it is not uncommon to have several crews working in one collection. Try to spread the assignments so the crews are not all using the same aisles, elevators, and other facilities.

2. In each crew, one person takes books from the shelf, hands them to the other unshelver, who puts them in the box, working from the back to the front of the box to the right. The front of the box is the end with the card pocket on it. Two people are more efficient when the

books are coming off the top or bottom shelves. When working from the midlevel shelves, crews often find it is easier for one person to grab an armload of books and put them directly into the boxes; the other sets up boxes, numbers, and stacks them. Don't be too rigid about the roles. The main idea is to provide the opportunity for a variety of lifting and turning motions. Because of the extra actions required for a box move (i.e., getting boxes from the factory, closing them or handling lids, and managing the much larger number of sequence cards), a person working alone is not very productive. Some crews do work best if one member does all the box filling and the other does all the ancillary tasks.

3. The crew fills one box at a time. Avoid the temptation to have each person filling a different box. The crew must pack the books tight in the boxes so they don't slide around. This is especially true for fiction and smaller books.

As the crew works along, they come to the waypoint flags inserted in the collection. They should take the flag along with the surrounding books and put it in the box exactly where it falls in the collection. Leave some portion of the flag sticking out so it is readily visible. Make a check mark or slash with a marker on the sequence card for every box that contains a flag. It doesn't work to mark the box. You are likely to recycle the boxes, using them several times. After a while, all of the boxes would be covered in marks.

4. Once the first box is filled, remove card number 1 from the pack and insert it in the card pocket. Pull the last two cards, marked "XXX," from the pack. Write the name of the collection and the call number of the starting waypoint on each card. Put these cards in the pocket as well with the XXX card showing.

5a. Using hand truck, pallet, or dolly, with boxes *not* to be restacked: Set the first box aside and fill the second box. Once four or five boxes are filled (whatever number you have agreed on as the height of a standard stack), put box 4 (or 5) in a convenient place and build up the stack in reverse order with box 1 on top. Then start another stack.

5b. Using hand truck, pallet, or dolly, with boxes being restacked an *even* number of times (i.e., once the unshelvers have built up the initial stack, the boxes are removed and restacked [the stack turned upside down] an even number of times somewhere along the route): This is the same process as 5a. Load up the agreed-upon number of boxes. Put the high number on the floor, pal-

TIP

It is essential that everyone all along the route understand how tall the stacks are to be and that no one deviate from that standard. Also, make certain to follow the proper loading order so that on every dolly or pallet the stacks are arranged the same way.

let, dolly, or whatever conveyance you are using and build up the stack in reverse order. The 1 box must be on top. Note that when the boxes are restacked the first time, or third, or fifth, box 1 ends up on the bottom. When they are stacked again, the even number, box 1 is on top, ready to reshelve.

5c. Using hand truck, pallet, or dolly, with boxes being restacked an *odd* number of times (i.e., once the initial stack is built, the boxes are removed and restacked an odd number of times): Load the first box, number it, mark the XXX cards, and pocket them. Put the 1 box onto the pallet, dolly, or other conveyance. Fill the next box, number it, and put it on top of box 1. Continue until you have built the stack to the agreed height. Then start another stack.

Depending on the unshelving and reshelving locations and the routes between them, one crew may be loading boxes 1-up while another loads 1-down. In a complex move, you may need to guard against confusion as you shift crews to new assignments. It helps to write the starting order on each collection flag. A simple "1-up" or "1-down" should suffice.

6. Pushers need to strap the boxes before moving dollies or pallets. Use a ratchet tie-down strap around the top layer of boxes. This prevents a stack from toppling as the load goes over a bump or incline.

If the pushers have to restack the books to put them onto a dolly, make sure you have counted this as the first restacking.

Pushers take the boxes to the elevator or to the loading dock. If there are any empties, they take a supply back to the unshelvers.

7. The elevator operator loads boxes onto the elevator, takes them to the loading dock level, and offloads them. If there are any empties, the elevator operator loads them and takes them to the floor(s) where they are needed. The elevator operator must be careful to get the lowest-numbered boxes of each color sequence onto the elevator first and to service all of the floors evenly.

8. The dock crew takes over next. They take the boxes from the elevator or the place where the pushers drop them onto the dock. They remove one of the XXX cards from the first box of each color and post it in a convenient spot. This provides a visible reference for what collections are in process at any time.

9. The dockmaster should establish some way to sort boxes on the dock so that it is easy to determine which are next to go on the truck. This may be as simple as a designated area for each color of boxes (each collection). The actual system develops through trial and error and is determined more than anything by the size and shape of your loading dock area. Here are some ideas:

One method is to designate an area for each color series using tape on the floor, caution tape on stanchions, or some other method.

Another is to establish one line for each color. The pushers drop the boxes at the tail of each line. Pushers need to be careful to drop the boxes in the proper lines.

A third method, useful when the dock is small, is to establish a single line for all collections. The line can run out of the dock and down an approach hallway. This reserves the dock space for offloading empties, supplies, and the like. With this method, it may be difficult to find a particular stack or pull it out of line if it is needed at the destination building or if you have to hold a color because it is backlogged at the destination.

With a small dock, the single- or multi-line options may be your only choice. They work best for dollies, less well for individual stacks, and not at all for pallets unless the aisle is very wide. If I were moving with boxes on pallets and had only a small dock area, I think I would establish a staging area in some open room near the dock where the pallets could be sorted more easily. I would pull onto the dock only those pallets I needed to fill the next truck.

10. Load the truck. If you are using dollies or pallets, it does not matter much in what order you put them on the truck. You do need to make certain to take the lowest-numbered boxes of each color, but they do not have to be in strict order on the truck. When they come off the truck, there will be a relatively small number of separate units, and the pushers can find the low numbers and take them in proper order.

With hand trucks, or if you are restacking boxes in the truck by hand, you should load the truck so you can control how the boxes are unloaded. We have used two methods:

a. Load the truck in blocks with all boxes of one color together. You unload one color at a time. The boxes still come off with the higher numbers first, but you quickly get to the low numbers for the first color and the pushers can get started moving them to the reshelvers while the dock crew unloads the next color.

b. Set up the destination dock with a separate space for each color. You can load the truck randomly, just so long as you take the low numbers of each color first. The sorting is done at the destination. The crew unloads the truck, at random, and puts all of the boxes of each color together in one area. The low-numbered stacks that went on the truck first come off last and so are toward the front of the staging area, ready for the pushers as soon as the truck is completely unloaded. This method is useful if the space at the origin dock is limited or if the dockmaster has had to establish just a single line for all collections leading into the dock.

10a. Load the truck, with dock plate. If you have a loading dock and a truck that nearly matches it in height, you can use a dock plate to roll the loads into the truck whether they are on hand trucks, dollies, pallets with a jack, or almost any other wheeled conveyance. This is by far the fastest and safest way to load a truck. A 4-by-4-foot plate of ½-inch plywood is large enough to make loading quick and safe, strong enough to bridge a gap of 6–8 inches between the truck and the dock.

Take any empty boxes and supplies off the truck and get them out of the way. If there are pushers available, they can start taking empties back to the unshelvers, but the first priority should be to get the truck reloaded and on its way.

Roll loads onto the truck. They do not have to go on in order, but it is vitally important that the lowest

TIP

Pushers should be trained to leave the sequence card end visible whenever possible. In most cases the dock crew takes the stacks in order, right down the line. However, if they need to hold a color, or advance the transport of another, the dock crew can walk along the row and pull out the stacks they need.

> **TIP**
>
> At some point, a dock crew may be tempted to just stack boxes in the truck as high as they will go to get more on the truck. After all, each box is numbered and color-coded, and they can be sorted out at the destination. Resist this temptation! I have seen this done several times. The resulting confusion at the receiving end and the staff and time needed to sort everything into order again outweighs any possible advantage at the origin.

numbers of each color sequence go before the higher numbers. If the crew skips a stack of boxes, the reshelvers have to wait for it. Worse, if the shelvers lose track of the numbers, they may just skip the forgotten boxes. If that happens, you have to shift anything they shelved until the mistake was caught or the next waypoint was reached.

10b. Load the truck, with ramp or liftgate. With hand trucks, you can load the truck using a ramp. Most rental trucks come supplied with a ramp. Dock crew should be able to pull a loaded hand truck up such a ramp. Be careful! These ramps have a particularly steep section at the very bottom. If you hit it too fast, you can bounce the stack of boxes and spill them. You will not be able to push a dolly up the ramp. It would be incredibly unsafe to pull a pallet up a ramp even if you could manage the weight.

If you try out a ramp with a test load, remember, it's not the first load that's the problem, it's the five hundredth.

A power liftgate should be safe if you are loading individual stacks with hand carts. The individual stacks are fairly stable unless you overloaded the boxes. You may be able to load pallets with a liftgate if you can set the pallet solidly on the lift and if the stacks are strapped together at the top. You would need another pallet jack in the truck to move the pallets off the gate and into position. *I do not believe it is safe to load a dolly or any other wheeled conveyance with a liftgate.* If the truck is parked on any angle, or if the gate is not dead level throughout its full range of motion, the dolly can roll off the edge and fall. The danger to the crew is too great to risk.

10c. Load the truck, with forklift. If your truck does not match the dock height, you need to load it with a forklift. You may be able to unload empties using the ramp supplied with the truck. If the ramp is not too steep, it is fastest to unload empties down the ramp.

Fastest of all may be simply to hand boxes down an armload at a time to the pushers and dock crew.

If you can, deploy the ramp and unload the empties. Then stow the ramp and load full dollies or pallets using the forklift.

With dollies, the most efficient way to load and unload is to put the forklift on the dock surface itself and use the forklift as a simple elevator, just as if you were loading carts. You can do this with dollies that have four swivel wheels; it is all but impossible when the dollies have two fixed wheels.

When you are loading pallets, the driver must turn and maneuver the forklift. Proceed in this manner:

The dock crew should spot the pallet in a convenient location, oriented so the forklift operator can approach it easily, then stand away. Drive the forklift under the pallet and lift until it just clears the dock. Turn the forklift to line up with the truck. Raise the forks just enough to clear the truck bed, move forward, and set the pallet into the truck. Use a pallet jack to move the pallet into place inside the truck. Move the forklift back and maneuver to pick up another pallet. Note that you have to approach the pallet from the front of the truck to pull the pallet into the truck, then either turn the pallet or pull it partway in, remove the jack, and maneuver to approach the pallet from the rear of the truck to set the pallet in the truck. At all times the forks should be kept as low as possible while they are carrying a loaded pallet. If it is necessary to keep the forks high to clear obstructions, all crew must stand out of the way during the operation. Any time the forklift is moving, it is essential that all dock crew and pushers stand out of the way.

There is another issue when loading pallets into a truck. Pallets are 48 by 40 inches. Most box trucks are 7½ feet wide. To load a truck full, you have to set a line of pallets along one side of the truck, then put another row in at right angles to the first. The problem arises because many pallets can be accessed only from the 4-foot side. To put the first row against the side of the

> **TIP**
>
> It is essential the forklift operator lift the loads high enough to clear. If you want to know what happens when a 5-ton forklift rams a 1-ton loaded pallet against a 10-ton truck, just type "immovable object—irresistible force" into your search engine.

truck, you have to drag the pallet into the truck, then turn it 90 degrees and set it in place. If you set all the pallets against the side wall first, it is almost impossible to negotiate a pallet down the remaining narrow aisle without catching on something. The only workable loading order is to alternate spotting pallets to the side and in the aisle, working toward the back of the truck.

The angle of the truck at the dock assumes major importance as the individual loads increase in size. With hand trucks, dock crews can negotiate almost any angle. Dolly wheels must be blocked if the truck sits on a slope. Your crew may not be able to push loaded pallets up or restrain a pallet going down a steep slope in a truck.

11. You need to restrain the boxes so they do not shift during transport. For dollies, you can use a heavy strap hooked to the sides of the truck and ratcheted tight or a cargo bar as we do for carts. If you load separate stacks of boxes, you have to restrain them so the top box does not slide off. Pack the boxes as tightly as you can to prevent sliding side to side. Ideally you want any void space at the side to be less than the *height* of a box; then even if a box slides it will not topple. You also need to prevent boxes from sliding to the rear. One or two straps near the top of the stacks prevent most problems. The light tie-down straps we use on dollies and pallets work for this use. To be extra certain, and especially if you cannot pack boxes tightly enough, you may install a restraining strap every three or four rows of stacks.

12. The driver takes the loaded truck to the destination building. Drive slowly and be careful on hills and at corners so boxes do not topple.

13a. Unload the truck, with dock plate. If you have a loading dock and a truck that nearly matches it in height, you can use a dock plate to roll the books out of the truck. It does not matter what conveyance you use. This is by far the fastest and safest way to unload a truck.

Load empty boxes, pallets, dollies, and such onto the truck. Make sure to include any straps, wheel chocks, or other reusable supplies. It is just as important to return empties and supplies as it is to move the books.

Strap or block empty dollies so they do not shift in the truck.

13b. Unload the truck, with ramp or liftgate. You can unload hand trucks using a ramp. Pushers or dock crew should be able to manage a hand truck down such a ramp with careful attention to safety. Never get in front of the hand truck; always let the truck precede you down the ramp. Be careful at the bottom of the ramp. If you are

 TIP

Think this through before you decide to use a liftgate to unload pallets. You have to have a way to move them onto the gate safely. If you approach a pallet from the back of the truck and pull it onto the lift, you have to have room to get the pallet, the jack, and the person pulling all on the lift, which is well up in the air. If you plan to approach the pallet from the front of the truck and push it onto the lift, how are you going to get in front of the row or two of pallets at the back of the truck?

going too fast when you hit the steep section at the bottom, you can bounce the stack of boxes and spill them or lose control of the hand truck entirely. Make sure you have the wheels lined up with the ramp; most ramps are only a little wider than the hand truck.

It is probably safe to unload individual stacks with a power liftgate. The stacks are stable and not overly dangerous even if one does topple.

It is not safe to unload dollies or pallets down a ramp. You may be able to unload pallets with a liftgate if you can set the pallet solidly on the lift and if the stacks are strapped together at the top. If the truck is parked on a slope or if the liftgate does not remain dead level throughout its full range of motion, any wheeled conveyance can shift and roll. This is extremely dangerous.

13c. Unload the truck, with forklift. If you are using dollies or pallets and your truck does not match the height of the loading dock, you may need to unload it with a forklift. The most efficient way is to put the forklift on the dock surface itself and use it just as an elevator.

With pallets, the operator must turn and maneuver the forklift. Proceed in this manner: The dock crew or driver uses a pallet jack to position a pallet at the rear of the truck. The forklift operator raises the tines until they just clear the truck bed, then drives the tines under the pallet. Lift the forks just enough to get the pallet off the truck bed and maneuver to set the pallet on the dock. Back up to pull the tines out of the pallet. One of the dock crew uses a pallet jack to move the pallet out of the way, and the forklift maneuvers to accept another pallet from the truck.

Use the forklift to load empty pallets or dollies onto the truck. Be sure to load any straps, wheel chocks, or other supplies.

14. Sort out the stacks and start them on their way. When the truck pulls into the dock, all available pushers should congregate at the dock.

Dollies and pallets come off the truck highest numbers first. The dock crew needs to organize them so pushers can determine the lowest-numbered stack, which is the one the reshelvers need first. Usually it takes only a few minutes to unload a truck; the dock crew can simply place the new loads aside with the sequence cards visible, and the pushers can take the low numbers once the truck has been cleared.

It is more difficult to sort when you have loaded the truck with individual stacks of boxes to be unloaded with hand trucks. Earlier I suggested two solutions: (1) loading the truck in blocks with all stacks of one color together and (2) establishing an area on the destination dock for each color.

If you used the first method, the dock crew should unload only one color at a time. When the first color is completely unloaded, the pushers have access to the lowest number and can begin taking this collection to the reshelvers while the dock crew unloads another color. This method has an advantage if you are using an elevator. You can fill the elevator with loads that are all going to the same floor. It is a bit more efficient than having multiple loads on the elevator.

With the second method, as they remove the stacks the dock crew sorts them by color and puts them in the designated area. Because the stacks come off the truck with the high numbers first, those stacks go into the back of the designated area, with the lower numbers in front. The pushers cannot begin to remove the stacks until the truck is completely unloaded.

Note: You should establish one or two overflow areas. Sooner or later the pushers will not be able to clear out an area before the truck returns with a new supply of boxes. If you load the new boxes in front of the ones already stored there, you bury the lower numbers.

> **TIP**
>
> If you have enough room in the general area where the reshelvers are working, you can create a final staging area there. In that case pushers can start taking loads as soon as they come off the truck and can do the final sorting away from the dock.

Unless the designated areas are large enough to give access to these earlier stacks, you should divert the later load to the overflow.

Remove the second XXX card from the first box in any collection and take it to the dispatch desk in the destination building. This serves as a notice that a new collection stream has arrived.

15. If you are using a dedicated elevator operator, that person takes the dollies or pallets to the appropriate floor and brings back any empties. With hand trucks, the pushers usually ride along with their loads. The elevator operator must make an effort to keep an even flow of work to all floors.

16. Take the boxes to the reshelving area. If there is an elevator, the dock crew is usually responsible for taking books as far as the elevator. Otherwise the pushers pick up their loads at the dock.

Pushers should leave boxes in an area very close to where the reshelvers are working. This spot moves as the shelvers progress, and the pushers need to plan ahead to place the stacks where they will be most convenient for the reshelvers. Stacks should be placed in a line, with the sequence cards visible. Pushers should make a last check to see that the sequence cards are in order and that the lowest-numbered box in each stack is on top.

Note: Supervisors should check occasionally that pushers are working to keep everything in order. I once discovered a pusher who, instead of restacking boxes, simply shuffled the sequence cards to get the lowest-numbered card on top. The retraining period was brief, but particularly intense, and was conducted entirely in words of one syllable.

Pushers return any empties to the dock area—or elevator—as soon as possible. Train the pushers that it is just as important to return all empties as it is to bring full loads to the shelves.

17. Reshelve the books. The reshelving crew must watch carefully the numbers of the sequence cards to make certain they unload the boxes in strict order. In addition, they must make certain to unload each box from left to right, just as if the box were a shelf. This should be ingrained in them through repetition and training.

Assign each reshelving crew a waypoint corresponding to the starting waypoint you assigned to the unshelvers for that crew. This spot is marked with a waypoint marker taped to the shelf where the first book is to go. The waypoint marker also indicates how much

TIP

If the boxes arrive stacked 1-down, call a supervisor right away. Someone miscalculated the number of restackings along the route. It is an easy matter for the supervisor to call back to the origin and have the unshelvers reverse the stacking order for this collection.

space the crew must leave empty on each shelf up to the next waypoint.

One person takes books from the box, starting with the first book at the left end of the box, and hands them to the other reshelver, who puts them on the shelf, leaving the amount of space indicated on the most recent waypoint marker. Provide each crew with a ruler or other way to gauge this distance.

Two people are more efficient when the books are going onto the top or bottom shelves of the stack. When the books and the boxes are at the same level, crews often find it is easier for one person to grab an armload of books and put them directly onto the shelves while the other person removes empty boxes and manages the sequence cards.

When the crew empties a box, they should remove the sequence card and keep it, in order, in a convenient place. The cards may be useful to diagnose a shelving error. A missing number might indicate a forgotten box; four or five numbers show a missed stack. Also, you may be able to recycle the deck of sequence cards to use on another collection if you have a large move.

18. As the crew works along, they come to the waypoint flags left between the books by the unshelvers. If you measured the collection and calculated waypoints accurately, the reshelving crew should reach the next waypoint on their shelves just as they reach the flag left in the books by the unshelvers when they loaded the box. In practice, because we measured growth to leave the collection a bit loose, they may reach the flag four to six boxes before they get to the waypoint marker.

If the crew gets to the flag before they reach the waypoint marker, they should skip to the marker, match the flag to the marker, and continue reshelving from that point. If they reach the waypoint marker on the shelves while they still have books left in boxes ahead of the flag, there is a problem and they must call for the move coordinator or their supervisor. See chapter 13 for the corrective steps.

19. If the boxes are not going to be reused, flatten and stack them for storage, resale, return, or recycling. It is usually easiest to do this at the destination loading dock. Assign one or two people to this task, more in a large move with many reshelving crews. Pile the flattened boxes on pallets and use strapping equipment, shrinkwrap, or tie-down straps to hold them in place.

USING BOXES TO STORE BOOKS DURING A MOVE

You may need to store books temporarily. Boxes are a useful way to store large numbers of books when you are remodeling or repainting shelves, or when you have to vacate one building before its replacement is completed.

You need sturdy boxes with either integral top flaps or separate tops. Open boxes don't stack well or support weight for any length of time. Closed boxes, on the other hand, support a stack four or five high for a year or more. The boxes I recommend for moving (specifications in appendix A) are suitable for storage. Using properly engineered boxes and tightly packed pallets, you can achieve high storage densities—up to 80,000 books in 1,000 square feet with pallets stacked on the floor. If you use industrial racking capable of holding the weight, you can store up to 150,000 books in 1,000 square feet of floor space.

How you load the boxes and organize the storage area depends on the space available. It is much less confusing if you can load and unload the collection in shelf order, that is, front to back. The lowest-numbered book is the first one packed and the first unpacked.

In a large storage room, you can load each collection in its own block and leave aisles so that you can access the first box of each collection. If you store on pallets, make sure the aisles are wide enough to maneuver a pallet and jack or a forklift. Figure 12.7 shows an arrangement of four collections in one large room. Each collection can be accessed from the front and back ends.

In a smaller room, you can lay out an arrangement so that the first boxes are stored near the door, immediately accessible, and the rest are loaded row by row into the room. With just a little creativity, you can design a layout that allows immediate access to both the first and last boxes, which provides ultimate flexibility when you retrieve the boxes to reshelve them. Figure 12.8 shows such

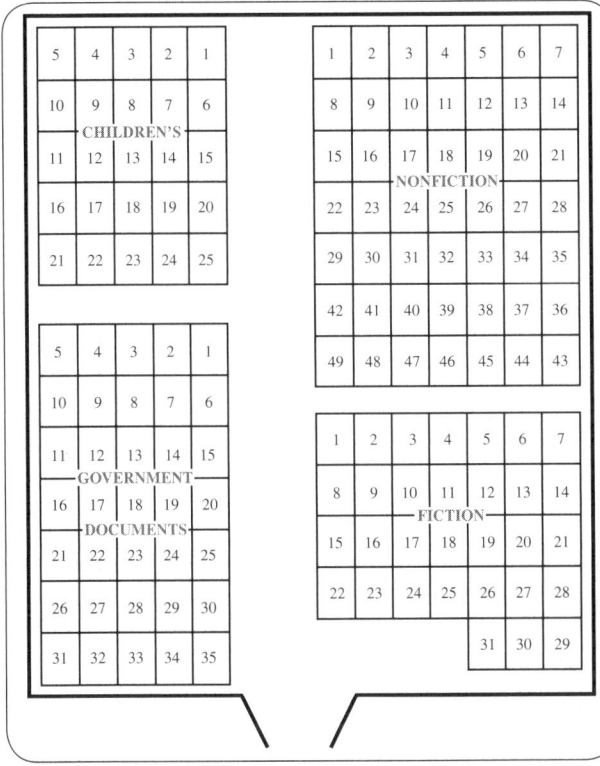

Figure 12.7 This arrangement permits access to front and back of all collections.

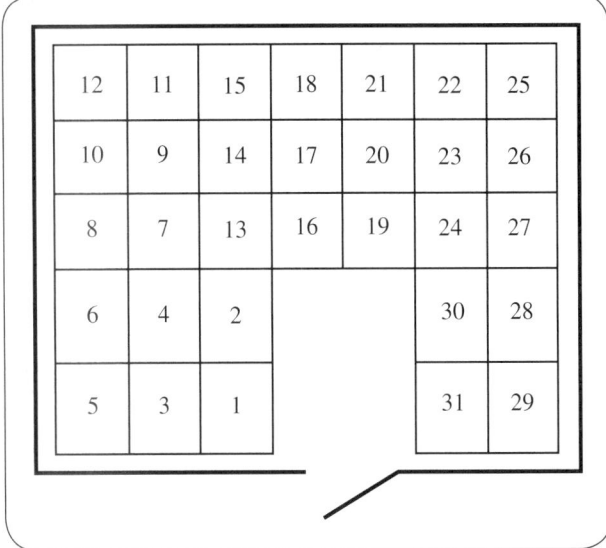

Figure 12.8 The first and last boxes of this collection are accessible at the doorway.

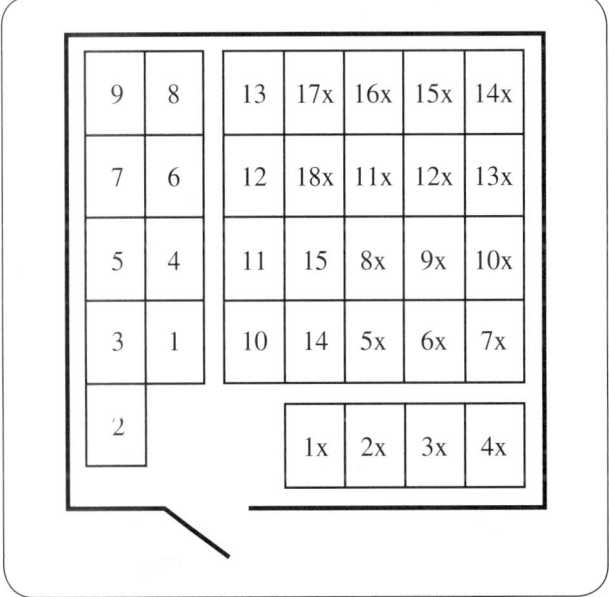

Figure 12.9 Box 1 of both collections is accessible at the door.

an arrangement. Figure 12.9 shows two collections in one room, both with box 1 immediately available. Your own layout will depend on the size and shape of your room and on whether you have two access doors or just one.

If you cannot design an arrangement that permits first-in, first-out access, you can always load the collection backward. The very last book in the collection goes into the first box packed, and the boxes are loaded first into the most inaccessible point in the room, working so the last box loaded, which contains the first book in the collection, is nearest the door.

However you organize the storage, make a drawing showing where each stack, or pallet of stacks, is to be placed. Post a copy of the plan in the room and require the people who are placing the books into position to note any deviations. Keep the marked-up copy of the plan for reference when you start unloading. Do not rely on memories or the "obvious" arrangement.

Consider how you will reshelve before you plan the storage. Several times I have been called in to plan a move and been told, "We have some books in storage." When I ask, "What books? How many? How are they arranged?" invariably I get blank looks and general descriptions. Makes it difficult to plan.

When you are planning the storage, plan ahead to prepare for moving, reshelving, and integrating them into the new space:

- Store boxes so you can get at the first and last books. You never know which way you will reshelve.

- Measure the collection before you box it. Shoot the shelves and strings and establish the waypoints. Do this separately for the books you are storing. If you are storing only part of a collection, measure each part separately. The Layout spreadsheet (appendix C) can merge them again if necessary.

In the worst case you are dividing a collection, part to storage, part to some other location, and you cannot effectively measure the storage portion while it is interfiled. You can still measure the stored books quite accurately, like this:

1. Establish waypoints before you divide the collection. Make two copies of each flag. Put one copy into the collection. Keep the other.

2. As you go through the collection to remove books for storage, include the flag you filed into the collection as you come to it. Yes, sometimes the two books adjacent to the flag are not chosen to be boxed. Never mind. Just pull the flag and put it in the box.

3. Number each box as you load it. For storage, when the boxes are not being reused many times, we do not use card pockets and sequence cards. Instead we number the boxes with a marker, 1 through XXX. Number an end and side so that one is visible no matter how the boxes are oriented in storage. When you come to a box that contains a flag, write down the box number and the call number from the flag. Write "FLAG" all over the box, top, sides, and ends, so it can be seen from any direction.

We usually number each collection separately, 1 through XXX. We add a simple prefix to denote the collection, such as "F" for fiction, "C" for children, "NF" for nonfiction. Sometimes we color-code the collections using colored markers. Write down the codes and what they mean. In a year or so they may not be so obvious.

TIP

If you are storing books over a concrete floor, carpeted or not, put pallets under the boxes if the books will be stored for more than a few weeks. The tightly packed boxes prevent airflow over the floor, and the cardboard wicks up moisture through the concrete, causing mildew. You can transport and store the books on pallets or, better yet, use pallets to create a raised subfloor and load the boxes in place.

TIP

If you are planning to store books on any other than a ground floor, get a qualified structural engineer to check the floor load capacity. Books in boxes stacked only four high are about double the floor load of the same space used for books on shelves with aisles. A space designed for a normal library floor load is not strong enough to hold books stored tightly packed in boxes.

With books boxed in this manner, getting a reasonable measurement is simple. You know how many boxes you loaded between each set of waypoints and how many inches of books fit in a box. Multiply the number of boxes by the inches per box and divide by 35.5 inches per standard shelf. That tells you how many shelves between the waypoints. Enter that on the appropriate Layout spreadsheet tab in the Shelves column.

4. Load everything as carefully as if it were going directly to the shelves. Load one row per box; don't fill up the empty spaces with extra books; load books upright, not spine up. This last is particularly important during long-term storage to prevent text blocks from sagging.

5. If you are loading in natural order, be sure to build stacks of boxes so that the lowest number is on top of the stack. To do this, fill as many boxes as there are in one stack, then put the highest-numbered box on the bottom and build up the stack to the lowest number. With most boxes, four is about as high as you can stack without having them sag, and five is the absolute maximum. For a high-density storage system capable of stacks to eight high, see "Long-Term Storage," below.

TRANSPORTING BOOKS TO STORAGE

You can move the books using any of the methods discussed in this book. I prefer to move the books on library or move carts and to box them, in place, at the storage location. To me, this minimizes the transportation issues and provides the tightest, most sturdy storage. It is easy to keep the books in order, and you need to staff and supply only one box factory.

You can use dollies or pallets to transport boxes as described above. You need to strap the boxes together during transport, but you should be able to remove the straps when the pallets are set in place.

You can use hand trucks, even if you are setting the stacks on pallets. When you approach a pallet, tip the hand truck back and set the edge of the bottom box or the lip on the bottom of the truck over the pallet. Swing the hand truck upright and slide off the stack of boxes. This takes minimal effort, especially compared to hand stacking. A person of average height and strength can do it easily. If you are moving within one building, the hand truck system can be quick and requires less effort to acquire equipment than other methods. And if you are staying in one building, consider the drag system. With the right route and floor surface, it could be the quickest and least expensive of all.

LONG-TERM STORAGE

You may need to store books for a period of several years. We used to do this in regular move boxes, but we found that many of the stacks collapsed over time. Also, we were limited to stacks only four or five high, which required considerable floor space.

In 2001 we moved Allen County Public Library into temporary quarters while the new building was constructed. The temporary building did not have room to hold all of our books. We had to put about a million items into storage, including the government documents and most of the periodicals as well as several hundred thousand books. We had limited ground floor space; the upper floors would not handle the load.

Thomas Kelly of Kelly Box and Packaging in Fort Wayne engineered a storage system using cardboard boxes to hold our materials on pallets, stacked seven high. We had over 35,000 boxes on almost eight hundred pallets. In five years, not one box collapsed or even sagged. Specifications for the boxes and other parts of this system are given in appendix A.

We began with a pallet to keep the boxes off the floor so they would not draw moisture from the concrete. We bought used pallets and got the supplier to fill in any gaps larger than about an inch to provide even support across the pallet. Over the pallet we placed a sheet of cardboard to provide a bit of padding and help even out differences in the thickness of the slats. We filled eight boxes and arranged them on the pallet in this order:

8	7	6	5
1	2	3	4

Over these boxes, we placed another sheet of cardboard 42 by 50 inches, which overhung the outside edges of the boxes by an inch or so.

We loaded eight more boxes, arranging them as a second layer, centered as nearly as possible over the first boxes. The interior intersections formed three pillars that extended straight down through the center of the stack and helped support the weight of the upper layers (figure 12.10).

Over the second row we put another cardboard sheet. These boxes did not have any tops. The sheets between the layers helped spread the load slightly and even out any minor misalignments of the pillars.

We continued building the stacks to seven boxes high, for a total of fifty-six boxes. Over the top we placed a lid (figure 12.11). The lid kept dirt out of the stack, and the sides of the lid helped hold the stack together at the top.

Figure 12.10 Box corners form pillars to transfer weight of upper rows all the way to the floor.

We wrote the call number of the first book on the front of the 1 box on the top course. We also kept a log that listed the pallet number, pallet location, and call number of the first book in the stack.

Each stack held about thirty-two full shelves of books and weighed upward of 2,000 lbs. The stacks were stable enough to be moved by forklift or pallet jack. We brought books from the origin building on carts and built the stacks in place. We loaded all of the collections backward, so the last book loaded could be the first out when we moved to the new building.

When we stored the books, we did not know which collection we would need to access first. We did not want to have one collection buried behind another. Our storage area was a complex of rooms, but it had only two entrances so we did not have direct access to several of the rooms. We solved the problem by loading most of the pallets into tight blocks but then running a "tail" from each collection back to one entrance. Because we loaded everything backward, the last pallet built contained the start of the collection.

As an additional check, we numbered each pallet, noted the beginning call number, and keyed its position to the blueprints of the storage rooms. In this way we were able to identify every pallet, measure the collection even though it was in boxes, and plan the return to the new building.

Figure 12.11 Finished stacks hold 1,100–1,500 books each.

Balancing the Move

Chapter 13

During the move, the primary job of the move coordinator is to provide balance, assigning people and resources to create a smooth, efficient flow of work, eliminating bottlenecks, and making the best use of the available people.

BALANCING THE COLLECTION

Under ideal conditions, each reshelving crew arrives at a waypoint marker on the shelves just as they get to the corresponding flag in their supply of books. In practice, however, the crew should run out of books a shelf or two short of each waypoint—that is, they should get to the flag a shelf or two before they get to the waypoint (figure 13.1).

This is intentional and is a result of the measuring and calculating process. When you are measuring the collection, you direct all errors and fractions toward overcounting the books and undercounting shelves. This is a deliberate attempt to introduce a little bit of looseness into the reshelving. It allows room for late purchases, extra returns, or minor errors by the reshelvers. If there are a few empty shelves scattered around the collection, you can use them for display, or shift a few books to fill the gaps, or just leave them to fill in naturally.

The problems arise when the reshelvers come up well short of a waypoint or blow past one. If the reshelvers are short of the waypoint (i.e., they loaded all of the books up to the next flag and still have empty shelves to the waypoint), what you do depends on how you moved and on how many empty shelves are left. The errors are more obvious and easier to explain if you are using move carts, so I start with those:

With Move Carts and Some Book Carts

- Short 1–2 shelves. Don't worry about it. They're doing fine.
- Short 3–4 shelves. Check the amount of space the crews have been leaving per shelf. They may have been shelving too tight. Have them leave a bit more space on the next set of waypoints.
- Short 8–10 shelves, or the equivalent of one cart's worth of books plus one or two shelves if you are using book carts. This error usually means a missed cart somewhere since the last waypoint. Check the carts

Figure 13.1 Shelvers should reach the flag just before they get to the waypoint marker.

sitting around for an out-of-sequence number. Check the pack of cards the crew removed from their carts to see if one is missing. If you do find a cart that was missed, you have to shift and interfile. Here is another advantage of frequent waypoints: you should never have to shift more than the number of shelves between the two adjacent waypoints.

Short 10 shelves or more, or if you do not find a missing cart. This is a more serious problem. It may be that a crew has ignored the last several waypoints, filling the shelves too tight. If so, retrain them. You can jump to the next waypoint and leave a section or more of shelves open for display or expansion. Alternatively, you can shelve a few books on each shelf and leave much more space per shelf for the next few waypoints until you catch up.

If the reshelvers go past the waypoint or have not yet reached the flag on the cart when they arrive at the waypoint marker on the shelves, we call this a "blowby." Here are your courses of action:

Over 1 or 2 shelves. Shelve a little tighter through the next waypoint. Use the ruler or gauge to be sure you are not leaving too much space on each shelf after that.

Over 3–5 shelves. Check if the crew has been leaving too much room per shelf. Have them shelve more tightly for the next waypoint if the collection is loose, the next two or three waypoints if it is tight.

Over 6–9 shelves, or the equivalent of one cart minus one or two shelves if you are using book carts. This could indicate a cart shelved out of order. Check the sequence cards pulled by the reshelving crew. Read the shelves to see if there is a sequence out of order. If so, you need to stop and shift right away. Usually you can just put the rogue books on a cart, mark it properly, and reshelve it in its proper sequence. If a backlog develops while you are doing the shift, you can do a skipahead with a new crew.

Over 10 or more shelves. Make sure the crew is following the shelving plan. An error of this magnitude usually indicates that the crew missed one or more sections of shelving, or possibly skipped the top or bottom shelves. This can happen easily if you are leaving the top or bottom open in one collection and using them in another. If the crew worked under one set of conditions, then was assigned to another, they may have gotten into a routine and missed the instructions on the waypoint marker. Also check to make certain someone did not add in a large number of books after you measured the collection. That happened to me one time.

With Boxes

If you moved in boxes, you are dealing with much smaller increments by which the collection can get out of order. Any time you are off by two or three shelves, you need to consider that a stack may have been missed or shelved ahead of its proper order. Because two or three shelves is within the normal error imposed by our attempts to introduce looseness into the collection and that introduced if a crew shelves too loose or too tight, it is difficult to determine the causes of such a small error. Even a perfect match of flag to waypoint could mean the crew left exactly the right amount of looseness but shelved in an extra stack of boxes that belong later in the collection. The only way to catch these small errors is by shelf reading. Nevertheless, there are some useful telltales:

Short 18–20 shelves. This indicates a missed pallet. Check for missing sequence cards in the stack removed by the reshelvers. Look around for a pallet containing the missing books. If you find a missed pallet, you have to shift and interfile. You should never have to shift more than the number of shelves between the two adjacent waypoints.

Short the equivalent of one dolly plus one or two shelves. If the dollies carry enough stacks, you may be able to use this clue. This would indicate a missed dolly. Proceed as described for a missed pallet, above.

Short more than about 10 shelves. If you do not find a missing dolly or pallet, check if the crew has ignored the last several waypoints, filling in the shelves that were supposed to be left empty at the waypoints. If so, retrain them. You can jump to the waypoint and leave shelves open for display or future expansion, or you can go on shelving with fewer books to each shelf for the next few waypoints until you catch up again.

Over 14–18 shelves. This indicates a pallet shelved out of order. Check the sequence cards for a card out of order. If there was a backlog along the route, the unshelvers may have run through a full pack and into another set of sequence cards of the same color. If so, the dock crew may have loaded from the later sequence first.

Do a quick shelf-read. An error of this magnitude is readily seen. You will have to stop immediately and do a shift. If a pallet was shelved before its proper place, I would shift the books onto open shelves as close as possible to their proper location and then shift again if necessary once the reshelvers have worked their way to that point in the shelves. Anything to avoid reboxing them. If a backlog develops while you are working out the problem, set up a skipahead to maintain workflow.

Over more than 10 shelves. Check that the crew is following the shelving plan. They may have missed one or more sections of shelving. They may have left the bottom or top shelf empty. This happens if you are leaving shelves open in one section and using them in another. The crew gets used to working with one set of rules and misses the instructions if they are reassigned. The waypoint markers indicate what shelves should be used or left open. Make sure the supervisors are training crews properly, especially when they make reassignments. Also make sure someone did not add a large number of books into one section after you measured the collection. It happens.

No matter how you moved, watch out for this serious error:

Over 50–100 shelves. The telltale here is that you are over by a whole waypoint worth of shelves. This almost certainly means that one waypoint did not get entered on the Layout spreadsheet. This qualifies as a major disaster. It is also the reason I suggest you check and recheck the collection measurements. At the very least, you have to go back to the Layout spreadsheet and recalculate all of the waypoints on that tab, from the point of the error to the end of that collection. If you are lucky and the collection is loose, you may be able to fit in the extra books by the end of the collection. If you can't fit the books into the remaining space, you have to recalculate the entire collection and shift books as necessary. In the absolute worst case you may have to allocate more shelves, which may even force you to relocate the collection. This could happen with a small collection where the effect of one missed waypoint would be a significant portion of the total.

I'll say it again. Check and recheck before you ever start moving.

BALANCING THE STAFF

As the move coordinator, you will likely spend more time assigning and shifting staff than any other activity. Here are some things to watch for:

Match the Speed of the Unshelvers and Reshelvers

Two really fast workers get more done than two slow workers. That one is obvious. Not so obvious is that two equally slow workers may get more done than one fast and one slow working together. Sometimes the faster worker ends up doing all the work. Other pairs seem to work at the pace of the slower worker. Some crews just cannot work at a reasonable rate, and you may need to reassign them to a different task.

TIP

Watch for the person who is not part of the move but wants to stand around and watch, talk to the crew, or, worse, superintend. This includes construction personnel still working in the building and library supervisors not working on the move. Get this person off the work site immediately. If the person is not under your authority as move coordinator, go to the person who does have authority and demand the offender be told to stay away. "An untrained person who has not had the safety training and who is on the work site is a danger to himself and to the workers." That's the argument I make, anyway. The real reason is that such a person can be a real morale killer.

Occasionally you find a person who prefers to work alone and who can maintain an acceptable rate of work. If so, remember that it is more important to get the job done than to enforce some preconceived work plan.

Often the fastest crews are the ones that are talking all the time. The faster they talk, the faster they work. Leave that crew alone. Other crews get so interested in talking that they stop working. You can try to "encourage" such a crew. A crew with a lot of camaraderie works well once you get them started. If not, you have no alternative but to break them up and reassign them.

Build Human Chains as Needed

When you cannot take carts all the way to the shelves, or when you have to move books up and down stairs, or if you have to do a shift, you may need a human chain. The balancing part comes in when you are using a chain to move books out of a narrow aisle. When the crew is working at the end of a range, you do not need extra people. As the working area moves down the aisle, you need to add one person for every two sections. Pull people judiciously so that you have enough to keep the chain moving but without having people standing around waiting the rest of the time.

Part of the art, not science, of being a move coordinator is keeping a mental picture of the state of the move at all times. If you can do this, you will know that the Red crew unshelvers are working faster than their reshelvers and could be pulled away occasionally to help fill out a chain. You will know that the Light Blue crew is now working close to the elevator, so their pusher could be reassigned to help out a crew with a long travel distance. You can keep track of carts, trucks, and underutilized staff and are able to move them around as needed. When you can do this, you have the move under control.

Elevator

Any elevator can be a choke point. If the elevator serves only the ground and one other floor, you may be able to let demand control its use. However, if a backlog develops at the elevator and interrupts the workflow, you may want to make some person responsible for controlling its use. This avoids having the elevator traveling up and

TIP

If you have an assistant to the move coordinator or a supervisor, that person should be authorized to establish skipaheads as needed.

down empty and means that the pushers do not waste time waiting for it to arrive.

Easing a Backlog: The Skipahead

Sooner or later a reshelving crew falls behind. A small backlog is not a problem. If it grows, you may need to restore workflow. Your first obvious solution is to assign faster workers. Sometimes, however, a crew is working in difficult conditions, tight aisles, or with a long travel path, and they cannot go any faster. Consider a skipahead. Look through the backlogged carts to find the next flag. Pull out that cart and any that follow it. Locate the waypoint marker that corresponds to that flag. Try to find a waypoint far enough ahead that you do not have two crews working in the same aisle. Assign a new crew to start reshelving at that point and go on from there. The original crew continues to work its own backlog up to the waypoint, then reports for a new assignment. No opprobrium is stated or implied.

Note: Because flags rarely fall at the start of a cart, the skipahead cart almost always has the first books after the flag and the last books before it. The skipahead crew should shelve from the waypoint forward and leave the remainder of the books on that cart to be shelved by the backlogged crew.

TIP

If you're confident, you can have the skipahead crew shelve the whole skipahead cart, working both ways from the flag. Match the flag and the waypoint and shelve from that point forward as you would normally. Shelve the books ahead of the flag backward, working from right to left, bottom to top, leaving the appropriate amount of space on the right side of the shelf. For this cart only, the *last* book you place on the shelf is the one on the TOP, BLACK, LEFT of the cart.

Cart Shelved Backward

What if someone shelved or unshelved a cart from the wrong end? Not a real problem. If you catch the mistake while the crew is still working on that cart, just move the misshelved books ahead a few shelves, then start shelving from TOP, BLACK, LEFT and shift the misshelved books to fill the gap, if any.

You may not find the error until the crew is well past the misshelved section. The telltale signature of a backward cart is that a range of books goes along in good order, then there is a disconnect to an earlier call number. The books go along in good order for four or five shelves, then jump to a later call number.

If you are using book carts, the disconnects are the same, but the disconnected section is as long as half the capacity of one cart.

To fix such sequence breaks, get a cart and locate the point where the first disconnect starts. Starting at that point, remove books from the shelves to a cart until you reach the next disconnect. You should find that you have exactly filled one side of a cart. Then shift books into the gap you just made, up to the point where the call number sequence jumps ahead. Check the first call number on the cart. That number should fall immediately after the highest-numbered book you just shifted. Load the books from the cart onto the shelves you just shifted from. Everything should fit exactly back into the same space.

The best advice I can give to help you, the move coordinator, establish and maintain workflow is to keep moving yourself. Observe everything. If you see a backlog building, work on it right away. Move people and resources where they are needed and don't get complacent. It really helps if you can keep a small number of people unassigned so you can attack problems as they develop. Efficiency is a moving target, but you can hit it.

TIP
Once the books have been reshelved, you can't know whether it was the unshelving or the reshelving crew who made the mistake. If you get multiple instances of the problem, you need to track it down and retrain somebody, but don't worry about an occasional happenstance.

Night Crew

On a large move it is useful to have a small crew who can work a second short shift after the rest of the crew has finished for the day. The night crew might

- finish loading or unloading the last few carts of a collection so the regular crew can be reassigned in the morning
- collect and return empty carts or boxes to the origin
- repair or reinforce wall and floor protections
- repair or do preventive maintenance on carts
- build a supply of boxes
- catch up on interfiling
- read shelves
- do anything else that helps keep the move in balance for the next day

The task list for the night crew is put together at the evening debrief meeting of the move team. The tasks may vary widely, and it is important to have a supervisor who can adapt to a variety of tasks. If the night crew includes someone who can drive the truck and someone qualified to operate the forklift if you are using one, you can assign the crew a wider range of tasks.

Even on a large move, four to six people seems to be the right number for a night crew. Four hours seems to be the right amount of time to complete the kinds of balancing tasks that usually get assigned to them.

Rain Delays

If you have an open dock, you are somewhat at the mercy of the weather. Rain is the worst problem because it can damage the books and cause excessive amounts of dirt to be tracked through your building. A brief summer downpour is not a problem. Wait it out. If a slight backlog develops, you can clear it in a reasonable time. Use skipaheads to assign extra reshelving crews or start an extra crew or two and new waypoints in the origin. If you have a lot of empties at the destination and few full carts or boxes at the origin when you resume operations, consider sending the truck back for another load of empties without waiting for a full load.

A daylong soaking rain is a different problem. If boxes get wet, they stay wet for days and transfer moisture to the books. You can try to cover move carts. Shrinkwrap doesn't protect well; water runs between the wrap and onto the books. A piece of waterproofed material or plastic draped over the whole cart does not work as well as it might seem. Water pools on the material and runs onto the books unless the cover is removed carefully. Unless the carts have side panels, water runs down the side of the covering and wets the books. You have to lay the material flat, wet side up, between uses, and when you put it over the cart you must be certain to keep the wet side up.

In a heavy, daylong downpour you may have no choice but to suspend operations. Consider carefully how you wind down the project. There is a temptation to load every available cart or box at the origin and reshelve everything possible at the destination to make up for lost time. If you do, you will have a huge backlog at the origin dock and no work for the reshelvers. The restart will be very inefficient, with many staff having nothing to do. As with breaks and lunch, it is usually best just to stop everything in place and pick up the smooth workflow again when you restart.

If you are moving with volunteers or paid hires, just send them home. If you are using staff, you could

- train them on features or equipment in the new building
- give them time to pack or unpack their offices and personal effects
- conduct building tours
- read shelves
- clean up cardboard, shelves, and move detritus
- just give time for some R and R

Moving Microforms

Chapter 14

How you move microforms depends on whether you replicate the filing order and growth space from the origin cabinets or calculate a new arrangement with additional or different growth space. Other factors may influence the plan of the move as well. If you reuse the microform cabinets, your plan must allow for some delay while the cabinets are moved. If you repaint the cabinets to match a new color scheme, the drying time may extend the delay over several days or a week.

If you have only three or four cabinets of film, don't bother to follow the detailed instructions in this chapter. Take the films out of the cabinets, in order. Load them onto move carts or book carts, in order. Remember the TOP, BLACK, LEFT rule. Move them to your new building and refile them. With so few films, it is relatively easy to arrange the films and organize growth space as you refile. Even if some films get out of order, it takes less time to refile and shift than to measure and calculate growth and to obtain the supplies you would need if you were doing a major move. The detailed descriptions in this chapter are for those who are moving a substantial film or fiche collection.

DELAYED MOVES

If you are refiling the films into the same cabinets they occupied in the old arrangement, there is a delay while the cabinets are moved and installed. Make sure you allow for this delay when you are planning the workflow. You would not want all of your carts or boxes tied up holding trays of film while you have move crews waiting to work.

Sometimes cabinets are repainted to match the new décor. Painting cabinets creates an additional delay of days or even weeks in the move. You may not have enough carts or boxes to use them for storage of film for an extended period at the same time you are moving books and other materials. There are three possibilities:

1. Move the film before or after the book move. Use all of your resources to unload, store, and move the film and treat it as a separate move. Make sure you have enough time to complete the film move before you have to start the rest of the project. (This option assumes that you can take the film out of service for some time while the rest of the library may be open.)

2. Store the film temporarily in boxes or trays stacked on the floor. If you load carefully, you can pile trays up to eleven high and boxes five high. Stack them against a wall

 TIP

If you are having cabinets painted, have the painter check carefully the drying requirements for the paint. Some paints give off fumes that can deteriorate microfilm in closed cabinets. These paints must be thoroughly dry and aired out before you load the film back in. You need to allow extra time for drying as you schedule your move. If you can smell even a hint of paint when you open a drawer, the paint is not dry enough to refile.

with each stack solidly against the next. Stacked in this manner and away from traffic, they will hold for several weeks without sagging.

Build each stack equivalent to one side of a move cart or a book cart if you plan to use those. The idea is to eliminate as much as possible errors caused by the extra step of storing the film. Determine how many trays you can stack on each side of whatever cart you are using. Put the first tray on the floor and stack each succeeding tray, in order, on it. The tray that is to go on the bottom of the cart should be on the top of the stack (figure 14.1, left). When you do load the cart, the first tray ends up on the top of the top shelf (figure 14.1, right).

Stack boxes no more than four high. Stack the boxes 1-up or 1-down, depending on the number of times they will be restacked before they get to the destination (see chapter 4).

3. Store trays temporarily on shelves. If you have some empty, flat shelves, you can store microfilms in trays there until you are ready to move them. If you can adjust your shelves so that back-to-back shelves are the same height, you can store up to three trays on each pair of shelves (figure 14.2). The important thing is to mark all the trays and keep them in some clear, logical order.

If you cannot adjust shelves, you must lay the trays on the shelves lengthwise.

MOVING IN THE CABINETS

You may be able to move the film without taking it out of the cabinets. In this case you really have nothing to measure. This may be the easiest of all the options, or it may be a total disaster. Let me emphasize the disaster possibility. Full cabinets are heavy, awkward, hard to move, and dangerous. They can overwhelm the tires on even a heavy refrigerator dolly. Moving them is best left to professional office movers who have the expertise and equipment to handle dangerous heavy loads.

First of all, check your warranty. Moving a loaded cabinet may void your warranty. Microform cabinets are built to hold a tremendous weight, straight up and down. They can easily become deformed if they are inclined, as when you move them on a hand truck. If they become

Figure 14.1 (left) Film stored in trays awaiting transport. (right) Ready for transport, tray numbers in order, ready to refile.

Figure 14.2 Store trays temporarily on shelves.

Figure 14.3 Microfilm overfiles weigh more than 700 lbs, empty.

MOVING IN CARTS OR BOXES

Measure the Collection and Calculate Growth

The first step is to determine how many feet of film you have and to determine how it will go into the new shelves.

Replicated Filing Arrangement

In this situation you are simply replicating the original arrangement and filing order of the films, in new or reused cabinets. You do not measure waypoints and you do not calculate growth. You only need to mark each row in the origin cabinets.

Get some 3-by-5-inch cards or cut 8½-by-11-inch paper into six pieces. You want the paper to be narrower but taller than a box of film. Insert one card as a flag at the end of each row. If a row is empty, you still put a flag in it, indicating a row of growth space. You may have several empty rows together. Put a flag in each of them. Do this before you start unfiling the films, not at the same time you are trying to pack.

Book-Type Collections

A few microfilm collections experience growth more or less throughout the collection, not necessarily just at the end of long title runs. Collections that are arranged by subject, that contain a high percentage of monographs,

deformed, drawers don't open and close properly. If moving the cabinets full voids the warranty, don't do it. If your cabinets are no longer under warranty, you may be tempted to move them full. It is certainly faster to do so. It requires fewer people and resources, although the work is harder.

In my experience, cabinets that are two rows wide can be moved full, inclined on a hand truck, without deforming. Good, solid three-row cabinets can be moved full; weak or flimsy ones cannot. Four- or five-row cabinets must be emptied. On a few occasions, I have been advised that wide cabinets may be moved with the bottom three or four drawers full.

It seems to cause less deformation if the hand truck approaches the cabinet from the back rather than the side.

If your cabinets are equipped with overfiles (figure 14.3), you need some sort of lifting machine to move them. Even empty, they are extremely heavy, too heavy to be handled without mechanical help.

> **TIP**
>
> When you establish a waypoint in a film drawer, tip the next film to its side so the label does not show or put a marker slip at the waypoint. This makes it easy to identify the waypoints when you go back to insert the waypoint markers.

some medical collections, and a few others may be filed in this manner. If you have such a collection, use the method described in chapter 4 under "Book Collections" to shoot shelves and strings for your collection. Also, consult the Layout spreadsheet instructions in appendix C. Make these adjustments to those instructions:

- When you measure strings, measure only the usable space in a row. Some drawers feature a sliding backstop that keeps the films tight to the front of the drawer. Slide the backstop all the way to the back and measure only the empty space in front of it.
- Use a Sheet tab to calculate growth, not the Microforms tab. Enter the length of one film row in cell C19 so the spreadsheet calculates for the shorter drawers, not for a full-length shelf.
- When you count the number of available rows, treat each cabinet as a range, each drawer as a section, and each row as a shelf. Enter these counts in the range and shelf columns on the spreadsheet tab.

Note that you can also use this method if you have a collection that normally grows only at the ends of the titles, but only if you have a lot of growth, 25 percent or more, in the new cabinets. This method allocates growth evenly throughout the collection instead of at the ends of the titles. However, the measurements and calculations are easier than for the title-by-title growth pattern, and the loose filing arrangement ensures that future shifts to accommodate new titles will be short ones.

Periodical-Type Collections

Most microfilm collections grow at the ends of the titles as do bound periodicals. There may be runs as long as one or more cabinets where no growth occurs, followed by many rows left empty for future growth. If the total growth space is tight, this type of collection requires detailed, title-by-title measurement and growth calculations.

Download the Layout spreadsheet from www.ala.org/editions/extras/fortriede09942, or use the paper copying master in appendix C. **WEB** Make enough copies of the Data tab to list all of your waypoints.

Start with a list of every title, in shelf order. Your computer system should be able to generate this; if not, make a manual list. If you are interfiling titles, merge the lists alphabetically into one order, but make a notation to tell you where the various titles originate. Enter all titles on a copy of the Data sheet.

Use the same type of tape you used to measure books. Measure each title separately. Record the length in feet in the Shelves column of the Data worksheet. You are not counting shelves or rows; with this method you measure the length of the title.

Next calculate the growth required for each title. Decide how many years of growth you want to allow; let's say ten years. Using a yardstick or ruler, measure the space required for the most recent ten years of the title and enter that number, in inches, in the Strings column on the Data sheet. If the title is closed or ceased, enter 0. Yes, some titles grow, cease, or condense over time, but we cannot predict these occurrences. This method gets you as close as possible based on the state of your collection today and allows you to make adjustments gradually over the years.

Click on the Microforms tab on the Layout spreadsheet. Enter the titles and measurements on the Layout spreadsheet. Enter the call number or title of every waypoint in column B. Enter the shelves and strings for each waypoint in columns C and D. If you have additional collections to interfile, the spreadsheet provides a space for these as well. See appendix C for more detailed instructions.

The spreadsheet is designed to calculate the total length of drawer space required for each title. In effect,

> **TIP**
>
> You can help the refilers identify the end of each title. Use colored cards, or cut up paper to use as flags. You want the paper to be narrower than a box of film but taller. Insert one of these flags at the end of each title. This gives the refilers a quick way to tell where each title ends.

it establishes each title as its own waypoint. Assign an experienced microforms librarian in charge of the reshelving crew. When you reshelve, work directly from a printout of the Microforms tab and fit each title into the allotted space. Pack ceased or closed titles tight and fill up the rows in the middle of a long run, leaving all of the growth space at the end of the open titles.

You may find it useful to start a particular title at the top of a cabinet, perhaps to avoid splitting a title. Treat the new cabinet as the start of a new collection. Use a new copy of the Microforms tab every time you start a title at the beginning of a cabinet. This may cause some cabinets to be relatively crowded while others are very open.

Next determine how much shelving you will have available. Measure a drawer and enter the length in cell C19. The default measurement is 26.5 inches. Count the number of drawers in each cabinet and the number of rows in each drawer, in the order in which you will file the materials.

If you did make subcollections, you need to count for each one separately. Use a separate Microforms tab for each subcollection, just as you did for the various parts of your book collection. Once you have calculated the growth, you may have to go back and reassign some cabinets to even out the available space.

Enter the number of drawers and rows in columns P and Q. If you left any rows unused, count them and enter the total for each cabinet *as a negative* number in column R. The spreadsheet calculates the rows in each cabinet and the cumulative number at the end of every cabinet. The total number of rows appears in cell M20 (in the Excel application, these are blue numbers on yellow fill).

Cell M19 (green numbers on blue fill) shows the number of rows you need to hold all of your films. At this point, with no growth yet calculated, this is the length of your current collection, packed tight.

The shelves available number should be larger than the shelves needed number. If it is not, your collection will not fit, even packed tight. In this case you need to allocate more cabinets for microforms. If you established subcollections, you may need to reallocate cabinets or even abandon the idea of starting some collections at the start of a cabinet if that means you have an excess of growth space in the preceding cabinet.

If the shelves available number is larger than the shelves needed, you have some excess capacity even above the growth space you assigned to each title. If you

> **TIP**
>
> If you have a series of complete or closed titles in a row and do not need growth space between them, you can treat the whole sequence as one title. Measure the total length of the sequence and record that in the Shelves column after the first title. Put only one marker slip at the end of the sequence. The growth in the Strings column is 0.

want all of the excess to fall at the end of the collection, skip the growth-rate step. Otherwise you can allocate the excess evenly into each of the rows. Over the years titles cease, you add new ones, your budget has ups and downs. You will have to do some shifting, but with growth evenly distributed the shifts can be small.

Enter the growth rate for the collection in cell C22 (red numbers on blue fill). The default is 1.0, no growth. Enter numbers in this cell in decimals greater than 1.0 until you find the magic number that makes the shelves needed equal the shelves available. The process is to pick a number that seems right, enter it, then adjust up or down until cell M19 and cell M20 both show the same number. As you get close, the growth rate you enter may become quite precise, extending to five or six decimals. Using the spreadsheet, this process takes only minutes.

Select some titles to serve as waypoints. Yes, every title is its own waypoint. However, when you refile, you adjust slightly one way or another to maximize the growth potential. It is convenient to have a few waypoints in fixed locations to limit an accumulation of errors in one direction. I like to set a waypoint about every twenty-five rows but at the end of a title. If you have a long run of a title, the waypoints may be much farther apart.

When you have finished, you have these calculations:

- your collection, title by title, with the growth you assigned to each title and with frequent waypoints where you can check your progress against the plan and make corrections without having to refile large runs of microfilm
- the number of the row where each title starts; for short runs, two or more titles may start in the same row
- the number of inches of growth to leave in each row

Flag the Collection

Unless you are moving in the cabinets or replicating the original filing arrangement, you need to make filing flags and insert them into the collection. Download an electronic copy of the collection flag in appendix D from www.ala.org/editions/extras/fortriede09942. [WEB] It is the page headed "Insert this flag immediately ahead of _____." Print enough copies for all of your waypoints. I like to use bright-colored paper so the flags are easy to see. From the spreadsheet, write the call number or title of each waypoint on a collection flag. Keep the flags in order if possible.

Shortly before you move, put the flags into the collection. Treat the flags as if they were rolls of film you were filing. Put the flag into place just in front of the film roll that has the matching title or call number. If the actual film you selected as the waypoint is out of the collection, just put the flag in its place. Fold the flag into thirds lengthwise and it just fits in a film drawer. If you tipped the boxes or put marker slips into the drawers as you measured the collection, this goes quickly.

Mark the Destination Cabinets

As with marking the drawers, you can skip this step if you moved in the cabinets or replicated the original filing arrangement.

Book-Type Collections

Download the waypoint marker in appendix D from www.ala.org/editions/extras/fortriede09942. [WEB] It is the page headed "Start _____ Here." Print enough copies for all of your waypoints. Using the spreadsheet, write the call number or title of each waypoint and the inches of growth on a waypoint marker. Keep the markers in order if possible. Pencil in the "starting row" number from the spreadsheet in the upper corner of the page; this helps you keep track of the last number you used.

Shortly before you move, put the waypoint markers into the destination cabinets. Remember, we are treating each cabinet as a range of shelves, each drawer as a section, and each row as a shelf. The spreadsheet gives the number of the row where the waypoint is to be located.

The starting waypoint is the front of the first row of the top shelf of cabinet 1. The number you wrote on the second waypoint marker tells you how many rows to count. The waypoint is the front of that row. To find the third waypoint, start with the second number and count until you get to the number on the third waypoint marker. Use this process to count out all your cabinets and mark the waypoints. Use the cumulative row numbers from the spreadsheet to maintain a check on your manual counts.

Confused? See the box for an abbreviated example.

Periodical-Type Collections

If you have a periodical-type collection, you do not have to place a waypoint marker in the cabinet for every single title. Select waypoints at the start of a long run of a title or in the middle of a series of several consecutive short runs. The spreadsheet calculates the growth needed for each title. With frequent waypoints marked, the refiling crew can use the spreadsheet to adjust between the waypoints to get the appropriate growth in the right places. I prefer to put an experienced periodicals librarian in charge of this work.

Pack and Move

You can move microfilm on book carts or move carts or in boxes. Place the film directly on carts or in boxes in a single row just as we do with books. This is a simple process and, once the movers have been trained to move books, requires no additional training. This is, however, not very efficient. With a single row on carts or in boxes, you end up moving a lot of empty space. There are ways to pack the films so that you can move more of them at one time.

Move in Trays

This is a convenient way to move microfilms on move carts. The carts can be loaded and unloaded in the natural order; that is, with the first film going onto and coming off of the top shelf.

Get some cardboard boxes 8½ by 26½ by 3 inches deep. The exact specifications are given in appendix A. These are called "trays" in the cardboard industry. A tray this size holds two rows of 35 or 16 mm microfilm in boxes or one row of microfiche or microcards. These boxes fit on most book carts and on move carts. Loaded with film in boxes, they can be stacked two or three high on each shelf (figures 14.4, 14.5).

COUNTING OUT THE ROWS: AN EXAMPLE

From your spreadsheet, you selected the following waypoints:

Title	Starting shelf
AAA Newsletter	1
Black Americana	31
Californian	59
Drummer's World	76

Your first three cabinets are of different sizes, arranged as shown here. The first waypoint is in drawer 1 at A. The second is at row 31. Count thirty-one rows (7 drawers of 4 = 28 plus 3 in the next drawer) and put the waypoint marker for *Black Americana* in drawer 31 (point B). I just roll up the waypoint marker and put it in the proper row. If your drawers do not have dividers, you can tape it in place.

A			4		42
			8		44
			12		46
			16		48
			20		50
			24		52
			28		54
		B	32		56
			36		58
			40	C	60
					62

				65
				68
				71
				74
		D		77
				80
				83

Starting from drawer 31, count through the rest of cabinet 1 and down through cabinet 2 to row 59. Put the *Californian* waypoint here. Then count out the rest of cabinet 2 and into cabinet 3 to row 76. Put the marker for *Drummer's World* here.

Figure 14.4 Load film trays two or three high.

Figure 14.5 Do not load trays higher than the end panel.

You can use either book carts or move carts for this move. Make sure to load the carts from the TOP with the BLACK end to the LEFT.

Decide how many trays you can stack on the top shelf of whatever cart you are using. Normally this is determined by the height of the ends above the top shelf. Make sure the ends are high enough to hold the trays on the cart.

For an example, let's assume you are working with a film cabinet five rows wide and eleven drawers high.

This is a large cabinet. Let's also assume that your move cart can hold two trays on the top shelf and three on each of the other three shelves.

Set up two trays to go on the top shelf of the cart. Get the tray properly oriented. As you stand facing the tray, the front—the place where you will write the number of the tray—is closest to you and the first row of film will go in the side to your left. Remove the boxes of film from the first row of the top shelf of the first cabinet and put them into a tray. Make sure the first film at the front of the row is at the front of the tray. Then take the boxes of film from the second row of the top shelf and put them in the same tray. Fill each tray completely.

As you come to marker slips or waypoint markers, put those into the tray just as they come out of the cabinets. If you are replicating the original arrangement, there will be a marker slip at the end of each row and there may be several slips in a row to indicate entire rows left open for growth. If you calculated growth across the entire collection or used a periodical-type calculation, the waypoint markers may be some distance apart. In any case pack all the markers just as you had them in the cabinet. Make sure the marker sticks up above the level of the boxes so the refilers can see it clearly.

Write the number "1" on the front of the first tray with a marker. Write small if you are going to reuse the trays. You will cross out this number and add another below it if you reuse.

Now fill the second tray in the same way and number it "2." Put the number 2 tray on the top shelf and set the 1 tray on top of it.

Now set up three empty trays for the second shelf. Remove the last row of film from the first drawer and put it in a tray, on the left side. Then take the first row of film from the second drawer and put it in the same tray, beside the first row. Label this tray "3." Put the second and third rows from this drawer into a tray labeled "4" and the last two into a tray labeled "5." Put the 5 tray on the second shelf of the move cart. Set the 4 tray on top of it and the 3 tray on top of both.

Continue like this until you fill one side of the cart, then spin the cart and load the other side. In our example, one side of a cart holds trays 1–11, the other side trays 12–22. Use the sequence card system to keep the carts in order. Number each cart as you finish loading it.

Two or three move carts should suffice for one large film cabinet. A cabinet only two or three rows wide fits on one move cart. It takes a larger number of book

 TIP

When you are filling two or three trays before stacking them on the cart, it is handy to have a place to spread out the trays. The most convenient way is to use the next film cabinet. Pull out a drawer at a convenient height and you have a ready-made table, right where you need it.

carts to move the same number of film rolls. How many book carts you need depends on the size and number of shelves on your carts.

Go on to the next cabinet and work through the entire collection. With a large collection you can have multiple crews working simultaneously. Start each crew at a waypoint (or in a new cabinet if you are replicating). Issue each crew different color sequence cards and notify the origin dockmaster and destination dispatch desk that a new sequence is on the way.

Move the carts of film just as if they were books. The sequence cards keep them in order. Be sure not to stack trays on the top shelf higher than the end panels of the cart or else the side panels or shrinkwrap may not be able to restrain them. Because a microfilm tray is shorter than most carts, the trays are more prone to slide around as the cart is moved. If your floor is rough or the path to the loading dock has turns, you may find it expedient to shrinkwrap the carts or install side panels and straps before you move the carts to the dock. If you are moving microfiche or other sheet material, you *should* apply the restraints at the loading site and remove them only when the carts are at the refiling location.

Move in Boxes

Trays are designed to be the same length as a full row of film in a standard cabinet. It is usually hard to find boxes this exact length, and such boxes would be difficult to

TIP

If you are replicating an arrangement, don't put film from two different cabinets on the same cart. Unless you are very short on carts, keeping each cabinet separate reduces confusion and allows you to treat each cabinet as its own waypoint. Also, you can assign each cabinet a letter and include that letter on at least the first and last few trays from each cabinet. This helps get films back into the proper cabinet.

lift in any case. It is also difficult to find boxes that are exactly wide enough to hold three or four film boxes without excessive space in which film boxes can slide around and get out of order. This is not a problem; we have a convenient work-around for it.

If you order boxes specifically for a film move, have them made about 12½ inches wide, inside diameter, and 12½ inches high. A box this size holds nine rows of film boxes in three layers of three rows, with very little space left over. For a fiche move, have them made 13¼ inches wide. Fiche boxes do not have to be more than about 6 inches tall.

One advantage of using boxes to move film is that you can store them for as long as necessary. This is particularly useful if you are painting your cabinets and need to allow for an extended drying time, or if you schedule the microform move separate from the book move.

Make sure to use boxes that are all the same size. Odd size boxes don't stack well and are more difficult to move. You can use the same boxes you use to move books. They are a handy size, have handholds, and are sturdy enough to be stacked. Put a book card pocket on the front of each box. If you use the standard move boxes, cut some sheets of cardboard slightly less than the height and length of your boxes. Also get a supply of newspaper. I'll tell you why later.

It is important to load all of the boxes in the same order so the refilers do not have to check each film as it comes out of the box. It seems to work best to have the films in the move box in the same orientation they go into the cabinets—that is, the film box closest to the front of the move box should be the one that goes closest to the front of the drawer.

The front of the box, arbitrarily, is the end that has the pocket on it. We train the pushers to set stacks of boxes with the sequence card visible so the refilers can see at a glance which box is next. This orientation also helps the refilers remove the films in the proper order without constant checking.

Most boxes can hold two or three rows of film, so it is important to establish which row goes into the box first and comes out last. Again, it seems to work best, but still arbitrarily, to designate the right-hand row in the box as the first in and last out. That is, as you face the box with the card pocket end toward you, the first row into the box goes on the side to your right. The next rows go beside it until the bottom of the box is full. The first films of the second layer go on the right side (as defined above) and so on until the box is full. Train all of your unfilers and filers to load every box in this specific order.

It is easiest and most certain in the long run to pack the boxes backward. The first item in is the last one out. This lets you pack the boxes full. It also lets the refilers work from the start of a cabinet, the start of a row, and the start of a title and makes it much easier for them to measure and configure growth space.

Because you are loading the collection backward, you start with the last film in the last row of the last shelf of the last cabinet in the sequence. That film goes into the *back* of the right-hand row in the move box. (This is exactly backward from the way we load carts. It is a felony violation of Rule Number One, but it works.) Put the next-to-last box of film in front of it. Continue to fill out the first row of film in the box. When you can't get any more film in that row, start a new row (figure 14.6).

When you have removed all of the film from the last row of your cabinet, go to the next to last row. Put the last box in this row (and the marker slip behind it if you are replicating) into the box immediately in front of the last box you packed. You do not need to start a new row. Make sure any flag or marker slip is visible above the top of the film boxes. If you have empty rows with marker cards in them, be sure to take all of the marker cards and put them into the box together, immediately in front of the last box you packed. When you refile, you can count the number of cards and re-create the number of empty rows that existed in the original cabinet.

With practice you can pick up and pack several boxes at a time. Be careful not to turn them around and so reverse their order. Some crews can pull a whole row of film boxes and get them into a moving box without dropping them.

Continue until you have built the first layer of films in the box. Resist the temptation to fit a few extra films

Figure 14.6 (top) Load the first film to the left in the row farthest from you. (bottom) Begin a second row with a marker slip.

into the box beside the last row if you have the extra space; this would almost guarantee some things getting out of order and causing extra work when the refilers have to decide exactly where they go. Yes, if you have a lot of room left over, the films could slide around when the box is moved. Patience, I'll get to that.

Once the bottom layer is filled, go on to the next layer. Again, start at the back of the box right above the first film you packed, compounding the felony. As you load the second layer, the film boxes cause the tops of the marker slips in the first layer to bend over between the layers. That's what you want. We do not want the markers to stick up and get caught between two film boxes in the second layer. If they do, the refilers may pick up several boxes together and inadvertently pull out a marker slip from the row below.

Continue until the box is filled. Do not fill a box above its top, even a little. If you do, the box gets rounded on top and it doesn't stack properly. Sooner or later a stack will topple.

When you have a box filled, you may have to brace the side to keep film boxes from sliding. If you have more than an inch of free space to the side, you should brace. Slide a piece of cardboard (the one you cut to the length and height of your box) into the box beside the stack of film. Wad up some newspaper and stuff that into the box to hold the cardboard against the film (figure 14.7). Don't skimp on the newspaper. It's cheap, and sorting film back into order is expensive. So now you know. Kind of a letdown, wasn't it?

Remove the *last* card from the deck of sequence cards. If you're playing with a full deck, it should be the number 100. Put this card in the pocket on the front of the moving box. Pull the last two cards marked "XXX." Write the name of the collection on both of them and put them in the pocket as well. The dockmaster and dispatch desk at the destination will use these cards as notification that a new collection is in the pipeline.

Start another box, always working from back right-hand side and loading from back to front. When this box is finished, stack it on top of the first box you filled and number it with the second-highest number in the deck, probably number 99.

Continue to stack boxes to the agreed height. Review the comments about stacking and restacking boxes in chapter 12. If you are restacking an odd number of times, reverse these directions and wait until you have filled the agreed

Figure 14.7 Cardboard braced with crumpled newspaper keeps films from shifting.

number of boxes before you build your stack 1-down. (In this case, specifically, that would be 97- or 96-down.)

When you have finished, you should have a row of stacked boxes, numbered up to 100, although they may not start from number 1. The last film you put in the lowest-numbered box should be the first film in your collection. If that lowest-numbered box is not full, stuff it with newspaper to keep the contents from shifting.

Write down the lowest sequence card number you used and make sure the move coordinator and the refilers know that this is the first box in this collection.

You can use multiple crews working simultaneously. Assign a different sequence card color to each crew and try to spread out the crews so that each has a relatively long run of contiguous cabinets. This minimizes disconnects, sequence color changes, and other disruptions. If you are replicating the original collection arrangement, each crew needs to mark the box to indicate the cabinet, row, and drawer from which they took that last film, the first to be refiled when they reach the end of their assignment (that would be the first box to be refiled). They should also mark the starting point in the cabinet itself. When you refile the films, you can match the starting box to the cabinet as a waypoint. If you are going to repaint the cabinets, make sure you put the starting mark inside the cabinet where it will not be covered by paint.

If you are doing a book-type or periodical-type move, assign the crew to stop at a specific waypoint. As they load the move boxes, they include each flag as they come to it. If a box contains a flag, the crew should make a check mark on the sequence card so the refilers can locate waypoints easily to check progress or to set up a skipahead. When the crew comes to the last waypoint, they should write the call number or title of the waypoint on the sequence card or just fold up the waypoint marker to fit and put it in the card pocket.

TIP

Before you start, you must know the number of boxes the movers can take in one stack and always stack boxes only to this height. If the movers pull off the top box or add one from another stack to make it easier to move, you end up with a collection that is way out of order. You must assume that movers do what is most efficient for them. Plan ahead to meet their needs as closely as possible.

TIP

If you have more than one hundred boxes, use a different color of sequence cards for every hundred boxes or make a double deck from 1 to 200 in a single color. Write down the order in which you used the colors and make sure the move coordinator and refilers know which color is first and in what order the others follow.

Move the stacks of boxes as you would books, on hand trucks, dollies, or pallets. Make sure that the boxes are kept in order as you stack and restack them.

Refile

It is easier to refile from trays on carts because the collection is moved in natural order. As soon as the first cart arrives, the refiling crew can go to work, starting at the first cabinet or waypoint. It becomes somewhat more involved to organize the refiling step when the films were moved in boxes. Crews are better able to judge growth space working in natural order from front to back but, because the boxes were filled starting at the end of the collection, the last few films arrive first.

If the collection is small enough, or the moving schedule allows, you may be able to pack all of the film and wait until it is all moved before you begin to refile. If so, refiling is easy. Start with the lowest-numbered box and work your way through the collection. You can start additional crews at any waypoint.

Make certain the refilers are trained to unload the move boxes in the proper order. The first film box removed should be the one nearest the card end of the move box, from the top row, to the left, facing the box. This should be intuitive, because they are working from left to right, the way materials are shelved normally, but I have seen many crews get confused, especially at the start. Also make certain that they watch the sequence card numbers on the boxes carefully.

If you have to begin refiling while other crews are still packing films, start the refiling crew at a title near the end and have them refile through to the end of the collection, then skip back to an earlier title and file through to the point at which they started. This requires a little extra work in the planning, but it is not hard. The packing crew should load three or four stacks of boxes until they come to a conveniently located waypoint, *then stop there*. Even though the last box may not be completely filled, number it and move all the boxes together. This lets the refiling crew start clean at the beginning of a title. They will still be skipping back and forth, but working from title to title with no leftover films.

Replicated Arrangement

When you are refiling these films, you are just trying to get them back into the cabinets in the same order in which they came out. No matter whether you used trays or boxes, there is a marker slip at the end of each row. Start filling the cabinets at the appropriate waypoint. Fill the first row until you come to a marker, then start the next row. Continue to the end. If you find two or more markers all together, you know to leave an extra row or rows open for growth. The first marker in the set denotes the end of the last row of film. Put each of the remaining slips into an empty row and recommence filing with the *next* row. If you put waypoints into the collection or marked the cabinet to show where a particular title starts, you should hit these markers exactly.

Remove the sequence card before you send the boxes back to be refiled. Keep the cards in order until you are sure you are hitting all the waypoints. You should be able to reuse these cards, even if a few of them are marked to indicate a flag in the box.

Book-Type Collection

In a book-type move, you are refiling with a constant amount of growth in each row between any two waypoints. If you used this method to add extra growth into a periodical collection, you will have some growth in each row in addition to that you assigned at the ends of the titles.

If you moved in trays, you can start at the beginning of the collection or at any convenient waypoint. If you moved in boxes, loaded from the back of the collection, you will likely start at a waypoint near the end of the collection and work in smaller, disconnected sections.

Periodical-Type Collection

We use this process when the growth is at the ends of the titles and the growth space is limited. The refiling part of the process requires some familiarity with the collection and with how periodical titles grow. I prefer to assign an experienced periodicals librarian to oversee this process. Such a person can judge how to arrange the films to best advantage between the waypoints.

The Layout spreadsheet tells you how much growth you have allocated to the end of each title. Pack each row full until you come to the end of the title. Consult the spreadsheet to determine the starting row for the next title. That may be in the same row you ended with, or it may be many rows away if the title has a lot of growth potential.

The waypoints you established throughout the collection give you a fixed point against which to identify any accumulation of errors before they require a major shift.

MOVING MICROFICHE

Microfiche, microcards, and other sheet goods require some adjustments to the microforms process. You can plan, count, measure, calculate growth, and lay out a microfiche collection just as you would for microfilms. You must decide which model best fits your collection, replicated, book-type, or periodical-type. Select the most appropriate model and follow the directions for microfilm.

Move in Trays

You can use the same trays I recommend for film. These trays are 8½ inches wide to accommodate two film boxes but hold only one row of fiche with some excess space left over. I have not moved a large collection of microfiche in this manner. For smaller collections, we have been quite successful using the film trays for fiche. If I were moving a large collection of fiche, I would have trays made 6½ by 26½ by 5 inches, specifically to fit the material.

Pack the fiche into the trays, front to back. Number the front of the trays and put them on the carts as you did with film. Make sure to load from TOP, BLACK, LEFT. You may get fewer trays of fiche on a cart than you can with film. Because a row of fiche is not particularly flat on top, I would not stack trays of fiche on top of one another unless I had some fool-resistant method to keep them from slipping. Install the sides and straps or shrinkwrap the carts before you move them to the loading dock. Leave the sides or shrinkwrap in place until the cart gets all the way to the refilers.

> **TIP**
>
> It takes two hours and forty-three minutes to refile one tray of microfiche once you have spilled it from the top shelf of a move cart. Personal experience. Very embarrassing. A word to the prudent.

Move in Boxes

It is somewhat more complex to move fiche in boxes. For one thing, you can put only one layer of fiche into a box without risk of serious disorder, so you move a lot of empty space unless you have boxes specially made for the purpose. For another, the packing process is fairly exacting.

The following assumes that you are using standard move boxes with a card pocket on the front end to pack the fiche:

Cut some strips of cardboard about 5 inches high and 10 inches longer than your boxes. Make sure the grain of the cardboard runs side to side, not lengthwise. We are going to bend the cardboard strips 5 inches from each end as we pack the fiche. Make sure the grain of the cardboard makes bending it easy.

It is easiest and more certain in the long run to pack the boxes backward. The first fiche in is the last one out. This allows you to build up a stack of boxes to a convenient height for moving without having to restack them.

Orient the boxes as for film, with the front toward you and the first fiche packed at the back of the row to your right. Start with the right-hand row of the bottom drawer of the last cabinet. Load the boxes from back to front. The front of the box is the end with the card pocket on it. You are loading exactly backward from the way we load carts. This is the exception that proves Rule Number One.

Load one row of fiche in the box. You are picking up more than one fiche at a time, so make certain you have not inadvertently turned them around, placing them out of order. When you have the first row almost finished, take one of the cardboard strips and bend it about 5 inches from each end. Slip the cardboard into the box so that the ends surround the row of fiche. The ends should not be so long that they extend past the end of the fiche, but they should fit fairly snugly against the ends of the box (figure 14.8).

Now fill out the rest of the row, packing the fiche fairly tightly. A tight pack and the cardboard surround help to keep the fiche from slipping around and provide a box-in-a-box.

Start a second row, again working left to right. Finish it with another cardboard surround. Put in as many rows as the bottom of the box can hold. If you have space left over, resist the temptation to fill it with fiche loaded perpendicular to the rows. It is inevitable that something will slip or the refilers will misinterpret the arrangement, and you end up refiling a lot of fiche. Instead, stuff the open space with newspaper to hold the last cardboard strip against the row of fiche.

I do not recommend putting more than one layer in each box. Yes, this is wasteful of space and you move a lot of half-full boxes. But there is no effective way to keep individual fiche from sliding down from an upper row and getting seriously out of order, unless you want to go to the trouble of having trays made to fit inside your move boxes. Besides, a box full of microfiche is heavy, and you do not want a box to be spilled, dropped, or, worse, have the bottom fall out.

When the box is loaded, number it. Loading backward, you remove the last card from a deck of sequence cards. If you're playing with a full deck, it should be number 100. Put this card in the pocket on the front of the box. Write the name of the collection on the two XXX cards and put them into the pocket.

Start a second box, to be numbered 99, and so forth. Stack each box on top of the preceding one to a predetermined height. Check with whoever will be moving the boxes before you start. Because of the weight of microfiche, they may want you to make shorter stacks than you would for books or microfilm.

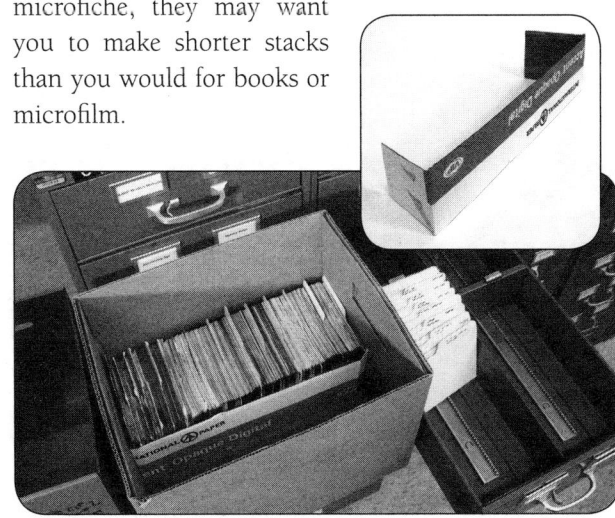

Figure 14.8 Cardboard dividers and newspaper keep fiche rows separated and stable.

Chapter 15

Special Situations

Books, periodicals, and microforms are not the only items a library has to move. Card files, loose magazines, valuable books, oversize books, odd-shaped items, and many other materials are included in library collections.

Also, some moves are very different from the typical shelf-to-shelf moves described in the previous chapters. The move may have to be interrupted so that the shelves themselves can be moved; the move may be over a distance so long that the carts, boxes, and other resources cannot be readily returned and recycled; or the library may be so small that the methods and techniques described earlier are too detailed and require more planning than can be justified.

OTHER MATERIALS

Card Files

Many libraries have catalog card files of one sort or another—if not the main catalog, then perhaps a shelflist or index to local records. For years we kept slides in an old catalog cabinet. If you have to move a card file, it is easily done using book carts.

It is not a good idea to move a full cabinet. It does not deform like a microfilm cabinet, but it is heavy and there is an excellent chance of spilling a drawer. The easy, safe way to move catalogs is to move the drawers separately and let the furniture movers take care of the cabinet. Here's how:

Number the cabinets 1 through X. Number each drawer in the cabinet.

Two stacks of drawers just fit on a 36-inch book cart or move cart with their handles interlocked (figure 15.1). On a 36-inch move cart, two pairs of drawers fit side by side, and it is safe to stack them two or three high. A single sixty-four-drawer cabinet fits on one move cart. It takes three or four book carts to move the same number of drawers. Try to load the drawers in a repeatable order, but so long as they are numbered it is easy to get them put back in the proper place.

With book carts, load the drawers lengthwise so they are supported under their full length and shrinkwrap them so they do not slide. You can fit more drawers on a book cart if you turn them sideways, but then it is difficult to shrinkwrap them securely. Load them sideways only for a move within a building (figure 15.2).

Figure 15.1 Two drawers fit on a 36-inch shelf if their handles are interlocked.

Figure 15.2 (top) Drawers supported full length are easy to wrap and safe to forklift. (bottom) Drawers loaded across the shelf are hard to wrap securely and may shift on forklift.

Figure 15.3 An occasional oversize book can be moved with the regular collection.

If your card drawers have retaining rods, by all means leave them in the drawers.

I have never tried to box catalog drawers. The box would be heavy. The drawers are likely to slide around inside, and a spill would be catastrophic. I see no advantage in boxes over book carts and none whatsoever compared with move carts.

Oversize Books

The occasional oversize book can be laid lengthwise at the head of the shelf of a move cart and between the rows on a book cart (figure 15.3). But when you have many large books (art collection, some periodicals, ledgers), you need a more concentrated way to handle them.

"Normal" oversize books can be moved upright on their bottom edge on book carts and on three-shelf move carts. Three-shelf carts handle books up to 15 inches tall. If the books are very tall, you may elect not to use the top shelf if the end panel is not high enough to support them.

You can also move oversize books, up to a point, in boxes. The problem is finding a box big enough to take the books and not too heavy to move. You may get only a few books in each box.

There are many ways to handle really large books:

- We have moved bound newspapers laid flat on dollies, strapped, or shrinkwrapped.
- You can remove the central keel on a move truck built to my design simply by removing a few (well, about twenty) screws. You are left with a cart that has four shelves 24 inches wide. We have used these to move a collection of heavy ledger books.
- For that matter, you can remove ten screws and four bolts from one of my move carts and slip off the whole shelf structure. You are left with a sturdy four-wheel dolly. Strap or shrinkwrap the books flat on this base.

You can move super-oversize books on book carts. Shrinkwrap each shelf separately and securely

TIP

If you take a move truck off its base, number the base and shelf unit so you can put them back together just the way you took them apart. You need to get the holes all lined up again.

(figure 15.4). Be careful if you have to forklift these; you do not want the part of the books that overhangs the shelf to be caught in the lift mechanism of the forklift.

Rare, Fine, and Valuable Books

If you have an extensive collection of rare books, you should consult a professional who specializes in this work. Don't do this at home, kids. Find a mover who has experience moving museums and other valuable collections.

We have moved "normal" rare books—valued to the hundreds and low thousands—upright on move carts with no problems. We used side panels and two or three straps per cart and sent a supervisor with every load of carts to make certain they were handled with special care. And to provide security, yes.

More delicate books we box, only a few to a box, and move on dollies, only a few to a dolly. We strap or shrinkwrap the boxes to the dolly at the unshelving location and unwrap them only at the destination shelves.

We wrap the most delicate and most valuable items in bubble or foam wrap without tape and pack them into boxes, then move the boxes on dollies or, one at a time, on book carts pushed by trusted staff. Some we wrap and hand-carry.

All persons working with rare, fine, and valuable books should be issued gloves. Leather gloves are too rough and could cause damage to fragile materials simply because they do not allow the delicate touch that may be needed. Jersey gloves are acceptable. Persons working with the most delicate books and particularly books with old, dry, leather bindings should be issued white cotton preservationist's gloves, which they should change frequently.

Consider the weather. If it is wet or damp, postpone the move.

Assign your most trusted staff not only to supervise but to carry out this move. The problem is not one of theft, although you must be on your guard; it is careless-

Figure 15.4 Overhanging books may be damaged by a forklift.

ness on the part of someone unfamiliar with the material and simply unaware that these "old books" may be irreplaceable.

I have twice moved substantial fine book collections. In both cases the books were to be shelved and displayed in a completely different arrangement in their new home, so there was no imperative to maintain strict order during the move. We packed those books according to what would best keep them safe. I think this is probably the approach to take in any move of valuable or irreplaceable items; safety first and Rule Number One second.

On another occasion I moved a smaller collection (2,500 volumes) of mixed rare and common books. Circumstances forced us to move quickly and to use move carts and boxes with little protection. Although we hand-carried a couple of real treasures, we kept the books nearly in order, which meant that old, delicate, and valuable items were on the carts next to quite ordinary volumes without any special protection. None of the books were damaged in the move.

Board Books, Multimedia Kits

Board books and other small, odd-shaped materials do not move well on carts and not much better in boxes. They are often small, and sometimes their shape is odd in all three dimensions so they don't pack tightly together and you have a lot of wasted space in the box or on the cart. Multimedia kits stored in plastic bags are even worse. In boxes they slide around and get out of order.

Typically we just bow to the inevitable: we pack them in boxes, full, more or less the same way they came off the shelves, and do not really try to keep them in strict order. In any case many libraries use a more relaxed shelving order for board books, so it does not take too long to reshelve them properly. Bagged media kits also move well, but not in strict order, in large canvas book bags and in office-size wastebaskets.

Vertical Files

File cabinets can be moved full but at considerable risk. Although their loaded weight is not as heavy as microform cabinets, neither is the construction of these cabinets, so they are easily deformed. The reason many file cabinet doors do not close properly is that, somewhere in their history, someone moved them with a hand truck. Many movers suggest that upright file cabinets may be moved with one or two bottom drawers full. Lateral files must be emptied.

Letter-size file folders can be moved like books on book carts and in boxes. The shelves of move carts are not quite deep enough to hold them. You can use move carts and they are efficient because they can handle the heavy weights, but you should shrinkwrap the carts instead of using the sides and straps. Letter-size folders fit easily across a book cart. They must be packed tightly so they do not slip around. In boxes, they must be packed lengthwise.

Legal and jumbo folders do not fit on move carts. They can be moved on book carts and in boxes. Book carts are more efficient. Pack them tightly and shrinkwrap the carts.

Film

Film in boxes can be moved like books. Round cans of 16 mm film are a particular problem. You can move them in boxes, but they are heavy and you usually cannot fill a box. The best way we have found to move film in cans is in heavy canvas book bags. Again, you don't move many to a bag because of the weight, but it is easier to handle them than any other way we have found.

Realia

Pack carefully in whatever box or crate fits. Better yet, let the office movers do it.

Unbound Periodicals

Periodicals in Princeton files, file cases, and some other containers can be moved on book or move carts just like bound volumes. They can be moved in boxes just like bound volumes, assuming you have large enough boxes.

Loose issues cannot be moved so easily. Typically they are flimsy and sag, bend, or slide around if you try to stand them on a cart shelf. Even if you lay them down on a shelf, they are likely to slide off before you can get them strapped or shrinkwrapped.

Periodicals tend to be just a bit thicker on the spine side, where they are stapled. You can reverse half of them to even out the stack, but that may require extra time and care at reshelving. A stack of periodicals all oriented the same way slants and slides away from the spine side. If you use book carts for your move, you can take advantage of this feature. Lay a stack of periodicals flat on the cart with their front edge against an end panel. Avoid building another stack in the middle of the shelf even if there is room; that stack would slide. If you shrinkwrap each stack to its shelf and around its end, they transport well (figure 15.5). Apply the shrinkwrap as soon as the stacks are on the cart, before you move it. To keep the loose issues in order, start at the end of your collection and work backward. Load the carts from the bottom up.

Move carts handle loose issues easily. Lay the magazines flat on the shelf, spine out, with the front edge against the keel, not the end panel (figure 15.6). On a 32 or 36 inch cart you should be able to get three stacks

Figure 15.5 Magazines wrapped in this manner don't slide.

to a shelf. Start at the end of the collection and load the carts from the bottom. Apply the sides and straps or shrinkwrap before you move them.

You can move loose periodicals in boxes. Lay them flat in the box, work backward and bottom-up to maintain order in the boxes, and use sequence cards to keep the boxes in order. Stack the boxes 1-up or 1-down depending on the conveyance you use to move them and on the number of times they will be restacked; see chapter 12 for details.

There is another, easier way to load magazines into boxes. Stand the box on end with the front (card pocket end) up. Start from the front of the collection and slide the magazines into the box with the top toward the open top of the box and the front of the magazine facing up (figure 15.7). Pack the box fairly tight to reduce sag. When you sit the box on its bottom, the magazines will be in shelf order. When you unload, make sure to start at the back (away from the card pocket) end of the box.

To load the collection backward, set the box with the card end down and load the periodicals facedown.

Finally, there is a very low-tech way to move magazines: Collect small office-type wastebaskets. If you used rubber wastebaskets as door protectors, use those. Wait until you are nearly finished with the move to address the loose magazines so you keep the protections in place. Lay the wastebaskets on their sides and slide the magazines in faceup. To keep them in order, number the baskets with a piece of painter's tape and a marker. Move them, unload them, and then distribute the wastebaskets to your staff.

Figure 15.6 The natural slant of magazines holds them on the shelf.

Figure 15.7 With this method, magazines don't slip when being loaded.

Newspapers and large-format periodicals present a more difficult problem. They can be moved on the wider book carts, shrinkwrapped to each shelf like loose periodicals. Newspapers usually do not transport well on a move cart because the individual shelves are too narrow. You can transport newspapers in boxes if the boxes are large enough. A box that is handy and the right size for books is too small for newspapers. You can tie up bundles of newspapers with twine or even shrinkwrap them.

Many libraries that have fifteen-day or thirty-day retention policies for newspapers simply discard most of the loose copies and start over in the new building.

OTHER MOVES

Interrupted Moves

The easiest moves to plan, equip, and carry out are those that go from the origin shelves directly to the destination shelves. Unfortunately, in many moves the books must be stored for some length of time before they can be placed in their final location.

The most common interrupted moves are those for which shelves are being reused. The shelves have to be cleared of books, removed, and rebuilt in a new location, either immediately or after being painted. Another common situation arises when a building project is phased. At some point it may become advantageous to move into the completed sections of the new building while the remainder is being finished. Some books may have to be moved into a temporary arrangement and shifted again later.

The problem with such moves is that it can be expensive to store the books for even a short time. In a shelf-to-shelf move, we may reuse a cart or box dozens, if not hundreds, of times. Once the initial cost or rental fee is paid, each additional use and recycling reduces the per-use cost. Allen County Public Library has move carts that have made more than a thousand trips back and forth. Their per-use cost is measured in pennies. On the other hand, if you have to leave books sitting on carts or in boxes even for a few days during your move, you need many more carts or boxes than for a straight shelf-to-shelf move, with considerably more expense to move the same number of books.

Let's look at some ways to reduce costs.

Jam and Cram

You may be able to cram all of the books into only a portion of the shelves while the rest are being installed, then spread them into final order after all shelves are completed. This method works only under specific, limited circumstances, but when it works it works well. You must have enough empty shelves to hold your collection, although you can pack the books as tight as possible knowing this is only temporary.

It is relatively difficult to plan a move in which books are to be packed tight. You have absolutely no leeway in calculating temporary waypoints. It works best if you can start at the beginning and load straight through using only one crew for the entire collection. If you do have to use simultaneous crews, use fewer waypoints and calculate as closely as you can to remove the looseness we try to build into normal waypoint calculations.

When all of the stacks are in place, lay out the collection over the entire space, if you have not done so already. Establish the normal number of waypoints every forty to seventy shelves and mark the destination shelves. Note that some of the shelves you are marking already have books on them—books to be moved to a new location. That's the tricky part about spreading out the books onto the full shelving arrangement: some of those books are going onto shelves that already have books crammed onto them. This is not a problem; you just have to give some thought to staging the move.

If you have a choice, you want the shelves you cram the books onto to be the ones at the back end of the eventual shelving arrangement. This allows you to move the first book forward, opening up a spot for a later book.

Consider a case in which half of your stacks are installed, ready to receive books. You load all of the books onto these shelves, packed as tight as possible. The construction crew installs the other half of the shelves "in front of" the initial shelves ("in front of" means earlier in the shelving scheme). The first book in the collection goes on the first of these new shelves.

Mark the waypoints on all the shelves. You can move half of the books into their final position on the newly installed shelves. Depending on the size of the collection, you could use multiple crews for this move, starting a crew at any waypoint. Now you have opened up another quarter of the total shelves. One half of the second half of the crammed books fits on these. Again you may be able to use multiple crews, but working in a smaller space. By the time you take half of the remaining quarter of the crammed books, you are down to one or two crews, even in a large collection. Eventually the last section of books moves only a few shelves. The last book doesn't move at all.

It is only a little more trouble if the new shelves are installed behind the crammed shelves:

Mark all the waypoints. Start as close as possible to the middle of the collection and move the second (back) half of the collection. Use multiple crews if you like. Then move the next quarter, half of the rest, half of what's left, and so on until all of the books have been spread into final position.

What makes the backward move a little more trouble is that you must always take *fewer than half* of the remaining books each time you pick a new starting point. As you get near the end, where you are working in smaller increments, you may have to do some shifting or store a few books on carts temporarily to make everything fit. If you take more than half at any one time, the first of those books must go onto a shelf that you have not yet opened. It's not a problem; it just takes planning.

Punctuated Move

You may be able to do an almost simultaneous move of books and shelves. This one takes some planning too, along with a lot of cooperation at the loading dock, but

> ### BUY NEW SHELVES OR REPAINT?
>
> It may not be cost-effective to reuse shelving if it is to be repainted. Against the cost of the new shelving, you have to set all of the costs of repainting:
>
> - Dismantling must be done carefully, parts must be sorted, especially similar ones. Parts must be packed for transport. All this takes more time compared to shelves torn down for metal recycling.
> - Transport. Unless painting can be done on site, there is one extra transport.
> - Paint. The cost of painting is substantial.
> - Drying time. If you have to store books while the shelves are painted, you may incur costs for boxes, longer cart rental, storage fees, and so forth.
> - More complicated move. You may recruit and train one crew to empty the shelves and have to recruit and train another to fill them again. You may not be able to retain them if there is no work for a week or so. If you have a time-critical move such as a university moving over a semester break, you may not have a window wide enough to get everything done in the time available.
> - Intangibles. Reused shelves may be less solid, have minor damage, rust, and the like. They may have no warranty.
> - Salvage value. If you buy new shelves, you may be able to trade in the old or recycle them as scrap metal. The value is an offset to the cost of new shelves.
>
> I was called into one move late in the process. The plan in place was to repaint approximately half of the periodical shelves and to move in two stages about a month apart. We ran into a construction delay that would have forced us to miss the first move date. Looking for an alternative, we evaluated buying all new shelves and, to our great surprise, found that for that library, in that situation, the all-inclusive cost of new shelving was no more than the cost of moving and repainting. If you are thinking about repainting to save money, don't just assume it will be cheaper. Do the math.

the ones I have seen have worked well. The essence of this move is that you move a few books out of the way. A separate shelf-moving crew dismantles the shelves, moves, and rebuilds them while the move crew unloads a few more shelves. "Few" here is a relative term. In a large move with many crews working, "few" could be a hundred sections or more.

This works best if you have at least some additional shelves in the new building. You start moving onto these shelves while the shelf movers work on the ranges you just vacated.

In the worst case you need to move the initial group of books into some sort of storage to get the starting ranges cleared, and you won't be able to move them out of storage until the last ranges have been moved and installed.

Give some thought to the sequencing of the move to be sure the shelves are always built in the place where the next books to be moved go. Also, take into account the different kinds of shelves. For periodical lift-up, CD/DVD, paperback, and other specialized types of shelves, you may have no choice except to store the materials until they can be returned to the same shelves from which you took them.

You should match the pace of the book movers as closely as possible to that of the shelf crew. Neither group can work any faster than the other.

The crews do not have to work simultaneously. I did two big jobs where we moved books all day and the shelf crew worked all night. The extreme example is when the shelves have to be taken off site and painted. It may take the shelf crew a week to tear down, move, paint, dry, and reassemble the shelves it took the book crew only a day to empty.

The Akron Alternative

Akron Public Library staff took the punctuated move to its extreme while they were building their new library. They built several hundred large move carts, five or six feet long. They put half their collection on the move carts, then moved the empty shelves to their temporary location, a former big-box home improvement store. They set up the shelves and moved the books back onto them.

Then they put the other half of the books onto the carts and arranged the carts, like shelves, in the temporary building. They left the books on the carts until it was time to move into their new building.

They spent a lot of money on the carts, but the move process must have been quite elegant.

Long-Distance Moves

Most library moves are over a relatively short distance, within a building, across campus, a few city blocks, rarely more. Over such a short distance, the coming and going of trucks is relatively constant and there is a smooth flow of books to and empties from the new building. The travel time is negligible and a smaller truck, faster to load and unload, actually improves the smoothness of the workflow.

As the travel time gets longer—several miles across town on busy streets—it makes sense to use a longer truck and take more materials each load. But it is more difficult to maintain a smooth, efficient workflow with the larger trucks. Loaded books pile up on the origin dock. If the dock is small or makeshift, the dock crew may not have room to sort and arrange materials. When the truck arrives with empties, it may be difficult to pass them through the dock to clear room to reload the truck.

The larger truck also leads to a somewhat punctuated move. There is a flurry at the dock when the truck arrives. The wave of activity spreads throughout the building to the elevator and to the unshelvers or reshelvers, dissipating as it goes. After the flurry, the dock crew may find themselves with little to do until the wave pulls back and floods their position again.

The move coordinator needs to pay particular attention to balancing the move. The transport step is the irreducible bottleneck. The crews at each stage should be sized so they are productively busy all the time and can just unshelve or reshelve one truck worth of materials in the time it takes to cycle that truck.

Say you have a truck that holds thirty move carts and it takes one hour to cycle the truck: load it, drive across town, unload, and drive it back. A crew can load seven move carts in one hour. You can have only four crews working simultaneously. Any more would just build a backlog at the dock and eventually the crews would run out of empty carts or boxes. Any fewer would require extra time as the truck waits for a full load. The same issue arises at the destination.

Though occasional rest periods may be appreciated, a constant shortage of resources, waiting for boxes, waiting for books, is a real morale killer. The speed that smoothness generates is lost, and idle crews can wander off in search of something to do, perhaps not something you planned for them to do.

In some cases it may actually be cheaper to use more, smaller trucks, even on the longer routes. The cost of the extra truck and driver is offset by the ability to run more crews simultaneously, which keeps the move short and reduces overhead costs by increasing productivity.

A really long move is another issue entirely. The only circumstances I can think of in which a move would be made over a distance so long as to obviate the advantages of a cyclic workflow is if a collection is to be sold or broken up or perhaps if a branch campus is closed and the books transported to be incorporated into the mother collection. There may be other circumstances, but such moves are rare. I have done one move of about 45 miles. That one was easy. We used a truck big enough to take everything in one load. The move crew rode out to the origin with the truck, loaded everything, drove back, and unloaded the next day. It was a very small move.

A large move would be much more problematic. First, a large, long-distance move would probably be done in boxes. Boxes can fill a truck more completely and are cheaper if they are not going to be recycled and reused. However, to get the most economy, the boxes have to be stacked taller than the stacks we take on a dolly or hand truck. This means that the integrity of the constant-height stack is lost and the boxes *do* get out of order. Given that, I would not worry about keeping boxes in order at the origin dock. I would number each box carefully, color-code any separate collections, and set up a sorting facility at the destination to get everything back in order before sending it to the shelves or storage.

The collection should be thoroughly measured before it is boxed. At least use frequent waypoints, every thirty to forty shelves. Depending on what is to be done

TIP

Most logging instructions say to log the beginning and ending call numbers of each box. I've never had any problem just logging the first number. If the log says box 256 starts with H37 and box 257 starts with H39, most people can figure out that H38 is in box 256.

with the books at the destination, you might log the contents of every box.

In a long-distance move there is little opportunity to establish a cyclic workflow and return empties for reuse. The effort should be to get a truck loaded full and dispatched at the origin and to get it unloaded and the boxes into usable order at the destination.

If the books change ownership as a result of the transfer, the move may be more like two separate events with separate crews and supervisors reporting to separate authorities at each building. The coordinator of such a move should concentrate on getting the work done in a timely manner and on making sure the collection is measured and logged in a manner that is useful to the receiving location.

Very Small Moves

The larger your move, the more books you have, the more crews you have working simultaneously, the more complete and detailed your planning must be. But what about the other end of the spectrum? Is there a point at which the efficiencies and security gained by careful planning and specialized equipment provide only diminishing returns?

Yes. Very small moves can be done with abbreviated planning, limited controls, and little or no specialized equipment. In fact, many quite large moves are done that way. Some are even successful.

I define a very small move as one with up to maybe 10,000 books. If your move is larger than that, you may be able to skimp somewhat on the details, but you still want to do a collection measurement and layout, use enough crew assigned to specific jobs, and design the move for optimum efficiency.

In a very small move the nature of the process changes. For one thing, you need only two or three people to do the whole job from end to end. For another, the consequences of error are much less. This is not to say that you can forget the planning part of the process and ignore Rule Number One, but you can scale down to a manageable minimum. Here's how to do a very small move:

1. Select a Method

With a very small collection in one building, consider the carry or drag option.

If you are moving within a single building, collect half a dozen good, strong book carts. If you don't have that many yourself, borrow them from a nearby library. You only need them for a couple of days.

If you are moving between buildings, use boxes unless you have a short, level path suitable for carts. If possible, get boxes all the same size, but take what you can get. Boxes must be sturdy and small enough to handle. Grocery store boxes are not strong enough, nor are copier paper boxes. You can get by with forty to fifty boxes; more is better. You can buy boxes from many mail-order or Internet suppliers. Price at this writing is a little more than $1 each in small quantities.

Borrow a hand truck or dolly to move the boxes. Use a van or pickup truck to move between buildings. You won't move enough boxes at one time to make it worthwhile to rent a larger truck.

Number every box, so you can hand-load them into the vehicle in random order. There will be so few of them at one time that you can readily sort them at the destination shelves.

If you have a very level path between buildings with no curbs, steps, or other obstructions, and good weather, then you can consider using book carts. You need a couple extra to accommodate the longer route.

2. Measure the Collection and Plan the Layout

If your collection has significant subcollections to be shelved separately, measure each one separately and allocate specific shelves for it. Otherwise you can plan a layout for up to 10,000 books with only four or five waypoints.

Measure your existing collection(s) in feet. Measure only the space taken up by books, not the empty spaces. Now measure the new shelving in feet. If your new shelves are all the same length, you can just count the shelves and multiply by the length of a shelf. If you have the collection divided into subsets, count separately the shelves you allocated to each.

Figure out how much growth space to leave on each shelf. Here's how you do it: Subtract the feet of books from the feet of new shelves. That is the total growth. Count how many shelves you will have. Divide the total growth in feet by the total number of shelves. That gives you the growth space to leave on each shelf. Multiply by 12 to convert that to inches per shelf.

You want to be sure this is right, so let's work through an example:

You measure 528 feet of books. You count 720 feet of new shelves.

720 − 528 = 192 feet of growth.

720 feet of shelving equals 240 shelves assuming your shelves are 3 feet long. You need to spread 192 feet of growth over 240 shelves.

192 / 240 = 0.8 feet per shelf. Multiply that by 12 to get 9.6 inches of growth per shelf.

3a. Move, on Book Carts

Use book carts to move within a building or between nearby buildings if you have a good, level path with no elevation changes—like steps or curbs—and good weather.

Mark one end of each cart with black tape on the end panel. Also tape an 8½-by-11-inch sheet of paper to the outside of that end panel.

Plan on a crew of one to four people. If you have one or two, they work together throughout the process. With three or four, you can assign one to unshelve, one to reshelve, one to push, and one to help out wherever needed.

Start at the beginning of a collection and load a cart, starting on the TOP shelf with the BLACK end of the cart to your LEFT. Load one side of the cart, top to bottom, then turn it around and load the other side. Write the number 1 on the paper taped to the end panel. Don't write too large; you're going to reuse the paper.

If you have a pusher, let that person take the cart to the destination. If not, push it out of the way and load another. As you load each cart, write the next higher number on the paper. When all of the carts are loaded, push them to the destination and shelve them. Take the empties back and load them again. When you reuse a cart, cross off the previous number and write down the new one.

If you have one person assigned at each end and one pushing, you can keep a constant stream of books going and empties coming.

As you reshelve, be sure to leave the amount of growth space you calculated on each shelf. It is okay to leave less, but if you leave more you run out of shelves before you get all of the books put away.

3b. Move, in Boxes

If you are transporting books between buildings, it is probably easiest to box them. Load the books into the boxes from left to right. Load only a single row. Do not fill up the empty spaces with books tucked in out of sequence. Stand the books on the bottom edge, just as if they were on the shelf. If you can't stand them up, put them in spine up. Do not lay them flat.

Close the box and number it starting with 1. Fill as many boxes as you have, numbering each one consecutively. Don't worry too much about stacking them in order.

Take the boxes to your loading dock (which just may be your door) and load them into a van or pickup truck. Again, don't worry too much about the order, but do try to get the low numbers before the higher ones.

Take the boxes to the destination, unload them, and move them to the reshelving area. Unbox the books and reshelve them. Watch the sequential numbers on the boxes to make certain you do not miss any or shelve a box out of order.

When all the boxes are empty, take them back to the origin to be reused.

If you are working with only one other person, you'll probably get done faster if you work together. If you have a crew of four you can assign one to unshelve, one to reshelve, and two to push. It takes at least two people moving the boxes to keep up with one unshelver.

When you reuse a box, cross off the old number and write the new one under it. Keep the numbers neat and in line so it is readily apparent which is the last number.

Assuming the prep work is done and all supplies are available, two people should be able to complete a 10,000-book move within a building in two days, including all the reshelving. It takes four people at least a day to complete a similar move between buildings. Smaller moves should take a proportionately shorter time. Cleanup, cart return, box recycling, and shelf reading will likely spill over to another day.

Chapter 16 Finishing Up

The cleanup process is much more than just picking up the trash. You need to allow time and allocate workers to this stage of the process. Cleanup takes more time and effort than you might think. For one thing, when the crew sees the last book move, they may feel the job is done and become motivated to do other things, like enjoy the new building. For another, cleanup tasks just seem to keep coming, and it seems you will never be done.

LEFTOVER COLLECTIONS

The first thing you are likely to find is that, even though the official, planned move is over, there are still materials left to be moved. You may find small collections, office or workroom collections, files that got missed, and other materials. Managers or administrators may reconsider collections they previously planned to abandon. Plan to keep one or two crews an extra day to deal with these materials. You should not need dock or elevator crews, but you may need the truck and forklift drivers, pallet jacks, dollies, or whatever moving equipment you were using.

Search the empty shelves for books left behind. You may find missed books lying flat on upper shelves. Someone needs to walk the aisles to look for these. This is a job for the tallest person on your crew. Also search at the bottom of the shelves for books that fell behind or between the stacks.

Assign another crew to walk the aisles in both buildings pulling flags and waypoint markers and collecting sequence cards, measuring blocks, and other supplies left on the shelves. This crew should wear plastic gloves; they will almost certainly find food and drink remnants on the shelves.

If you moved with boxes, you need a crew to collect and prepare them for recycling. The best place for this crew to work is usually the loading dock in the destination building. If nothing else, this location saves transporting the empty boxes one more time. The number of people you need for this crew depends on the size of your move and how quickly the job needs to be completed. Teams of two or three people work well. Supply the crew with leather gloves to prevent paper cuts. If you taped the boxes, the crew needs box cutters or other safety knives. Flatten the boxes and stack them on a pallet, then strap them down with ratchet straps, twine, or industrial strapping equipment. You should be able to stack boxes about 4 feet high if you strap them tightly.

TIP

Don't recycle all of your boxes. Keep a supply, broken down and stacked on pallets for easy moving. You may find lots of uses for them. If you ever have a flood or sprinkler malfunction, you will be happy to have a supply of boxes readily available. The recommended first response with wet books is to pack them in cardboard boxes, laid flat, and get them into a very cold freezer as quickly as possible.

TIP

If you bought good, sturdy boxes for moving books, offer them to your office mover. They may offer you a better deal, in cash or services, than a recycler. If you bought pallets, you should be able to resell them as well. Call a pallet supplier and ask if they will purchase your used pallets. They won't pay much, but they will haul them away, saving you that cost.

If your office mover loaned you boxes, you need to stack those separately. They are customarily returned to the mover, who will reuse them.

Assign another crew to collect all of the emptied carts and move them to a central area to be returned to their owners. The actual return of the carts may be a project in itself. If you rented carts, notify the rental or shipping company to make a pickup.

You may also need to assign a crew to remove the various wall and floor protections. Plan sufficient resources for the job. This crew may need heavy dollies if they are removing plywood floor coverings. You may need to give this crew some instruction on how to remove tape residue or other specific techniques. Check with your contractor to determine if there are any cleansers the crew must use or must avoid, especially where finishes are new and may not be firmly set. Make sure the contractor has no further need of any of the protections before you remove them.

You will have to do a lot of general cleaning. Moving a library generates a regular blizzard of crumbs, those little bits of paper, wood from the floor protections, pieces of tape, labels, flags, waypoint markers, and other trash. Allow time for a thorough cleaning before you open to the public. This work will likely fall to your housekeeping staff. Because of the amount of work a move causes, you may need to assign extra help to complete the job in a timely manner.

SHELF READING

Earlier I have recommended that you use the weeks just before the move to do everything possible to get your collections in order, interfile as many items as possible, and eliminate any small collections that have to be interfiled. The whole plan of the move is designed to keep the books in the same order they were in on the origin shelves. The move cannot make them better; it can make them much worse.

Ideally you will read the shelves before you open to the public. Especially if your previous shelves were crowded, out of order, or fractured, your patrons and staff are looking forward to a nice, clean, orderly arrangement. A careful shelf reading ensures this.

Shelf reading is time-consuming, and most staff can do it effectively only for short periods at a time. Assign as many staff as possible to the project and rotate them frequently.

Now a confession: I have not done a single move in the past half-dozen years where we read the shelves before we opened. Sometimes that was because we were pushed up against a tight opening deadline and simply didn't have time to get that task done. More important, even when we had the time, we did not have the need to do an immediate, thorough, book-by-book read to get the shelves into acceptable order. At most we read relatively small sections of books that had been in poor order prior to the move.

How did we get away with it? All of these moves were done on nice, big move carts. The smaller the number of books you can move as one unit, the greater the chance that any one of them will get out of order.

Consider the ultimate small-unit move, the walk-in-line method. Remember this one? Each worker grabs a double handful of books and walks to the new shelves. If everyone stays in line, the books stay in order. Every time someone stops to tie a shoelace, walks too fast or too slow or alongside a friend, drops a book, or any of a hundred other things, something gets out of order. A thorough shelf reading by dedicated staff is an absolute necessity.

A move in boxes is a little better, and a move with book carts is better yet. It takes sixteen boxes to move

TIP

Assign the shelf reading project to people who have to use the shelves to find books for patrons. They have every motivation to get it right. Keep reminding your staff that the books are now in the same order they were on the old shelves. "Garbage in, garbage out" applies here, with a vengeance.

the equivalent of one move cart. Assuming the same level of care by the crews, you are sixteen times more likely to have a unit out of order with boxes. The odds that a box will get out of order go up every time it is restacked. Because a box holds only about half a shelf of material, it requires as close reading of every shelf to catch a mistake.

With move carts, we are dealing with units of 250–400 books. A supervisor can see at a glance if carts are being loaded or unloaded in proper order. TOP, BLACK, LEFT is very obvious. It is much easier to keep the books in order and to identify any that do get out of proper order. If a crew loads or unloads a cart from the wrong end, the disconnect is not one or two books, nor half a shelf, but five or ten shelves. You need to check only two or three books on one shelf out of every four to catch this error.

If the books were in reasonable order on the origin shelves and if you used move carts, the books should be in good, usable, not perfect order at the end of the move. You should still read shelves, but it won't have to be done as a hero project before you can reopen. If the origin shelves were not in such good order, you have to allow time and assign staff to do a book-by-book read.

STACK SIGNS

If you are going to use end-of-range signs with the call numbers of the books on each range, you should assign a crew to this task. This is a good job for employees who want to help but are not able to do the book-moving tasks.

It is not necessary to wait until the very end of the move. As soon as the reshelvers are finished with a range, the signage crew can go to work. It may help the move crews to have signs on the stacks as soon as possible. The signage crew may detect out-of-order books as they are gathering data, and while there is still time to correct the error. Supervisors can check the progress of the work easily, and crews interfiling returned books can find their way more easily. A crew of three people is sufficient and can keep up with as many as twelve to fifteen reshelving crews.

Prepare a signage template well in advance of the need. You can use almost any word processing, database, spreadsheet, or publishing software with which you are familiar.

- Determine the appropriate font, layout, and size of sign.
- Determine how specific the signs should be. Do you list the entire call number or a specific number of characters? 921.723418 or 921.7? E178.25 .D37 2003 or E178.2?
- Do you show only the starting number of each range or include the ending number as well?
- Is there a collection identifier such as "Reference" or "Fiction" on each sign?
- Are the stacks numbered? If so, is the number included on the sign?
- Are the signs color-coded?
- Is there a separate sign on each side of the end panel or a single sign that references both sides?

Make up a worksheet with columns for all of the variables—call number, stack number, color, and any other necessary information. During or after the move, two of the signage crew members record the starting (and ending?) call numbers and other variable information. If you use two people, one can read the call numbers while the other records the information. The two can check each other. A third person can be tasked to produce the labels.

As each batch of labels is finished, the data collection team installs them. In a large move with many crews working, the finished shelves are scattered at first, then the gaps are filled in as crews complete their assignments. The signage crew skips around to follow the shelvers. On a small move, it is reasonable to wait until the reshelving is completed.

> **HERO PROJECT**
>
> This is what most moves are. The term comes from the old Soviet Union. It describes a seemingly impossible project accomplished against all odds only by the hard, dedicated, manual labor of a large group of people, all of whom are then considered heroes. The reward is usually a gold star.

Specifications for Boxes

Appendix A contains drawings and specifications for four different cardboard systems: moving boxes, in two styles; high-density storage system; film/fiche trays; and side panels for move carts. These plans were provided to me by Tom Kelly of Kelly Box and Packaging Corporation in Fort Wayne, Indiana. Mr. Kelly graciously gave me permission to publish his proprietary designs. With these designs as a guide, a box manufacturer should be able to provide you with the boxes you need for almost any materials. The information in this appendix is available in electronic format at www.ala.org/editions/extras/fortriede09942. WEB

You can buy ready-made boxes from many sources including mail-order and Internet suppliers. In small quantities this may be the most cost-effective plan. You'll have to take a standard size—and there are thousands to choose among—but you don't have to pay a setup charge. Many of these suppliers do custom work as well. For a large move, it is almost certainly more cost-effective to have boxes made for you.

If you do buy ready-made boxes, make sure you order corrugated cardboard; there are some boxes advertised with the term "cardboard" that are light-duty, single-ply boxes not much stronger than a clothing store gift box. Pay particular attention to the crush weight of the box. This is a measure of the strength of the cardboard used. The overall strength and weight-carrying capacity of a box depend on the type of construction—glued, stapled, folded, and so forth. For a given construction, a box made with cardboard of a higher crush weight is stronger.

MOVING BOXES

Figure A.1 is a standard box with integral top and bottom flaps. The drawing is for the box used for oversize books. The same design is used for standard-size books but with the 14-inch dimension reduced to 10 inches. The recommended crush weigh is 275 lbs/sq. ft.

The manufacturer cuts the box to this pattern, then bends the right and left panels and glues the tab on the right panel to the left panel. To construct the box, you form it with pressure on the outside corners, then fold in and tape the bottom flaps.

Figure A.2 is a plan for a strong, no-tape box with an integral bottom and triple-wall end panels. This drawing is for the standard-size box; for oversize books, increase the 10-inch dimension to 14 inches. The crush weight is 275 lbs/sq. ft.

This is my preferred moving box. Building the box is quick and easy and requires no tape. Fold the sides up, then bend the ends over and lock the little tabs into place. The triple-wall end panels and handholds provide a safe, strong, almost comfortable way to handle the boxes. The downside is that this box requires a separate lid.

Figure A.3 is the lid for the folded box, called a "tray" in the box profession. This particular drawing is the lid for a midsize box we had built to move a large periodicals collection. Adjust the dimensions up or down to fit standard or oversize boxes. The lid should be made with a 275-lb/sq. ft. crush weight.

To build this lid, fold up the two long sides. Then fold up the ends, fold the tabs on the end panels, and tape them to the sides. Always put the short flap on the outside of the lid. It keeps the inside of the lid smooth and makes it much easier to fit the lid on the box.

HIGH-DENSITY STORAGE SYSTEMS

Figure A.4 is the box. The manufacturer glues the tab on the end panel to the side. When you make the box, you fold and tape the bottom flaps. The top is open. The crush weight is 275 lbs/sq. ft.

Figure A.5 is a plain sheet of cardboard. Put one sheet over a pallet to even out irregularities in the pallet boards. Center another one fairly exactly over each course of boxes. You want the cardboard to cover all of the sides and ends of the boxes. The crush weight is 200 lbs/sq. ft.

Figure A.6. is the top cover for the stack. It is another big tray. Build it by folding down the sides and ends and taping the tabs on the ends to the outside of the side panels. Tape in both directions along the side and over the side panel to the inside. Staple the flaps if you have a heavy-duty stapler. The strength of the sides of this top cap is what keeps the stacks of boxes from pulling apart at the top.

FILM/FICHE TRAYS

Figure A.7 is the tray we use to move microfilm or microfiche. The tray holds two rows of film in boxes or one of fiche. You can customize the tray for fiche by reducing the 8-inch dimension to 6½ inches and increasing the depth of the sides to 5 inches. Check the length of a drawer in your cabinets and adjust the 26½-inch dimension to hold one full row. The crush weight is 200 lbs/sq. ft.

Build the tray by folding up the sides and ends and tape the tabs on the end panels to the outside of the trays. If you have a suitable stapler, reinforce the tape with staples. These trays take a lot of abuse. Make them as strong as possible.

SIDE PANELS

Figure A.8 is the piece used to construct the side panels for move carts. Two pieces this size are used per panel, but cut with the corrugations running in opposite directions. The drawing shows the dimensions for a panel for a 32-inch cart. Adjust the 31-inch dimension so the panel makes a tight press fit into the sides of your book carts. The shelves and base on the cart are recessed inside the end panels to receive the cardboard sides. The crush weight of the cardboard is 275 lbs/sq. ft.

Corrugated cardboard is strong in one direction but bends easily in the other. The manufacturer glues two of these panels together with the grain running at right angles. The result is a light, strong side panel.

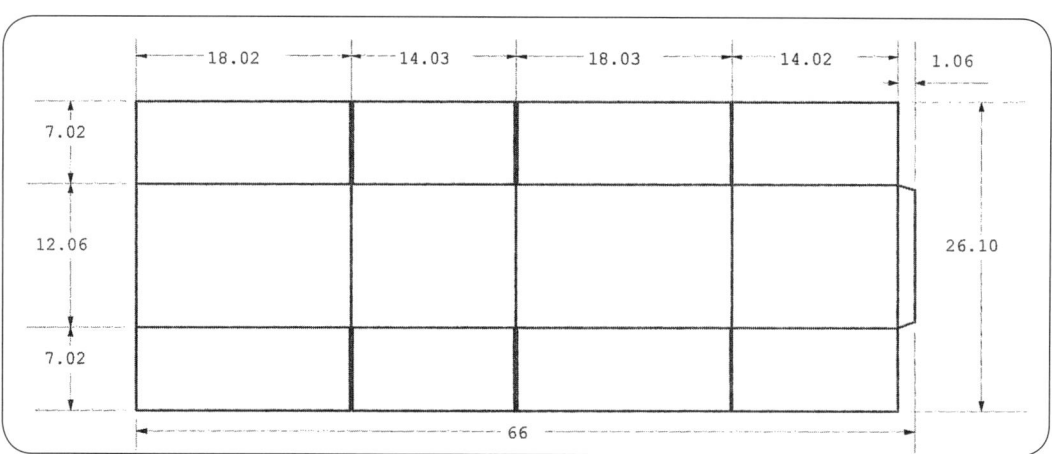

Figure A.1

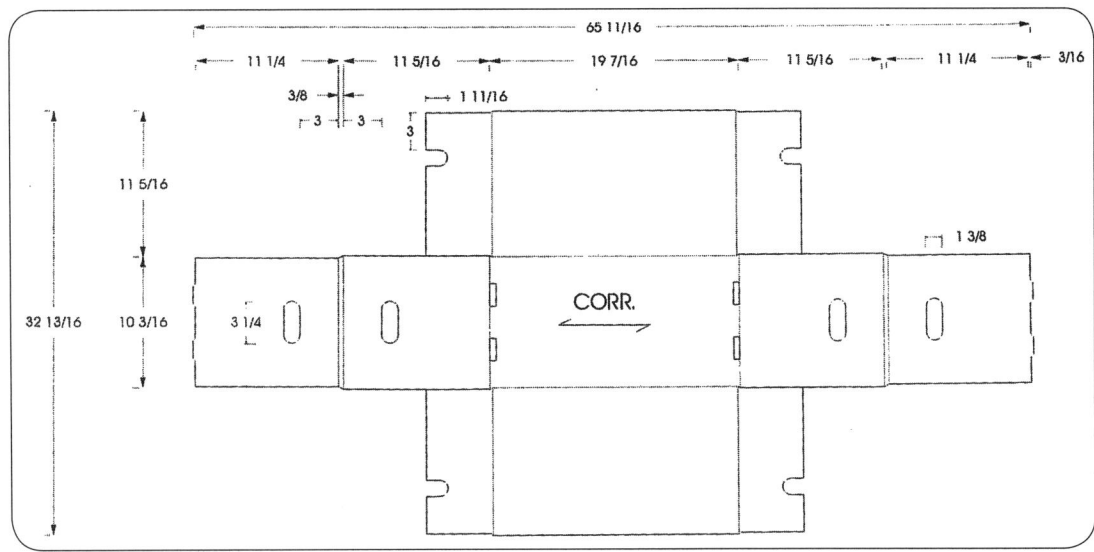

Figure A.2

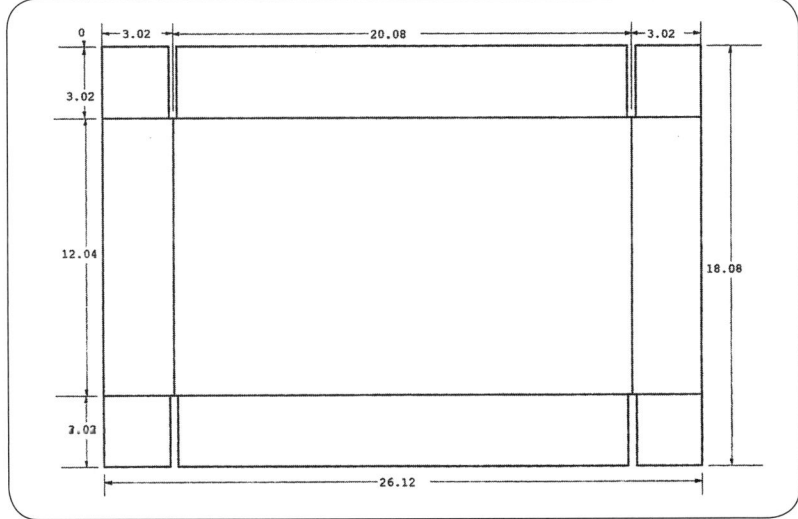

Figure A.3

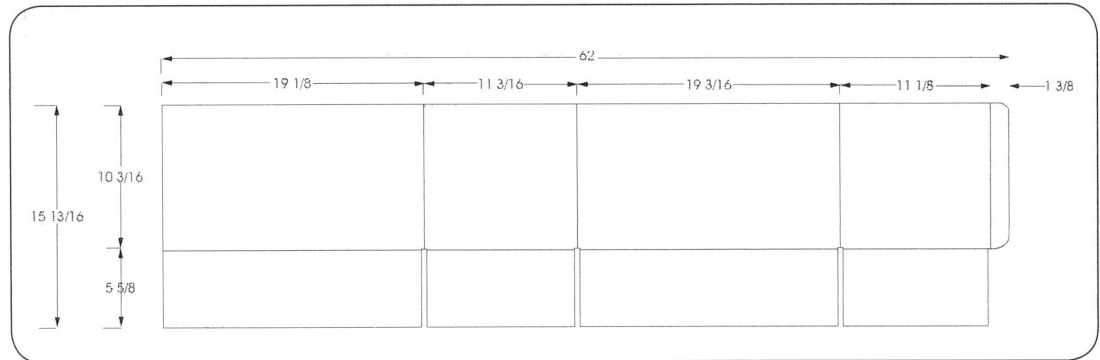

Figure A.4

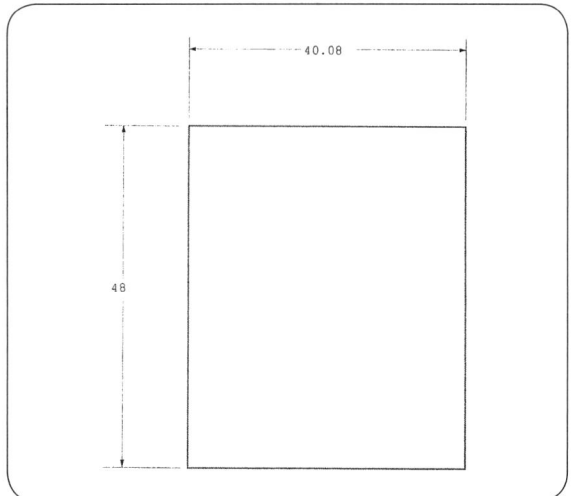

Figure A.5

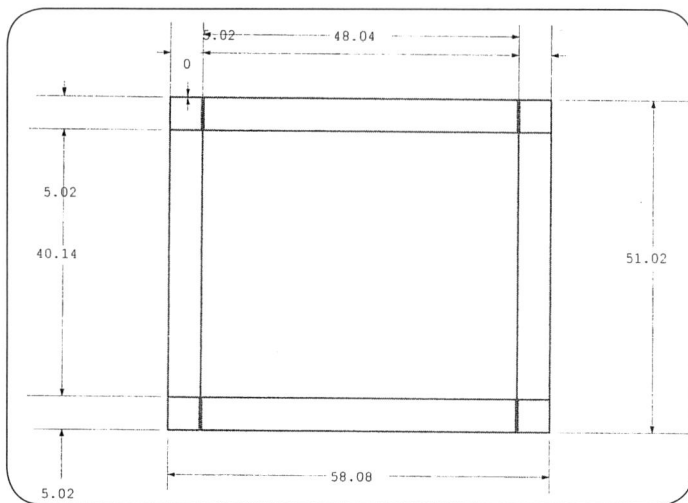

Figure A.6

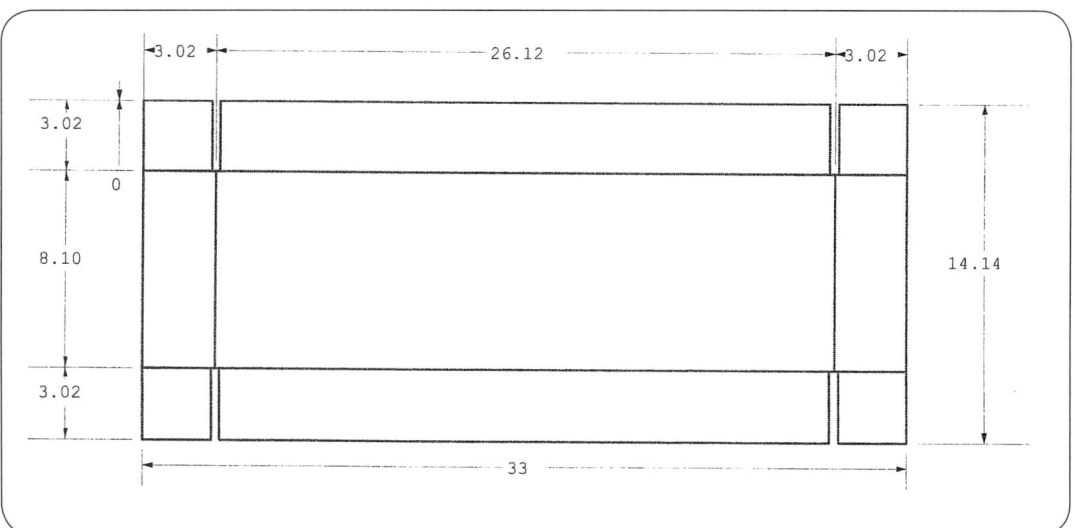

Figure A.7

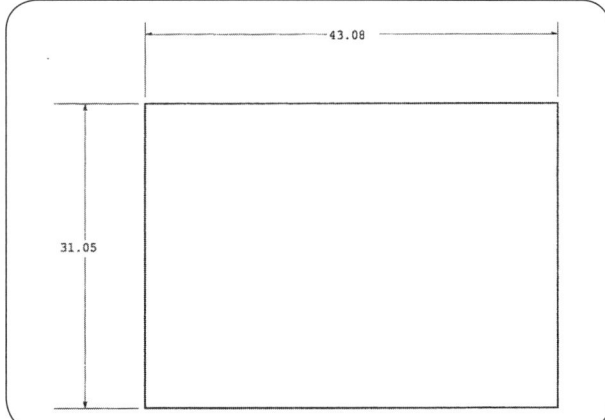

Figure A.8

Specifications for Move Carts and Sorting Trays

Appendix B

Appendix B contains a set of specifications and construction notes for carts designed especially to move library materials and to be forklifted onto a truck or dock if necessary. It also contains a sheet that describes the trays we use for sorting or interfiling books. The information in this appendix is available in electronic format at www.ala.org/editions/extras/fortriede09942. WEB

The carts are designed to be rugged and easy to maneuver, not pretty. Construction does not require a full woodworking shop. My builder works in a garage. The only specialized equipment required is a table saw large enough to handle 4-by-8-foot sheets of plywood. A drill, stapler, hammer, screwdriver, and some wrenches are the other tools. An electric screwdriver is a real bonus. You can keep the cost low if you can find a home handy person who can build the carts for you.

The dimensions shown are for a cart that spins inside an ADA-minimum 36-inch aisle. If your aisles are wider in both buildings, you can make the carts longer with more capacity. The maximum is about 4 feet. Beyond that, the carts become too heavy for one person to push, and the strength required for the wheels raises the costs significantly.

If your new building is under construction, talk with the project carpenters. They have equipment on site and may be able to build carts for you during downtimes in the building construction.

The important things to stress with whoever builds the carts are the wheels and the base construction. The wheels specified are rated for 255 lbs each. From experience we know they can support a 1,500-lb cart with ease. Cheap casters from most hardware and home improvement stores are not strong enough; heavy-duty ones are expensive in the small quantities most of those stores have available. Plan ahead and order from a professional supplier. If your carts are longer than 36 inches, upgrade to a wheel rated for 300–350 pounds.

Get 5-inch hard rubber wheels, ball bearings, full swivel casters, and strong construction throughout.

The base is designed with two side rails and four transverse members of two different lengths. It would be easier and cheaper to construct the carts by cutting all four transverse members to the same length and nailing them inside the side rail. But this construction has proved to be weak and often fails when the cart wheels hit an obstruction. Build the base as shown, with one transverse member across the ends of the side rails to act as a bumper.

It is often useful to purchase a few extra bases. Inevitably some get damaged, and it is not hard to replace one. One extra base per twenty carts is plenty.

The sorting trays are even easier to construct. The most important issues are to make sure the sideboards are set high enough in the end panels that a book will not drag on the table through the gap and that the overall length will fit comfortably on whatever tables you have available.

SPECIFICATIONS AND INSTRUCTIONS
PURCHASE OF LIBRARY MOVING CARTS

_____ Library will received sealed quotes for library move carts until _____ a.m./p.m., ____ (date) _____. Quotes must be delivered in a sealed envelope marked "Move Cart Quote" mailed or delivered in person to _____.

Quotes must be submitted on the enclosed Quote Form, signed by a responsible agent of the person or corporation submitting the quote.

The Library intends to purchase _____ 4-shelf carts and _____ 3-shelf carts. The actual number may vary. The unit price must be guaranteed for at least 180 days. In addition, the Library will purchase approximately _____ extra bases without base shelves or casters as replacements for bases that may become broken during use.

Submittal Checklist

1. The enclosed Quote Form properly filled out and signed.
2. Evidence of ability to perform the project in a timely manner, including but not limited to references to projects similar in type of construction or scope.
3. Specifications, model numbers, or cut sheets showing details of the casters proposed to be used on this project.
4. A statement of changes from, exceptions to, or other deviations from the specifications.
5. A proposed delivery schedule.

Construction Specifications

Project is a mobile bookshelf/cart capable of moving 1,000–1,250 pounds of books smoothly over smooth surfaces and carpet and of being forklifted into a truck. Construction is heavy-duty throughout. Shelves, including the base shelf, are inset ¼" inside the limit of the structural base and end panels to allow a cardboard side panel (by owner) to fit inside the end panels. A retainer made of aluminum threshold extrusion holds the cardboard panel at the bottom and a ratcheting tie-down strap (by owner) retains the panel at the top. Casters must allow the cart to rotate 360° in its own length.

Plywood is ¾" nominal BC grade SYP, unfinished. 2" x 4"s are #2 or better without knots or splits that will affect structural integrity. Casters are 5" hard rubber wheels, 360° swivel, with ball bearings, and rated for a minimum load of 255 lbs per wheel, equal to or better than Global Caster wheel HR 50 GB on arbor 5050-03-YAN. This is a 5" x 1¼" hard rubber wheel with ball bearings and a $^3/_8$" axle.

Grain of end panels must run vertical. The top of each end panel is covered with a 4" x 36" 20 oz. cotton duck canvas, centered and glued to the end panel with corners mitered and stapled as necessary. One end of every cart is topped with black canvas. On 4-shelf carts the other end is white canvas. On 3-shelf carts, it is yellow. Before installing the canvas, break the sharp corners of the end panels.

Shelves must be installed with the B side up. The screws that hold the base shelf to the structural base must be countersunk below flush. There must be no screws in the tops of any of the other shelves. Shelves are rabbeted ¼" into the end panels and set on supports screwed to the keel.

End panels are fastened to the structural base with #7 deck screws and with two 2½" x $^5/_{16}$" bolts located as far apart as is practicable, bolted through the structural base and finished with washers as needed to avoid crushing the wood, lock washers, and nuts.

The base must be built as shown. The two transverse 2" x 4" members are of different lengths. The outside member must run the full width of the base. The inside member must run between the longitudinal members.

All wood is unfinished. Splinters, snags, and other sharp points should be removed or sanded down.

Delivery is to be according to the following schedule

_____

All carts to be delivered to _____

_____

MOVE CART QUOTE FORM

The undersigned agrees to provide move carts and bases according to the accompanying specifications at the prices quoted below:

PRICE EACH

4-shelf carts, per spec $ _____

3-shelf carts, per spec $ _____

Extra structural bases $ _____

Name of Individual or Corporation _____

Address _____

City, State, Zip _____

Telephone _____

Signature of Responsible Officer _____

Date _____

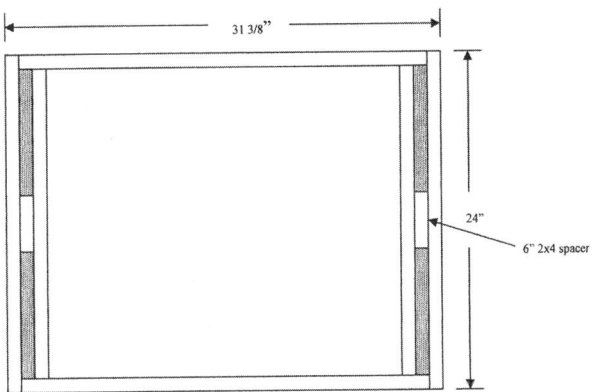

Base of 2x4 SPF, nailed with 16d CC sinkers

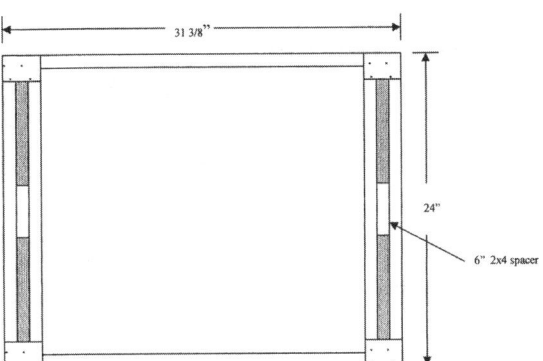

Bottom view of base. Casters are lag bolted to structural base with ¼" x 1 ½" lag bolts with flat washer. Nails holding structural base should be off-center toward the top side of the base to avoid splits and weakening of the joints.

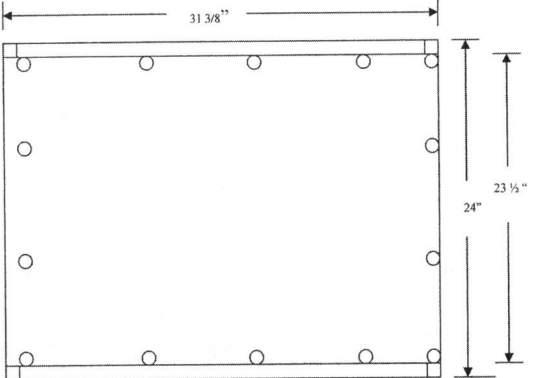

Base shelf of ¾" SYP, centered on base with ¼" of 2x4 base exposed on either long edge. Screw to base with 14 #6 1 ¼" drywall screws, countersunk below flush.

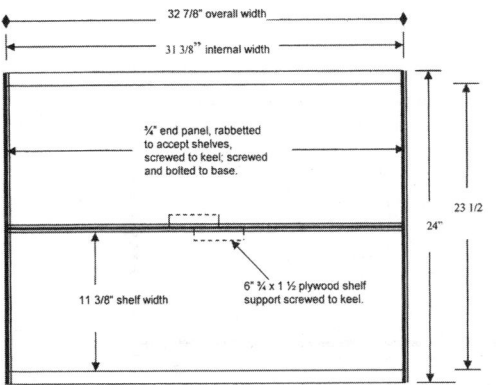

Top view showing keel and recessed shelves.

MOVE CART QUOTE FORM *(cont.)*

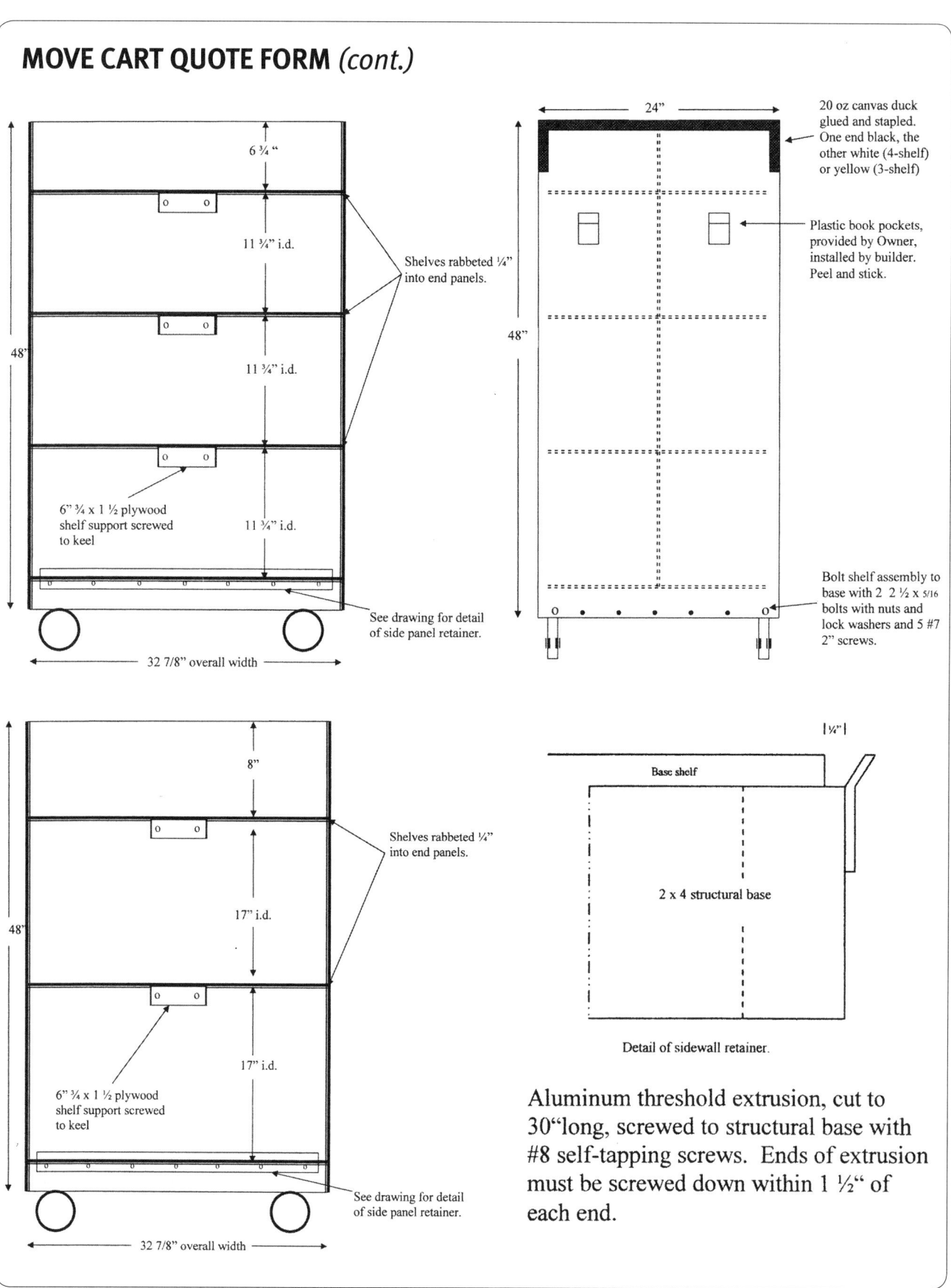

SORTING TRAY

The sorting tray is a longer version of the old-fashioned desktop book holder often found in libraries. It consists of two 1-by-8-inch boards held together at right angles by two 1-by-8-inch end pieces. The books sit at an angle with their spines readily visible. The angle of the support helps keep the books upright without a separate bookend.

Use good-quality boards without snags or splinters; ¾-inch plywood will work. Sand the edges and corners to remove splinters and sharp points that could snag a book or cause injury.

Do not paint the trays. Paint rubs off on the books. If you like, put two coats of a clear finish on the boards. If you use plywood, you must add the finish to seal the grain. Sand between coats and make sure the finish is fully dried before you use the trays.

Size the trays about 6 inches shorter than the tables you will be using so they do not slip off the ends of the tables. A tray 5½ to 7½ feet long is a good size to work with.

The end panel should be about 16 inches long. This length provides stability and allows two sorters to sit comfortably on even a 30-inch-wide table as the ends overlap slightly.

Fasten the boards to the end panels with nails or screws. Leave a gap of an inch or two between the two boards at the bottom. The books stand up better and slide more easily with the gap. Do not make the gap so wide, or set the boards so low on the end panel, that the corner of the book drags on the table underneath. The boards should be at right angles to one another to hold the book squarely and at 45 degrees to the end panel.

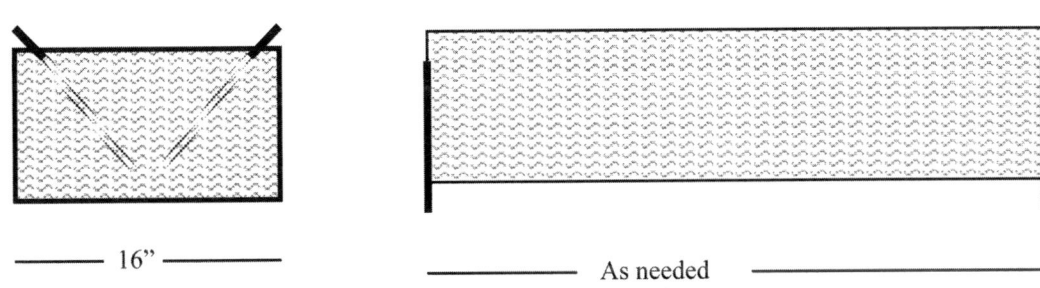

———— 16" ————   ———————— As needed ————————

Appendix C

Worksheet to Calculate Shelving Layout and Growth Rates

The Layout spreadsheet contains tabs for four separate kinds of Excel spreadsheets:

The Data tab is a form you can print out and use to record the measurements of the shelves using the shelves-and-strings process. You do not enter any data in the electronic version of this worksheet. The instructions on the sheet are set up for a relatively large Dewey-classified collection. You may need to modify the specific instructions to match your own collection

There is one Master Layout tab and fifteen copies, marked Sheet 1, Sheet 2, etc. Use one copy for each of your collections. Rename the Sheet tabs to identify each of your collections. At the same time, enter the name of the collection in cell B30 so it shows on the printed copies of the sheet. In a large library with many collections, you need additional copies.

Enter the information you have recorded on the Data sheet into the appropriate sheet, which you use to calculate growth, waypoints, and shelving layouts. Each copy also contains a section that calculates an exact count of the shelving assigned to each collection.

There is a tab customized to calculate Periodicals layouts.

There is a tab customized for Microforms.

In some instances you use one of the Sheet tabs for periodicals or microforms, depending on how you measured those collections.

The entire Layout spreadsheet with all of the tabs is available in electronic format at www.ala.org/editions/extras/fortriede09942. [WEB]

Each of the spreadsheets is protected using Excel's internal Protect function. The cells in which you enter information are unlocked; the rest are not readily accessible. This is to prevent an accidental erasure or loss of a formula.

You can remove the protection. There is no password. Click on the tab you want to unprotect. Click Tools, then Protection, then Unprotect Sheet. You must remove the protection if you add columns to interfile four or more collections. I strongly recommend you reinstall protection as soon as possible. One corrupted formula can render your entire shelving plan inaccurate and might require you to shift your entire collection.

To reset protection, click on the tab you want to protect. Click Tools, then Protection, then Protect Sheet. In the drop-down box check "Select unlocked cells," "Format columns," and "Insert columns." Those functions are necessary if you add columns for interfiling or for data entry.

INSTRUCTION CHECKLIST

Measure the collection
- ☐ Click on the Data tab.
- ☐ Print copies of the Data sheet, enough to record shelves and strings for all waypoints in all of your collections.
- ☐ Shoot the shelves and strings and record the information on the Data sheet. Measure periodicals as described in chapter 4 and microforms as described in chapter 14.

Prepare the tabs for each collection
- ☐ Rename the sheets to match your collections. Do not use the Master tab. Keep that as a reference in case you inadvertently change a formula elsewhere.
  - ☐ Right click on each tab for Sheets 1 through 15.
  - ☐ Click Rename and type in the name of your collection. Do this for every collection, even those so small they have only the starting waypoint. You still need to calculate growth for the small collections, and there is value to having every collection in the same format.
  - ☐ Also enter the name of the sheet in cell B30.
  - ☐ If you do not need all fifteen worksheets, just leave the unused ones unnamed.
  - ☐ If you need more than fifteen worksheets, go to www.ala.org/editions/extras/fortriede09942 and download another Layout spreadsheet. [WEB] Each download includes one Data, one Master, fifteen sheets for books, one Periodicals tab, and one Microforms tab.
- ☐ Adjust the number of columns for interfiling collections. The tabs are set up with extra columns to allow you to calculate and interfile up to three collections. You can adjust the number as needed:
  - ☐ If you are not interfiling, Hide columns E, F, G, and H.
    - ☐ Click on the tab you want to adjust.
    - ☐ Click a cell in columns E, F, G, and H—Format/Column/Hide.
  - ☐ If you are interfiling only one collection, Hide columns G and H.
    - ☐ Click on the tab you want to adjust.
    - ☐ Click a cell in columns G and H—Format/Column/Hide.
  - ☐ To interfile four or more collections, add two new columns for each additional interfiled collection.
    - ☐ Click on the tab you want to adjust.
    - ☐ Beginning at column I and, moving right, highlight two columns for every additional collection—Insert/Columns.
    - ☐ Label the new pairs of columns "Shelves" and "Strings" to match the three sets I provided.
    - ☐ Adjust the formula in column I. Note that the original column I now has a new letter designation, depending on how many columns you added. For consistency, I continue to refer to it as column I.
      - ☐ Unprotect the worksheet—Tools/Protection/Unprotect Sheet.
      - ☐ Go to cell I34, or whatever its new designation may be.
      - ☐ The formula in this cell has two main elements. The first is (G34+E34+C34). Add the cell references to the new "Shelves" columns. They should be columns I, K, M, O, etc. If you added one more set of columns, the adjusted first element now reads (G34+E34+C34+I34).
      - ☐ Add the cell references to the second element (D34+F34+H34+???).
      - ☐ Protect the worksheet—Tools/Protection/Protect Sheet.

Note: If you are expanding the Periodicals or Microforms tab, the formulas are slightly different in both elements. Follow the formulas as they are shown on those tabs.

For Books and for Periodicals or Microforms Measured as Books in Shelves and Strings

Enter measurements from the Data sheet
- ☐ Click on the tab for the collection you are going to enter.
- ☐ Starting at cell B34, enter the call number at each waypoint and the number of shelves and strings counted for each. You can have up to two hundred waypoints on each tab. Two hundred

should be sufficient for up to 500,000 books in the main run. If you need additional waypoints for a very large collection, break it into parts and calculate each part on a separate tab.

- ☐ If you are interfiling into this collection, enter the shelves and strings for those collections in the appropriate pair of columns. Remember that you used the same waypoints for all of the interfiled collections.
- ☐ If you were unable to measure a collection, enter the estimated total length, in feet, in cell C17.

Determine the growth factor

- ☐ If you want to distribute growth evenly over the whole collection, skip this step. Otherwise work with each collection separately. Decide what growth applies to the materials in each waypoint. Rate each waypoint on a scale from 1 to 5: 3 is average growth; 1 is 25 percent slower than average; 2 is 10 percent slower; 4 is 10 percent faster than average; 5 is 25 percent faster.
- ☐ Click on the tab for the collection you want to adjust.
- ☐ Enter the growth factor for each waypoint in column J. 3 is the default.

Determine how many shelves you have available

- ☐ Count the number of shelves on each side of each range, in the order in which you will shelve the materials. A detailed explanation of this process is illustrated in chapter 4.
- ☐ Enter the data, range by range, on the tab for the collection to which the shelving is assigned. This data entry section is to the right of the growth calculation section.
- ☐ Enter the numbers of sections and the shelves per section for each range. If some shelves are missing or are to be left unused, enter the number of such shelves as a *negative* number in column R. If there are extra shelves, enter that number as a *positive* in column R.
- ☐ Do this for all, and only, shelves assigned to this collection.

Determine the actual growth for each shelf

- ☐ Measure an average shelf and enter the length in cell C19. The default is 35.5 inches, the actual capacity of a standard 3-foot cantilever shelf.
- ☐ Make sure you have assigned enough shelves: Compare cell O19 to cell O20. If the number in cell O20 is larger than the one in O19, proceed. If O19 is larger, you need to allocate more shelves to this collection.
- ☐ Enter a number greater than 1.0 in cell C23. Cell O19 changes. If cell O19 is still smaller than cell O20, try a larger number (in the form 1.XXX) in C23. If O19 is larger than O20, try a smaller number. You may have to enter a number out to several decimals to get an exact match.

This whole process may seem complex, but it can be very fast once you have detailed waypoint and shelf count information entered. On one of my moves, we had already loaded the first carts of a 10,000-volume periodicals collection when the powers-that-be decided to remove one entire range. We zeroed out that range in the shelf counting section, tried a smaller growth factor, calculated new waypoints, printed out new waypoint markers, and remarked the shelves. It took less than half an hour. Once you have the data set up, you can make major changes with only a few keystrokes.

For Periodicals Measured Title by Title in Feet and Inches

If your shelving is tight and you measured your periodicals so as to assign growth at the ends of open titles, use the Periodicals tab. The difference between this and the Book tabs is that the Periodicals tab is calibrated in feet and inches. The instructions in chapter 4 explain how to do this measurement.

The spreadsheet allows you to calculate for up to 400 titles. If you have more than 400 titles, go to www.ala.org/editions/extras/fortriede09942 and download another Layout spreadsheet. **WEB** Each download includes one Periodicals tab with space for another 400 titles.

To adjust the number of columns for interfiled collections, use the instructions above.

Enter measurements from the Data sheet

- ☐ Click on the Periodicals tab.
- ☐ Starting at cell B32, enter the title or call number of each periodical, the length in feet of each title, and the growth in inches you assigned to each title You can have up to 400 titles.
- ☐ If you are interfiling into this collection, first enter all of the titles in column B, then enter the measurements, in feet and inches, in the appropriate pair of columns.

☐ If you were unable to measure a collection, enter the estimated total length, in feet, in cell C17.

Determine how many shelves you have available

☐ Count the number of shelves on each side of each range, in the order in which you will shelve the materials. A detailed explanation of this process is illustrated in chapter 4.

☐ Enter the data, range by range, in the Periodicals tab. This data entry section is to the right of the growth calculation section. The number of sections in the range goes in column P and number of shelves per section in column Q. If some shelves are missing or are to be left unused, enter the number of such shelves as a *negative* number in column R. If there are extra shelves, enter that number as a *positive* in column R.

☐ Do this for all, and only, shelves assigned to periodicals.

Determine the actual growth for each shelf. Even though you assigned a specific amount of growth to each title, you may have additional growth capacity available. This step distributes that growth over all of the shelves, making reshelving easier and allowing growth flexibility in the future.

☐ Measure an average shelf and enter the length in cell C19. The default is 35.5 inches, the actual capacity of a standard 3-foot cantilever shelf.

☐ Make sure you have assigned enough shelves: Compare cell M19 to cell M20. If the number in cell M19 is larger than the one in M20, proceed. If M20 is larger, you need to allocate more shelves to periodicals.

☐ Enter a number greater than 1.0 in cell C22. Cell M19 changes. If cell M19 is still smaller than M20, try a larger number (in the form 1.XXX) in C22. If M19 is larger than M20, try a smaller number. You may have to enter a number out to several decimals to get an exact match.

For Microforms Measured Title by Title in Feet and Inches

If your shelving is tight and you measured your microforms so as to assign growth at the ends of open titles, use the Microforms tab. The difference between this and the book tabs is that the Microforms tab is calibrated in feet and inches. The instructions in chapter 14 explain how to do this measurement.

The spreadsheet allows you to calculate for up to 400 titles. If you have more than 400 titles, go to www.ala.org/editions/extras/fortriede09942 and download another Layout spreadsheet. **WEB** Each download includes one Microforms tab with space for another 400 titles.

To adjust the number of columns for interfiled collections, use the instructions above.

Enter measurements from the Data sheet

☐ Click on the Microforms tab.

☐ Starting at cell B32, enter the title or call number of each microform, the length in feet of each title, and the growth in inches you assigned to each title. You can have up to 400 titles.

☐ If you are interfiling into this collection, first enter all of the titles in column B, then enter the measurements in the appropriate pair of columns in feet and inches.

☐ If you were unable to measure a collection, enter the estimated total length, in feet, in cell C17.

Determine the space you have available in the new cabinets. Remember that we are treating cabinets as a range, drawers as a section, and rows as a shelf. Use the Data sheet and count the number of drawers and rows in each cabinet. Count each cabinet in separately and in the order in which you will file the microforms. A detailed explanation of this process is illustrated in chapter 14.

☐ Enter the data, cabinet by cabinet, on the Microforms tab. This data entry section is to the right of the growth calculation section. The cabinet name or number goes in column O. The number of drawers in the cabinet goes in column P and number of rows per drawer in column Q. If some drawers are missing or are to be left unused, enter the number of such drawers as a *negative* number in column R.

☐ Do this for all, and only, shelves assigned to microforms.

Determine the actual growth for each row. Even though you assigned a specific amount of growth to each title, you may have additional growth capacity available. This step distributes that growth over all of the rows, making refiling easier and giving you growth flexibility in the future.

☐ Measure an average row and enter the length in cell C19. Measure only the holding capacity of the row. Some drawers have integral supports that reduce their capacity. The default is 26.5 inches.

☐ Make sure you have assigned enough shelves: Compare cell M19 to cell M20. If the number in cell M20 is larger than the one in M19, proceed. If M19 is larger, you need to allocate more cabinets to microforms or reduce the number of years of growth you allocate to each title.

☐ Enter a number greater than 1.0 in cell C22. Cell M19 changes. If cell M19 is still smaller than M20, try a larger number (in the form 1.XXX) in C22. If M19 is larger than M20, try a smaller number. You may have to enter a number out to several decimals to get an exact match.

In the growth portion of the spreadsheet, you now have calculated

- The shelf number (row) on which each waypoint (title) starts.
- The number of inches of growth to leave on each shelf (row). This number varies depending on the total growth you have available and on the growth factor you assigned to each waypoint. With a tight periodical collection, all of the growth may be concentrated at the ends of the titles with nothing left on the intervening shelves.
- The "Natural Growth," which is the actual, precisely calculated growth space. The recommended "Leave XX inches" amount is always a bit less. This deliberately makes the shelved collection a bit loose and provides just a little extra space for the reshelvers. Use the "Leave XX inches" number when you fill out the waypoint markers.
- For book collections only, cells D25 to D29 show the actual growth rate for factors more or less than the average.

In the shelf counting portion, you have

- A virtual collection map.
- The cumulative number of assigned shelves at the end of every range or each microform cabinet. Use this number to help you lay out a paper collection map.

PRINT WAYPOINT AND SHELF COUNT LISTS

When you have finished entering all of the collection measurements and shelf counts and have calculated the growth rate, and you are satisfied that everything is correct and will fit in the assigned space, you are ready to print. There are two useful printouts. One is the master list of waypoints to be used to fill out waypoint markers and collection flags and to prepare the collection map. The master list is used as a reference as questions arise during the move, so make one or two extra copies and keep them at the destination dispatch desk. The other printout is used when you mark the cumulative shelf counts on the floor plan before you make the collection map.

You will have a master list and a shelf count list for each collection tab that you used.

Click on the tab for the collection you want to print.

Unprotect the worksheet
  ☐ Tools/Protection/Unprotect sheet

Print the master list of waypoints
  ☐ Hide columns C, D, E, F, G, H, I, and J. You do not need this information, and leaving it out allows the printout to fit on one page. Highlight these columns, then use Format/Column/Hide.
  ☐ Highlight from A30 to O234, or as far down the sheet as you have entered data.
  ☐ File/Print/Selection/OK.
  ☐ Unhide columns C, D, E, F, G, H, I, and J. Highlight columns B and L together, then use Format/Column/Unhide.
  ☐ Hide column K. This column is used for an internal calculation to simplify a later formula. It does not display during use of the spreadsheet. Highlight column K, then use Format/Column/Hide.

Print the shelf count list
  ☐ Highlight from Q30 to V234, or as far down the sheet as you have entered data. File/Print/Selection/OK.

Reset protection on the sheet
  ☐ Tools/Protection/Protect sheet

CREATING YOUR OWN WORKSHEETS

You can create your own worksheets instead of downloading them. Copy the text, prompts, instructions, and other printed matter as they are shown on the printouts.

Copy the formatting where it is visible. Where formatting is not obvious, and is important, it is noted below. The formulas are as follows:

Data Tab (Figure C.1)

There are no formulas. This is simply a printing master.

Master Tab (Figure C.2)

These formulas also apply to Sheets 1 through 15.

Cell	Formula
B32	=NOW()
I34	=(((G34+E34+C34)*$C$19)((D34+F34+H34)*12))/12
	Replicate to I234
K34	=LOOKUP(J34,$C$25:$D$29)*I34
	Replicate to K234
	Hide column K
L34	=K34/$C$19*12
	Replicate to L234
M34	1
M35	=M34+L34
	Replicate to M234
N34	=INT(O34-.025)
	Replicate to N234
O19	=SUM(L34:L234)+((C17+0000001)/3)
O20	=V20
O30	=B30
	Merge cells O30 through R30
O34	=((L34*$C$19)-(I34*12))/(L34*$C$19)*$C$19
	Replicate to O234
U34	=R34*S34+T34
	Replicate to U234
V20	=MAX(V34:V234)
V34	=U34
V35	=V35+U34
	Replicate to V234

Lock all of the formulas and protect the worksheet.

Periodicals Tab (Figure C.3) and Microforms Tab (Figure C.4)

B28	Periodicals (or Microforms)
B30	=NOW()
I29	=SUM(I32:I432)
	Hide this cell
I32	=(((G32+E32+C32)*12)-((D32+F32+H32)*12))/$C$19
	Replicate to I432
J	Hide column J. It is not used.
K32	1
K33	=K32+I32
	Replicate to K432
L32	=INT(M32-0.25)
	Replicate to L432
M19	=I29*$C$22
M20	=T20
M32	=($C$22-0.9999999)*$C$19
	Replicate to M232
O28	=B28
	Merge cells O28 through R28
S32	=(P32*Q32)+R32
	Replicate to S232
T20	=MAX(T32:T232)
T32	=S32
T33	=T32+S33
	Replicate to T232

Start a new count at each break in the collection and at each Dewey 100, i.e., fiction, reference, 400s, oversize, etc.
Enter the call number of the first book and count over 10 sections. Count and enter the number of shelves under "Shelves."
Measure the empty space on the shelves in that section. Enter the cumulative number of feet of space under "Strings."
Go to the first book in the next set of 10 sections and repeat.
If you have fewer than 10 sections left, that's okay. Just count the shelves and strings that you have.
When you come to a collection break, put a note in the call no. cell so we will know what part of the collection you are surveying.

Beginning call no.	Shelves	Strings			

Figure C.1

Layout Spreadsheet

INSTRUCTIONS: Use this spreadsheet to calculate growth rates and waypoints.

There are 15 copies of this spreadsheet. Use a different spreadsheet tab for each collection. Use the worksheet labeled "Master" to make additional spreadsheets if you need them. RENAME each worksheet for the collection it represents. Also enter the collection name in cell B30 so it will show on the printouts.

There are enough rows on each spreadsheet to calculate 200 waypoints. If your collection requires more than 200 waypoints, put any extras on a separate worksheet.

There are enough columns to calculate waypoints for a main run and two interfiled collections. If you do not need to interfile, you can HIDE columns E & F and G & H. If you must interfile more than three collections, see the instructions to learn how to modify the spreadsheet to accommodate the additional collections.

If you have a collection to interfile and you were not able to measure shelves and strings, enter your estimate of the total length in cell C17. (See chap. 12.) Enter the length of a single shelf in cell C19.

				Total number of shelves you need	0
				Total number of shelves you have	0

What is the estimated total length in feet of any collections you were unable to measure?

35.50

What is the length in inches of most of your shelves?

1

Enter growth rate options in cell C23 (red number) until the number in cell O19 equals the number in cell O20 to spread growth over your entire collection.

1	0.75
2	0.9
3	1
4	1.1
5	1.25

9/14/2009 14:08	Main Run		Interfile Collection #1		Interfile Collection #2		Total	Enter Growth Factor	Total Shelves/w	Start @	Leave	Natural
	Shelves	Strings	Shelves	Strings	Shelves	Strings	in Feet	(1 - 5)	Growth	Shelf	xx Inches	Growth
Beginning call no. of waypoint												

Figure C.2

Shelf Counting Section

INSTRUCTIONS: Use this section to count out your available shelves.

Count each side of each range, in the order in which you will shelve the books.

Enter the number of sections in each range in column R and the number of shelves in each section in column S.

Count any shelves you left unused for display or any other purpose and enter the total as a NEGATIVE number in column T.

Print this section and use the cumulative shelves number to help you lay out your collection map.

Total shelves available 0

Range	Number of sections	Shelves per section	Adjust for unused shelves	Number of shelves in this range	Cumulative shelves at the end of this range
0				0	0
				0	0
				0	0
				0	0
				0	0
				0	0
				0	0
				0	0
				0	0
				0	0
				0	0
				0	0
				0	0
				0	0
				0	0

Figure C.2 (continued)

Layout Spreadsheet for Periodicals

INSTRUCTIONS: Use this spreadsheet to calculate waypoints for periodicals where the collection is tight.

There are enough rows on each spreadsheet to calculate 400 waypoints. If your collection contains more than 400 titles, put any extras on a separate worksheet.

There are enough columns to calculate waypoints for a main run and two interfiled collections. If you do not need to interfile, you can HIDE columns E & F and G & H. If you must interfile more than three collections, see the instructions to learn how to modify the spreadsheet to accommodate the

If you have a collection to interfile and you were not able to measure it, enter your estimate of the total length in cell C17. (See chap. 12.) Enter the length of a single shelf in cell C19.

What is the estimated total length in feet of any collections you were unable to measure?		
What is the length in inches of most of your shelves?	35.50	Total number of shelves you need: 0
Enter growth rate options in cell C22 (red number) until the number in cell M19 equals the number in cell M20 to spread growth over your entire collection.	1	Total number of shelves you have: 0

Periodicals

9/14/2009 14:11	Main Run		Interfile Collection #1		Interfile Collection #2					
Title or call number	Length in Feet	Growth in Inches	Length in Feet	Growth in Inches	Length in Feet	Growth in Inches	Total Shelves	Start @ Shelf	Leave xx Inches	Natural Growth
							0	1	-1	0.00
							0	1	-1	0.00
							0	1	-1	0.00
							0	1	-1	0.00
							0	1	-1	0.00
							0	1	-1	0.00

Figure C.3

Layout Spreadsheet for Microforms

INSTRUCTIONS: Use this spreadsheet to calculate waypoints for microforms only when you measured the collection in feet and inches.

There are enough rows on each spreadsheet to calculate 400 waypoints. If your collection contains more than 400 titles, put any extras on a separate worksheet.

There are enough columns to calculate waypoints for a main run and two interfiled collections. If you do not need to interfile, you can HIDE columns E & F and G & H. If you must interfile more than three collections, see the instructions to learn how to modify the spreadsheet to accommodate the extras.

If you have a collection to interfile and you were not able to measure it, enter your estimate of the total length in cell C17. (See chap. 14.) Enter the length of a single row in cell C19.

What is the estimated total length in feet of any collections you were unable to measure?	
What is the length in inches of most of your shelves?	26.50
Enter growth rate options in cell C22 (red number) until the number in cell M19 equals the number in cell M20 to spread growth over your entire collection.	1

| | | | Total number of rows you need | 0 |
| | | | Total number of rows you have | 0 |

Microforms

9/14/2009 14:14	Main Run		Interfile Collection #1		Interfile Collection #2		Total Shelves	Start @ Shelf	Leave xx Inches	Natural Growth
Title or call number	Length in Feet	Growth in Inches	Length in Feet	Growth in Inches	Length in Feet	Growth in Inches				
							0	1	-1	0.00
							0	1	-1	0.00
							0	1	-1	0.00
							0	1	-1	0.00
							0	1	-1	0.00
							0	1	-1	0.00

Figure C.4

Signage

Appendix D

You may need various signs and other printed materials for your move. This appendix shows samples of some of the most commonly used. Full-size templates are available online at www.ala.org/editions/extras/fortriede09942. [WEB]

INSTRUCTIONS TO UNSHELVERS

Load carts starting from the **TOP**, with the **BLACK** end of the truck to your **LEFT**.

Number each cart using the pre-numbered sequence cards provided. There are 100 cards in a pack. If you load more than 100 carts, start the numbering over with a new pack of the same color.

When you finish an assignment, return any cards you have left over and report to the Dispatch Desk for a new assignment.

Make sure you keep carts exactly in order.

Stay with your team. Don't "help out" another team. If they get behind, we'll assign them extra help.

Instructions to Unshelvers

INSTRUCTIONS TO RESHELVERS

Unload carts starting from the **TOP**, with the **BLACK** end of the truck to your **LEFT**. Unload every cart **TOP, BLACK, LEFT**.

Keep carts exactly in order. Keep checking the sequence cards on each cart to be sure.

Waypoints are marked on the shelves. When you receive your assignment, you will be told at which waypoint you are to start. The waypoint marker will tell you how much room to leave on each shelf.

Watch the call numbers as you shelve so you know when to jump to the next section. Keep the sequence cards in order as you remove them from the carts.

When you finish an assignment, report to the Dispatch Desk for a new assignment. Turn in the sequence cards you have saved.

Stay with your team. Don't "help out" another team. If they get behind, we'll assign them extra help.

KEEP EMPTY TRUCKS MOVING BACK TO THE UNSHELVERS.

Instructions to Reshelvers

INSERT THIS FLAG IMMEDIATELY AHEAD OF

_____

DO NOT REMOVE THIS FLAG. LEAVE IT IN PLACE AND SEND IT WITH THE BOOKS.

LOAD ALL TRUCKS FROM THE **TOP** WITH THE **BLACK** END TO YOUR **LEFT**.

Collection Flag

Load all trucks from the **TOP** with the **BLACK** end to the **LEFT**

Origin Building Reminder

Unload all book trucks from the **TOP** with the **BLACK** end to your **LEFT**

Destination Building Reminder

START
_____
Here

Leave _____ inches per shelf

If you still have books left to shelve when you reach the next waypoint, call a supervisor before you proceed.

Unload all book trucks from the **TOP** with the **BLACK** end to your **LEFT.**

Waypoint Marker

MAXIMUM

2

Loaded carts

Elevator Load Limit

182

Safety Concerns

We want everyone to be safe throughout this move. There are a number of things YOU can do to ensure your own safety and that of your coworkers. Among these are:

Wear good, protective shoes. Tennis shoes are all right, but stronger shoes are recommended. Open-toed shoes are not acceptable under any conditions.

Be careful pulling, pushing, lifting, etc. Use your body weight and leverage.

Be careful when pushing carts. They are heavy. It is hard to get them moving, but once they are rolling, they move very smoothly. Watch out when approaching a corner. Don't get your fingers pinched between carts, or between the cart and a wall. When you are walking, watch out for oncoming carts, particularly at corners.

Trade out jobs. This is the responsibility of the team leader. Change the work you are doing to avoid repetitive stress.

Work smoothly. We need to work fast, but you will find that the best way to achieve speed in this kind of work is to get into a rhythm and stick with it. Smooth makes you fast. Fast just makes you tired. Tired makes mistakes.

Work carefully.

Safety Concerns

Sequence Cards

Appendix E: Sample Request for Quotes for an Office Move

REQUEST FOR QUOTATION

The _____ Library is seeking quotations from qualified persons or companies to move its offices, library furniture, equipment, and supplies.

Scope of Work

The library will move from its temporary location at _____ (Origin) to its new location at _____ (Destination), a distance of about 4 blocks. The move will be done during _____(date)_____ and _____(date)_____, according to a schedule to be worked out between the library and the selected contractor. The work does not include moving the books or the bookshelves.

The library has purchased new furniture and equipment for its new building. As a result, we will move limited quantities of furniture out of the Origin. Items to be moved are listed in the attached Inventory.

We are asking for a price to move the items on the Inventory list, plus approximately 2,500 boxes of office files, personal effects, supplies, and other materials from the Origin to the Destination.

The amount of noninventoried material to be moved was calculated as the equivalent of 2,500 boxes 12 inches wide, 12 inches high, and 20 inches long. This number is approximate and represents our best estimate. A list showing the calculation is enclosed, and potential responders are welcome to check it or to make their own calculations. This is an estimate of volume only. Responders must make all calculations based on the size and capacity of the actual containers they plan to use. About 300 boxes of materials are already boxed in sturdy cardboard containers and will not be reboxed. These containers may vary slightly from the 12-by-12-by-20-inch dimensions.

Conditions of Work

The loading area at the Destination has a 6-inch curb wide enough for two trucks, but no loading dock. Trucks longer than 26 feet or heavier than 46,000 lbs cannot use this loading area. The Destination has a pull-off lane long enough for a 53-foot van to be unloaded, although not without blocking at least one lane of traffic. There is a pull-in area along Ewing Street that is suitable for a single tractor and 53-foot van. The entry from this point requires a step down inside the building. The responder must inspect the various options and determine which are suitable. The responder is responsible for providing all walkboards and other unloading equipment necessary.

The Origin location has a 32-inch-high dock, wide enough for a single truck. The dock must be shared with shelving and book movers and possibly other trades. The Origin building has several available street-level entrances.

The Destination location has a freight elevator about 5 by 8 feet and several smaller elevators. The Origin location has a freight elevator about 10 by 16 feet and four large personnel elevators. Responders should perform an on-site inspection and note the difficulties inherent in moving large quantities of furniture and equipment vertically in the Destination location. The elevators must be shared with shelving and book movers and possibly other trades.

The move will be phased to reduce disruption to library services. The library will be open to the public during some portions of the move. The specific schedule will be worked out in concert with the library, the shelving contractor, and the move contractor. Dock space, elevators, and exits will be assigned to each function to minimize conflicts and waiting time. At this time, the move is expected to take place during the first or second week of _____(date)_____.

Library staff will box their personal effects and most supplies and other materials used at personal, workroom, or reference desks. Contractor will box, wrap, or otherwise package as necessary any other furniture and equipment.

Library staff will label each box and each piece of unboxed furniture or equipment. The label will show the room number to which the item is to be delivered. Where appropriate, library staff will be assigned to direct movers to specific locations within the numbered rooms.

Weekend work will be permitted but not required unless necessary to complete the move in the required time frame.

The contractor will be required to clean up and remove, or dispose of, all trash, packing material, leftover parts, and other debris at the Destination location.

The contractor will be required to protect furniture and equipment from damage during disassembly, transport, and reassembly and to protect the finishes and furnishings of the Origin and Destination locations from damage during transport and installation.

The contractor must provide evidence of insurance including workers' compensation to cover all of the contractor's employees, property damage in an amount of at least $1,000,000, to cover loss or damage to library property, and general liability for any acts or omissions of contractor or contractor's employees while working on this project. The contractor will be required to hold the library harmless from all effects of action, inaction, or omission on the part of the contractor or contractor's employees.

Walk-through Dates

On _____(date)_____ at 1:00 p.m. and _____(date)_____ at 9:00 a.m., library staff will be available to walk through the buildings with potential responders. We explain the move as we see it and answer any questions. Attendance at at least one of the sessions is mandatory. No quote will be considered unless a representative of the responder has attended at least one walk-through session.

Submitting a Quotation

Submit the following documents:

- A completed Quotation Form (enclosed), signed by a responsible officer or agent of the company. The price quoted must be valid if accepted by the library at a time before _____(date)_____.
- A completed Contractor Information Form (enclosed), with the additional references and work plan as requested.

The Quotation Form requires three amounts:

- A fixed price for moving all of the furniture and equipment listed on the Inventory; plus approximately 2,500 boxes of materials.
- An alternate price if the library supplies cardboard boxes for the move.
- A per-hour rate for moving furniture, equipment, and other materials not listed on the Inventory or not included in the office/employee moves.

Submit both documents, together, by mail or in person to:

_____
_____
_____
_____

Quotes are due no later than 2:00 p.m._____(date)_____.

Questions, requests for clarification, and scheduling of site visits should be directed to _____ at 999-999-9999 or by e-mail at _____.

Contract Price

If the quotation is accepted by the library, the quoted fixed-price amount will become the Contract Price. Ten Percent, 10%, of the Contract Price will be retained by the library until the move project is satisfactorily completed. The contractor may invoice for work performed and for time-and-materials work, at any convenient interval, subject to the 10% retainage.

We are aware that the estimate of 2,500 boxes of material is only an estimate and that the actual number of boxes may vary from that estimate. Prior to awarding a contract, the library will negotiate with the responder an adjustment formula to be applied if the actual number of boxes of material moved is substantially different from the estimate.

Room-by-Room List of FFE to Be Moved

Floor		1	1	1	1	1	1
Item	**Size (L-W-H-D)**	Check-in Clearing-house	Children's Playscape Area	Children's Services Reference Desk	Circ Services Desk	Readers' Services Public Area	Readers' Services Workroom
Book dump							
Magazine rack	26 X 26 X 72				2	10	
Table < 12 sf			2			12	
Table 12-16 sf				4		2	
Table 17-24 sf				3		2	
Table 25-32 sf							
Table	4' X 10'						
Nonstacking chairs		3	7	45	8	16	
Stacking chairs						146	
Lounge chair						12	
Couch							
Refrigerator, full-size							
Refrigerator, half-size							1
Microwave							1
Coffeemaker							1
Podium							
Movable whiteboard							
Wall-hung whiteboard			1			4	
Clock		1		2	1	2	
Computer table—single				1	1	3	1
Computer table—double						2	1
Reference desk				2		3	
Reference desk modules					2		
Locker							
File cabinet—letter						1	
File cabinet—legal						2	
Fille cabinet—jumbo						18	
File cabinet—lateral							
Card catalog						3	
Microfiche viewer						9	
Microfilm viewer	< 22 X 25 X 40"					11	
Microfilm cabinet	< 25 X 28 X 42"					28	
Microfilm overfile							
Fax machine—tabletop						1	
Paperback rack				1		20	
Newspaper rack						7	
Atlas stand						4	
Map case						6	
Bench							
Trash container	16 X 16 X 40"	1		1		1	
Literature display				2		1	
Change machine						2	
Cash register					1		
Floor fan							
Flat file							
Index table						2	

Index

Note: Illustrations are indicated by the page number followed by *f* (e.g., 72f).
Tips are indicated by the page number followed by *t* (e.g., 73t).

A
"acceptance" of the building, 11
Akron Public Library alternative move, 154–155
art works, 91

B
backlogs and restoration of workflow
    at elevators, 132
    and mismatched speed of crews, 131–132
    reassigning workers, 132
    skipaheads, 35t, 131, 132
backup plans, 10t
balancing. *See* workflow balancing
bids for moving office contents
    conditions of the move, 92–93
    inventory of, 91–92
    sample, 184–185
    walk-through, 93–94
    See also request for proposal for professional movers
black tape, 70
blowbys, correction of, 130
board books, 150
book card pockets, 70, 80, 84, 105
book carts
    advantages and disadvantages, 30–31, 32
    loading on truck, 105
    microforms, 141–142
    number required, 31
    preparation of, 70–72
    safety with, 104
    unloading from truck, 110
    wheel chocks for, 74t, 109t
    See also carts; move carts
book trucks. *See* book carts
bookends, installation of, 83
box assemblers, 84
box factory, 84, 85t, 99
box lids, 29–30, 84t, 162f
box moves
    failure to meet waypoints, 130–131
    for microfiche, 147
    probability of errors in, 159–160
    reshelving, 123–124
    small moves, 157
    workflow for, 112–128
    See also cart moves
boxes
    advantages and disadvantages, 28, 32
    assembly of, 84
    breaking down of, 124
    equipment for moving, 30, 72–73
    loading of, 105
    microform trays, 77–78, 136, 140–142, 146, 162, 164f
    for microforms, 140–145
    move boxes, 76–77, 161–162, 163f
    number of pushers required for, 102
    packing and stacking, 115–117
    preparation of, 84–85
    preplacement of, 84, 99
    recycling and reuse of, 158
    storage, 77, 162, 163f, 164f
    types of, 28–30
boxes, collections in, measurement of, 40–42
boxes, methods of using
    advantages and disadvantages, 28–30
    dolly or cart, 113–114
    hand truck, 113
    hand-carry, 112–113, 156
    hybrid systems, 115
    pallet, 114–115
box-moving equipment, 30, 72–73
budget
    estimated, 12–13, 14f, 15f
    paying costs directly vs. paying consultant, 17t

187

building completion
    and authorization for move, 11–12
    and certificate of occupancy, 21
building protection during move, 85–88
buildings and grounds representative, 8

C

canopy tops on shelving, 43t
card files, 148–149
card pockets, 70, 80, 84, 105
carpet protection, 85
carry option. *See* hand-carry option
cart moves, 31–33, 106–111
    failure to meet waypoints, 129–130
    very small moves, 157
    See also box moves
cart routes, 85, 88, 96, 104
carts
    advantages over boxes, 115, 116
    capacity of, 71–72
    hand position for pushing, 104
    length of, 70
    loading technique, 105
    number of pushers required for, 102
    preplacement of, 99
    probability of errors in, 160
    signing of by workers, 25
    sources, 71
    TOP, BLACK, LEFT reminders for, 99, 105, 182
    workflow using, 106–111
    See also book carts; move carts
carts, machine, 71
carts shelved backward, 133
catalog card files, 148–149
caution tape, 81, 84
celebration of completed move, 25–26
certificate of occupancy (C of O), 21
checkout-and-return method, 33
children's collections, 68, 72
chocks for wheels, 74t, 109t
cleaning books before move, 20
cleaning the new shelves, 21, 50, 83
cleanup after move, 158–159
collections
    identification of, 35
    order of moving, 101–102
combining collections. *See* interfiling
communications system, 79, 84
communications with staff, 22–23
competition, encouragement of, 4
completion of move, 25–26
computer room during move, 20
computer technicians, 8. *See also* IT staff
computers, 93
conditions of the move in bids, 92–93
consistency in loading book carts, 31
consolidating collections, 59. *See also* interfiling

construction delays and timing of move, 11
contractor's representative, 8
control, definition, 7t
conveyors, use of, 28
copiers, 93
crush weight, 162

D

diesel trucks, 74t
director of library
    participation in move as morale factor, 22
    support for move coordinator, 7, 9
disasters, planning for, 10t
dispatch desks
    assignments for crews, 102
    description, 67
    organization of, 79
    setup of, 99
dispatchers, job description for, 67
display shelves, 44, 51
dividing collections, 59–61, 126. *See also* weeding before move
dock, origin building
    arrangement of carts at, 107, 108f
    in workflow for boxes, 120
dock crew, 66, 107
dock plates, 74, 75f, 107, 109, 120, 122
dockmaster, destination building, 65–66
dockmaster, origin building, 65, 107
docks
    arranging for use of, 83
    choice of, 19t
    and professional movers, 17
    safety, 105
    and size of trucks, 73, 74
    supplies for, 99
    telephones for, 79, 84
    workflow at, 108–109
dollies
    and loading the truck, 120, 121
    number of pushers required for, 102
    safety with, 104
    space required for maneuvering, 116
    specifications, 72–73
    use of, 113–114
drag system, 112–113, 127, 156
drinking fountains, 87
drivers, job description for, 66–67
drywall dust, coping with, 21, 50, 83
duct tape, 80

E

early timing for move, 12
edge protectors, 78, 87
elevation changes, 86, 87–88
elevator lockout key, 82–83, 99
elevator operator

    job description for, 66
    in workflow for boxes, 119
    in workflow for carts, 107
    workflow maintenance by, 110
elevators
    backlogs at, 132
    inspection of before move, 21
    lack of, 27, 28
    load limit signs in, 78, 99, 182
    protection for, 78, 87–88
    repairs to, 82
end of move, 25–26
equipment. *See* FFE (furniture, fixtures, and equipment)
equipment, rented, 12
errors. *See* shelving errors
"everybody loads" start, 100

F

fast workers and slow workers, 101
FFE (furniture, fixtures, and equipment)
    coordinator for, 7–8, 24
    labeling and packing of, 94–95
    moving of, 89–96
    weeding of, 23–24
fiction collections, 68, 72, 119
file cabinets, moving of, 91, 94–95
film, 151
fines, forgiveness of during moves, 19, 20t
finishing up, 158–160
fire extinguishers, protection for, 87
flagging the collection
    in box moves, 117
    for interfiling collections, 53
    microforms, 137, 138t, 140, 141t
    printing the flags, 49t
    procedure, 49, 181
    timetable for installation of flags, 83–84
floor load capacity for stored books, 126t
floor plans
    checking against actual construction, 42
    on moving day, 95
    and shelving map, 48, 49f, 174
    in supplies, 81
floor protection
    installation of, 78, 85, 87f
    moving carts over, 110t
    removing, 159
foam insulation as wall protector, 78, 86, 88
food, provision of, 79–80
forklift operator, job description for, 66
forklifts
    in box moves, 121
    and carts, 31, 32

Index **189**

charging of, 99
and height of loading dock, 73
and large books, 150
safety around, 105
specifications, 75–76
in unloading operation, 109
in workflow, 108
fragile books, 20. *See also* rare or valuable materials
furniture, fixtures, and equipment. *See* FFE (furniture, fixtures, and equipment)

G

games for celebration party, 25–26
gloves
  for box assemblers, 84
  for box disassemblers, 158
  for moving rare books, 150
grand opening ceremonies, 12
grand opening date as deadline for move, 11
growth factors
  microforms, 139
  periodicals, 172
  in planning, 10–11
  procedures, 43, 44–48
  too much growth space, 48t

H

hand trucks
  and height of workers, 101
  and loading the truck, 120
  microforms, 137
  number of pushers required for, 102
  and ramps, 122
  specifications, 72–73
  use of, 113
hand-carry option
  rare books, 150
  small moves, 112–113, 156
handle for dragging boxes, 112–113
hands
  position on carts, 104
  preventing strains, 104–105
hero projects, 160t
hills, loading on, 109t
human chains
  as moving method, 27–28, 32
  for narrow aisles, 102
  sources of workers for, 132
hybrid systems for moving boxes, 115

I

insurance company
  additional insurance, 93t
  approval of right to move in, 11
  coverage of volunteers, 63
  and use of professional movers, 16, 93
interfilers, job description for, 64–65

interfiling, 52–61
  books in no useful order, 52–53
  inserting entire collections into main collection, 59
interfiling (cont.)
  before move, 35, 40, 55–56, 84
  no time for, 55–58
  returned materials, 59
  and shooting shelves and strings, 37
  small collections, 58–59
  two or more collections, 53–55
  use of spreadsheet, 40–42, 171
  worksheet, 57f
interfiling station, 53, 54f
interrupted moves, 152–153
inventory of furniture, 90–91, 96
IT staff, 93. *See also* computer technicians

J

jam and cram reshelving, 153
job descriptions, 63–68

L

layout planning
  responsibility for, 24
  for storage during a move, 124–126
layout spreadsheet
  and combining collections, 40–42
  data entry into, 37, 42t, 171
  master tab, 36, 175, 177–178f
  use of, 45, 47 fig. 4.7
leased equipment, moving of, 93
leftover collections, 158–159
length of move, planning for, 12. *See also* timetable
liability issues. *See* insurance company
librarians
  in periodicals moves, 39, 64
  as supervisors, 64
library carts. *See* book carts
liftgates on trucks
  in box moves, 121, 122
  and carts, 74
lifts, operation of, 28
loading dock. *See* dock
loan period during move, 19t
long-distance moves, 155–156
lunchtime check-in sessions, 25. *See also* food, provision of

M

machine carts, 71
maintenance-of-service officer, 9
managers and administrators in layout planning, 24
measurement of collections, 34–42
  layout spreadsheet, 35–37, 170–175, 176f, 177–178f, 179f, 180f
  microforms, 137–139, 171–174

periodicals, 39–40, 171–173
  in preparation of RFP, 17
  shooting shelves and strings, 37–40, 138–139
  before storage, 126
  stored collections, 40–42
  very small moves, 156–157
  See also waypoints
measuring blocks, 81
meetings, 25
mental fatigue, 54, 58, 64
microfilm. *See* microforms
microform cabinets
  in furniture inventory, 90
  marking of, 140
  painting of, 135t
  reuse of in new building, 135–136
  weight of loaded cabinet, 136–137f
microform trays, 77–78, 136, 140–142, 146, 164f
microforms, 135–147
  boxes for, 162, 164f
  delayed moves, 135–136
  on layout spreadsheet, 36, 175, 180f
  measured in shelves and strings, 171–172
  measured title by title in feet and inches, 173–174
  moving in cabinets, 136–137
  order of moving, 101
  periodical-type, 138–139
  refiling, 145–146
  replicating current arrangement, 137, 143t, 146
milk crates, 30
missed books, 158
missed carts, signs of, 129–130
moldy books, 105
morale
  and nonworking staff as observers, 22
  and prizes, 8, 80
  See also personnel and morale officer
move carts
  advantages and disadvantages, 31–33
  loading of, 105
  microforms, 141–142
  for really large books, 149, 150t
  safety with, 104
  sides for, 72, 107, 168
  specifications for, 70–72, 165–168
  as temporary shelving, 154–155
  unloading from truck, 110
  See also book carts; carts
move consultants, 13, 17–18
move coordinator
  and planning of building, 12
  responsibilities of, 7, 67–68
  tasks during move, 24
  working with professional movers, 16

move crates, plastic, 30
move day
    introductions, 102–105
    preparations, 99–102
Move Olympics, 25–26
move (planning) team, 4, 6–9, 22, 24–25
move within a building, 69
movers, professional
    and FFE coordinator, 8
    for loaded microform cabinets, 136–137
    for moves of furniture and equipment, 89–90
    and rare or valuable books, 150
    requests for proposal, 18, 90–94, 184–186
    services offered by, 13, 16–17
moves between buildings, 32, 69
moves while building is still under construction, 21
moving methods, 27–33
    carts, 106–111
    checkout-and-return, 33
    hand carry, 112–113, 150, 156
    human chains, 27–28, 32, 102, 132
    stack movers, 27, 32
    walk-in-line, 33, 159
    See also box moves; cart moves; small moves
multimedia kits, 150–151

N

newsletter for move, 23
newspapers
    bound, 149
    unbound, 152
night crew, 68, 133
night moves, 18

O

odd jobs for staff, 21
office contents, inventory of, 91–92
origin dispatch desk, 24
origin shelving plan, 99
overflow areas, 123
overplanning, dangers of, 9–11
oversize books, 101, 116, 149–150

P

packing
    microfiche, 147
    microforms, 143–145
painter's tape, 80, 84, 87
painting
    microform cabinets, 135t
    shelves, 154t
pallet jacks, 72–73, 102, 115

pallets
    under books stored on concrete, 126t, 127
    and loading the truck, 121, 122t
    selling of, 159
    space required for maneuvering, 116
    specifications, 72
    unloading, 122
    use of, 114–115
parties as celebration of completed move, 25
pedestrians in cart route, 87, 104
periodicals
    and expertise of periodicals librarians, 39, 64
    on layout spreadsheet, 36, 175, 179f
    measured in shelves and strings, 39–40, 171–172
    measured title by title in feet and inches, 172–173
    microform, 138–139, 140
    moving time for, 68
    reshelvers for, 64
    unbound periodicals, 151–152
personal effects of staff, 12, 24, 91–92, 95
personnel and morale officer, 8, 24, 68
physically limited workers
    as guides, 95
    jobs for, 20–21
    as sign makers, 160
planning of building
    move coordinator on, 12
    shelving layouts, 42
planning team. *See* move (planning) team
preparations
    basics, 82–88
    checklist, 99
prizes, 8, 80
publicity and public relations
    and donation of boxes, 30
    and donation of food, 80
    and extended loan periods, 19t
    and loans of carts, 71
    move as opportunity for, 4
    for mover of furniture and equipment, 90
    and walk-in-line method, 33
punctuated moves, 153–154
pushers
    job description for, 64
    numbers required, 68t
    requirements for, 101–102
    and unloading a truck, 110
    in workflow for carts, 107

Q

quote request sample for professional movers, 16, 184–185

R

rain. *See* weather
ramps, 75, 86, 108, 109–110, 122
range, definition, 36t
rare or valuable materials
    in contract with professional movers, 16
    fragile books, 20
    handling of, 150
    moving of as task for library director, 9
realia, 151
recycling of boxes, 158
reference services during move, 19–20
renewals during move, 19
repainting. *See* painting
repairs to damaged equipment, 81
request for proposal for professional movers, 16, 17, 184–185. *See also* bids for moving office contents
reserves pickup during move, 19
reshelvers, job description for, 64
reshelving, 110, 123. *See also* waypoints
restraining straps
    for boxes, 114, 119, 122
    for carts, 72, 109
    in truck, 75, 109
returned materials during move, 19, 59, 84
room numbering, 95
routes for carts, 85–88, 96, 104
rumor control, 23

S

safety
    introductory lecture on, 21, 100, 104–105
    and liftgates on trucks, 74
    in loading boxes, 121
    pedestrians on cart routes, 87, 104
schedule slips and professional movers, 16
schedules
    communication with staff about, 22
    and number of book carts needed, 31
    packing of furniture and equipment, 95
secretary, role of, 8
section, definition, 36t
semester breaks as time for move, 11
sequence card numbering system
    in box moves, 116–117
    in cart moves, 31, 106–107
    in instructions, 105
    in interfiling collections, 54
    in loading of truck, 108
    in preparation for move, 99
    in unloading a truck, 110

sequence cards, 78–79, 183
service points during move, 18–20
shelf reading
    after move, 159–160
    before move, 20, 35
shelf-to-shelf moves, 118–124
shelves and shelving
    cleaning of, 21, 50, 83
    empty shelves before a waypoint, 129–130
    reuse of, 153–154
    signing of by workers, 25
    spacing of, 83
    temporary shelving, 153
shelves to be left empty, 84
shelving errors
    with box moves, 130–131
    with cart moves, 129–130
    cart shelved backward, 133
    probability of, 159–160
    responsibility for, 133t
shelving expert on planning team, 9
shelving installers, 42, 43, 83
shelving layout, design of, 42–51
    allocation of shelving for each collection, 43–44
    calculation of available shelving, 42–43, 172
    finished layout, 45f, 46
    rough layout, 43–44, 45f
shelving map
    collections to be interfiled later, 57–58
    construction of, 48–49
shifting. *See* shelving errors
shoes, open-toed, 99, 104
shooting shelves and strings, 37–40, 138–139
short distances and human chains, 32
shotgun start, 100
shrinkwrapping
    of book carts, 31, 72
    technique, 107
    unbound periodicals, 151–152
    vertical files, 151
sides for move carts
    specifications, 168
    use of, 72, 107
signage
    examples, 181–183
    for move, 78–79, 84, 99
    on moving day, 95
    for new shelving, 160
skipaheads, 35t, 131, 132
slides, use of, 28
small collections
    growth rate calculation, 44
    order of moving, 101

small moves
    book carts for, 32
    boxes for, 30, 32
    methods, 112–113, 156–157
    microforms, 135
    moves of furniture and equipment, 89
soft opening, definition, 12
sorting trays
    in interfiling collections, 53
    specifications for, 169
space on shelves, planning for. *See* growth factors
spilled microfiche, refiling, 147t
spreading a collection out, 153
stack movers (equipment), 27, 32
stacking
    microform boxes, 144–145
    miscalculations in, 124t
    starting order, determining, 119
    for storage, 126
    techniques for, 117–118, 119t
    terminology, 51t
    in truck, 121t
    in workflow, 119
stacks, stability of, 83
staff
    balancing allocation of, 131–134
    communications with, 22–23
    and computer moves, 93
    as interfilers, 64
    move traumatic for, 8
    nonparticipating, 20–22, 62, 131t
    numbers required, 68–69
    packing of furniture and equipment, 91, 94–95
    personal effects of, 12, 24, 91–92, 95
    role in move, 4, 62
    and use of professional movers, 16
    See also workers
staging areas, 123t
starting the move
    everybody loads start, 100–101
    phased-in start, 101t
    shotgun start, 100
    with two start times, 100t
staying open during move, 18–20
step stools, 81, 84
storage, long-term
    boxes for, 77, 162, 163f, 164f
    stacking for, 127–128
storage, transporting books to, 126–127
storage during a move
    cost of, 152–153
    for microforms, 135–136, 137f, 143
    using boxes, 124–126
stored collections, measurement of, 40–42
straps. *See* restraining straps
streets, closing of, 11–12

strength of workers, 101
students as workers, 63
study areas during move, 20
supervisors, job description for, 64
supplies
    obtaining early, 11
    weeding of, 23–24

T

tape measures, 37
tapes
    black tape, 70
    for boxes, 29
    caution tape, 81, 84
    duct tape, 80
    painter's tape, 80, 84, 87
telephones, 79, 84, 99
temporary services agencies, 63
temporary shelving, 153
theft, possibilities of during move, 18
timetable
    for dividing collections, 60–61
    flexibility in, 10–11
    interfiling collections, 53–54
    for move, 11–12
    for moving furniture, 96
    in preparation of RFP, 16, 17
    and professional movers, 16
toolbox, 81
tools and supplies, 70–81, 84
TOP, BLACK, LEFT principle, 99, 105, 106, 182
tops of boxes, 29–30, 84t
tours of building for staff, 22
tours of building for workers, 25
traffic wardens, 18
training for workers, 23, 100–101, 105
training videos, 23
transport safety, 104
trays, microform. *See* microforms
trucks (automobile)
    diesel trucks, 74t
    loading of, 107–108, 120, 121, 122t
    rental of, 73, 82
    specifications for, 73–74
    stacking in, 121t
    unloading of, 109–110
    See also book carts; hand trucks; move carts
trucks, book. *See* book carts
trucks, hand. *See* hand trucks

U

unshelvers, job description, 63–64

V

vacuum cleaner for elevator, 83
vending machines, 93
vertical files, 151

vests for building guides, 95
videos for training, 23
volunteers
    and human chains, 27–28
    and walk-in-line method, 33
    as workers, 63

W

walk-in-line method, 33, 159
walk-through with movers, 93–94
wall protection
    installing, 78, 86–87
    removing, 159
wastebaskets
    as bumpers, 78, 86–87
    as magazine containers, 152
waypoints
    on books, 49
    in box moves, 119, 123–124
    for collections being divided, 126
    for combining collections, 40
    definition, 35
    microforms, 138t, 142
    missed, 130
    monitoring of, 24
    in periodicals collections, 39–40
    selection of, 39t
    on shelves, 50–51, 182
    on shelving map, 48–49

timetable for marking, 84
    in unshelving, 106
weather
    light rain, 109t
    rain delays, 133–134
    and rare books, 150
    and timing of move, 11
weeding before move, 23–24. *See also* dividing collections
wheel chocks for book carts, 74t, 109t
whiteboard, use of, 24, 79, 99
work crew, definition, 63
workers
    matching speeds of, 131–132
    numbers required, 66
    paid nonstaff, 63
    physically limited workers, 20–21, 95, 160
    recruitment of, 62–69
workers, job descriptions for, 63–68, 104t
    box assemblers, 84
    dispatcher, 67
    dock assistants, 66
    dockmaster, destination building, 65–66
    dockmaster, origin building, 65
    driver, 66–67
    elevator operator, 66

    forklift operator, 66
    guides for professional movers, 95
    interfilers, 64–65
    move coordinator, 7, 12, 16, 24, 67–68
    night crew, 68
    personnel and morale officer, 8, 24, 68
    pushers, 64
    reshelvers, 64
    supervisor, 64
    unshelvers, 63–64
workflow
    for boxes, 118–124
    for carts, 106–111
    restarting after delays, 134
workflow balancing
    collection, 129–131
    in long-distance moves, 155
    staff, 131–134

X

XXX cards, use of
    destination dispatch desk, 110, 123
    loading dock, origin, 107, 120
    microforms, 144
    unshelving, 106–107, 119

TH 435 .B86 2013
Assemblies cost data

WITHDRAWN

NOV 2012

Don't Miss Your Free Quarterly Cost Data Updates!

Stay up-to-date throughout 2013! RSMeans provides free cost data updates four times a year. Sign up online to make sure you have access to the newest data.

For Free Quarterly Updates, Register Online Now at:

www.rsmeans2013updates.com

Parkland College Library
2400 West Bradley Avenue
Champaign, IL 61821

DATE DUE

APR 29 2015
JUL 29 2015
MAY 0 8 2015

PRINTED IN U.S.A.

For Your Convenience: Bookmarks with special offers and useful tips and information on the back...

REFER-A-FRIEND AND SAVE

10%

Your referred friend saves 10%
You save 10% on your next purchase

Go to www.rsmeans.com with promotion code:
REFR-FRND

Offer expires 8/1/13

RSMeans®

OVER 50 SELECTIONS!

Find them at:
www.rsmeans.com

Try RSMeans Online

25% OFF

You've got the book, now get the matching online data!

Gain the benefits of online data!
Access data from the web — anywhere, anytime!

Call 1-800-334-3509 ext.1 to order!

Tips for Customizing Your RSMeans Cost Data By Location

The cost data found throughout the book reflects national averages.

Customize your cost data for over 930 locations throughout the U.S. and Canada.

- ☑ To adjust costs to your region, use the Location Factors found in the back of the book.
- ☑ To compare costs from region-to-region, use the City Cost Indexes found in the back of the book.
- ☑ For additional guidance, refer to the How RSMeans Data Works section towards the front of the book.

Metric Conversion Formulas

Length

cm = 0.3937 in.	in. = 2.5400 cm.
meter = 3.2808 ft.	ft. = 0.3048 m.
meter = 1.0936 yd.	yd. = 0.9144 m.
Km. = 0.6214 mile	mile = 1.6093 km.

Weight

gram = 15.4324 grains	grain = 0.0648 g.
gram = 0.0353 oz.	oz. = 28.3495 g.
kg. = 2.2046 lbs.	lb. = 0.4536 kg.

Area

sq. cm. = 0.1550 sq. in.	sq.in. = 6.4516 sq. cm.
sq. m. = 10.7639 sq. ft.	sq. ft. = 0.0929 sq. m.
sq. m. = 1.1960 sq. yd.	sq. yd. = 0.8361 sq. m.
hectare = 2.4710 acres	acre = 0.4047 hectare
sq. km. = 0.3861 sq. mile	sq. mile = 2.5900 sq. km.

Weight, cont.

kg. = 0.0011 ton (short)	ton (short) = 907.1848 kg.
ton (met.) = 1.1023 ton (short)	ton (short) = 0.9072 ton (met.)
ton (met.) = 0.9842 ton (large)	ton (large) = 1.0160 ton (met.)

Common Units of Measure

Abbreviation	Measurement	Formula
SF	Square feet	Length (in feet) x Width (in feet)
SY	Square yards	Square feet / 9
CF	Cubic feet	Length (in feet) x Width (in feet) x Depth (in feet)
CY	Cubic yards	Cubic feet / 27
BF	Board foot	Length (in inches) x width (in inches) x thickness (in inches)/144
MBF	Thousand board foot	Board foot / 1,000
LF	Linear feet	12 inches of the item
SFCA	Square foot of contact area	A square foot of concrete formwork
SQ	Square	100 square feet
Ton	Ton	2,000 pounds